SAGE was founded in 1965 by Sara Miller McCune to support the dissemination of usable knowledge by publishing innovative and high-quality research and teaching content. Today, we publish over 900 journals, including those of more than 400 learned societies, more than 800 new books per year, and a growing range of library products including archives, data, case studies, reports, and video. SAGE remains majority-owned by our founder, and after Sara's lifetime will become owned by a charitable trust that secures our continued independence.

Los Angeles | London | New Delhi | Singapore | Washington DC | Melbourne

CHINA and INDIA

Thank you for choosing a SAGE product!
If you have any comment, observation or feedback,
I would like to personally hear from you.
Please write to me at **contactceo@sagepub.in**

Vivek Mehra, Managing Director and CEO, SAGE India.

Bulk Sales

SAGE India offers special discounts
for purchase of books in bulk.
We also make available special imprints
and excerpts from our books on demand.

For orders and enquiries, write to us at

Marketing Department
SAGE Publications India Pvt Ltd
B1/I-1, Mohan Cooperative Industrial Area
Mathura Road, Post Bag 7
New Delhi 110044, India

E-mail us at **marketing@sagepub.in**

Get to know more about SAGE

Be invited to SAGE events, get on our mailing list.
Write today to **marketing@sagepub.in**

This book is also available as an e-book.

CHINA and INDIA

History, Culture, Cooperation and Competition

EDITED BY
Paramita Mukherjee
Arnab K. Deb
Miao Pang

Los Angeles | London | New Delhi
Singapore | Washington DC | Melbourne

Copyright © Paramita Mukherjee, Arnab K. Deb and Miao Pang, 2016

All rights reserved. No part of this book may be reproduced or utilised in any form or by any means, electronic or mechanical, including photocopying, recording or by any information storage or retrieval system, without permission in writing from the publisher.

First published in 2016 by

SAGE Publications India Pvt Ltd
B1/I-1 Mohan Cooperative Industrial Area
Mathura Road, New Delhi 110 044, India
www.sagepub.in

SAGE Publications Inc
2455 Teller Road
Thousand Oaks, California 91320, USA

SAGE Publications Ltd
1 Oliver's Yard, 55 City Road
London EC1Y 1SP, United Kingdom

SAGE Publications Asia-Pacific Pte Ltd
3 Church Street
#10-04 Samsung Hub
Singapore 049483

Published by Vivek Mehra for SAGE Publications India Pvt Ltd, typeset in Times New Roman 10/12 pts by Zaza Eunice, Hosur, Tamil Nadu, India and printed at Saurabh Printers Pvt Ltd, Greater Noida.

Library of Congress Cataloging-in-Publication Data

Names: Mukherjee, Paramita, editor. | Deb, Arnab K., editor. | Miao, Pang, editor.
Title: China and India : history, culture, cooperation and competition /
   edited by Paramita Mukherjee, Arnab K. Deb, Pang Miao.
Description: Thousand Oaks, Calif. : SAGE, 2016. | Includes bibliographical
   references and index.
Identifiers: LCCN 2016023052| ISBN 9789385985690 (hardback : alk. paper) |
   ISBN 9789385985683 (epub) | ISBN 9789385985706 (ebook)
Subjects: LCSH: China—History. | China—Foreign relations. | China—Economic
   conditions. | India—History. | India—Foreign relations. |
   India—Economic conditions.
Classification: LCC DS35.2C455 2016 | DDC 303.48/251054—dc23 LC record
available at https://lccn.loc.gov/2016023052

ISBN: 978-93-859-8569-0 (HB)

SAGE Team: Shambhu Sahu, Sandhya Gola, Mayukh Lahiri and Ritu Chopra

Contents

List of Tables	vii
List of Figures	ix
List of Abbreviations	xi
Preface	xv
Acknowledgements	xvii
Introduction	xix

Part I: History, Culture and International Relations

1. Indus Civilisation and Ancient Shu Civilisation: A Comparative Study — *Zou Yiqing* … 3
2. Unfolding the Westerly Transmission of Chinese Silk — *Duan Yu* … 16
3. Sino-Indian Cultural Differences and Their Impact on Tourism — *Xiang Baoyun* … 24
4. India, China and Beyond: Tagorean Insights into Culture, Leadership and Human Development for Management — *Sanjoy Mukherjee* … 37
5. China and India: Cultural and Religious Exchanges in the 15th Century — *Huang Weimin* … 58
6. China's Enlightenment by Indian Strategies of Cultural Soft Power — *Jian Li* … 72
7. Driving Force and Constraints of BCIM Economic Corridor — *Li Jingfeng* … 83

8. The US 'Pivot to Asia' and China–Pakistan Relations: Implications on China–India Relations 93
   Chen Jixiang

9. China and India Cooperation in Afghanistan 108
   Xie Jing

Part II: Economy and Business: Comparative Focus

10. Multiple Paths to Globalisation: The India–China Story 121
    Sriparna Basu

11. Regional Inequality over the Post-globalisation Era: A Study on India and China 133
    Arindam Banik and Arnab K. Deb

12. Manufacturing Policies and Strategies across China and India: A Comparative Analysis 153
    Prageet Aeron and B.A. Metri

13. Corporate Social Responsibility Practices: A Comparative Study of India and Asia 169
    Paramita Mukherjee and Rajashri Chatterjee

14. Health Care Sectors of India and China: A Comparative Study of Performances and Challenges 188
    Paramita M. Nag

15. Social Responsibility Strategies in China and India: A Comparative Exploration 203
    Tirthankar Nag, Arindam Banik, Miao Pang and Chen Jixiang

About the Editors and Contributors 215
Index 223

List of Tables

3.1	China's World Heritage Sites	28
3.2	India's World Heritage Sites	29
3.3	Number of Indian Tourists to China 2006–12 (in ten thousands)	30
3.4	Number of Chinese Tourists to India 2006–12 (in absolute figures)	30
3.5	Top Tourist Destination Countries and Regions for Chinese and Indian Tourists, Respectively	32
3.6	Numbers of Outbound Tourists from China and India from 2006–12 (million)	33
5.1	Chinese Envoys to the Indian Kingdoms	61
5.2	Indian Kingdoms Paying Tribute to China	62
11.1	Disparity in Per Capita GSDP: Weighted and Unweighted Indices	139
11.2	Per Capita SDP and Growth in SDP for Select States	141
12.1	Contribution of PRD Towards Overall Production from China (2000)	159
12.2	Manufacturing Growth Phases (China)	161
13.1	Trend in GDP Growth and Human Development Index in Select Developing Countries	171
13.2	Summary of Findings on CSR Spending by Indian Companies during 2012–13	180
13.3	Top Three Companies Countrywise from ASR 2014 Ranking	184
14.1	Summary of Historical Developments	192
14.2	Performance of Key Health Indicators	193
14.3	Mortality from Infectious and Non-communicable Diseases	194

14.4	Policy Factors Impacting the Chinese and Indian Health Systems	199
15.1	Firms in India and China Selected for Understanding CSR Investments	210
15.2	CSR Activities in Selected Chinese and Indian Firms	211
15.3	Firms Reporting CSR in Shanghai Stock Exchange [Companies Reporting CSR (% of Total Sample in Sector)]	212

List of Figures

11.1	Inter-state Inequality in Per Capita Consumption Expenditure	140
11.2	Interprovincial Inequality in Per Capita GDP, 1978–2006	145
11.3	Decomposition of Interprovincial Inequality, 1978–2006	146
11.4	Per Capita GDP of China and Its Three Regions, 1978–2006	147
11.5	Decomposition of Intraregional Inequality, 1978–2006	148
12.1a	Percentage Share of GDP from Industry and Service	154
12.1b	Share of China in World GDP	154
12.2	Various Clusters in PRD	163
13.1	Number of Companies Contributed in Different Sectors	181
13.2	Distribution of Top 100 Companies	182
13.3	Sectoral Distribution of Top 100 Companies	183
15.1	CSR Reports Issued in China	207
15.2	Percentage of Companies Reporting CSR in China and India (100 Largest Companies in Countries)	209
15.3	Percentage of Companies Reporting CSR (100 Largest Companies in Countries)	210

List of Abbreviations

AD	Anno Domini
AIIB	Asian Infrastructure Investment Bank
ANSF	Afghan National Security Force
ASEAN	Association of Southeast Asian Nations
ASR	Asian Sustainability Rating
BC	Before Christ
BCIM	Bangladesh, China, India and Myanmar
BCIM-EC	Bangladesh, China, India and Myanmar-Economic Corridor
BJP	Bharatiya Janata Party
BRICS	Brazil, Russia, India, China, and South Africa
BRR	Business Responsibility Report
BSE	Bombay Stock Exchange
CDC	Centres of Disease Control
Chindia	China and India
CMS	Community Medical System
CNPC	China National Petroleum Corporation
COPD	Chronic Obstructive Pulmonary Disorder
CPC	Communist Party of China
CPI	Communist Party of India
CPI(M)	Communist Party of India (Marxist)
CRT	Cathode Ray Tube
CSR	Corporate Social Responsibility
CV	Coefficient of Variation
ESG	Environmental, Social and Governance
ETIM	East Turkestan Islamic Movement
FDI	Foreign Direct Investment
FKI	Federation of Korean Industries
FSC	Financial Supervisory Commission
FY	Financial Year

GATT	General Agreement on Tariffs and Trade
GDP	Gross Domestic Product
GIS	Government Insurance Scheme
GNP	Gross National Product
GRI	Global Reporting Initiative
GSDP	Gross State Domestic Product
HIV	Human Immunodeficiency Virus
ICCR	Indian Council for Cultural Relations
ICT	Information Communication Technology
ICWA	Indian Council of World Affairs
IDSA	Institute for Defence Studies and Analyses
IMF	International Monetary Fund
IT	Information Technology
ITES	Information Technology Enabled Services
LBW	Low Birth Weight
LIS	Labour Insurance Scheme
MCA	Ministry of Corporate Affairs
MNC	Multinational Corporation
MW	Megawatt
NATO	North Atlantic Treaty Organization
OECD	Organisation for Economic Co-operation and Development
OOPs	Out-of-pocket Payments
PAT	Profit after Tax
PC	Personal Computer
PHC	Primary Health Centre
PPP	Purchasing Power Parity
PRC	People's Republic of China
PRD	Pearl River Delta
RBC	Responsible Business Conduct
SAARC	South Asian Association for Regional Cooperation
SASAC	State-owned Assets Supervision and Administration Commission
SAW	Spirituality at Work
SCO	Shanghai Cooperation Organization
SDP	State Domestic Product
SEBI	Securities and Exchange Board of India
SEZ	Special Economic Zone
SOE	State-owned Enterprise
SQ	Spiritual Quotient

LIST OF ABBREVIATIONS

SRI	Socially Responsible Investment
TPEx	Taipei Exchange
TPP	Trans-Pacific Partnership
TTIP	Transatlantic Trade and Investment Partnership
TV	Television
TWSE	Taiwan Stock Exchange
UK	United Kingdom
UN	United Nations
UNESCO	United Nations Educational, Scientific and Cultural Organization
US	United States
USA	United States of America
USD	US Dollar
VCD	Video Compact Disc
WBCSD	World Business Council for Sustainable Development
WHO	World Health Organization
WTO	World Trade Organization
YRD	Yangtze River Delta

Preface

Since time immemorial, China and India have had cultural and economic exchanges. The historical account of such exchanges as well as social linkages has immense importance in understanding their current development process. With this as the backdrop, we felt it would be an interesting idea to cover the aspects having significant impact on the growth the two economies have shown in the recent past.

The remarkable emergence of these two big developing countries from a long period of self-imposed seclusion from the rest of the world is the most distinctive feature of the modern era of globalisation. Many believe that global economy is on the verge of an 'Asian Century' which will be significantly dominated by Asian economics, politics and culture. Beginning in the 1980s both of these Asian giants continued the process of economic liberalisation and exposed their economies to foreign technology and knowledge transfers. However, instead of following one straight path out of economic misery towards economic prosperity, these two countries have taken different routes towards the destination that unfolds an interesting lesson for other emerging economies. This divergence reflects how nation-specific ideas, norms and institutional lineage interact with the process of globalisation. Despite being different in focus and implementation of the type of policies, these two countries, moving fast on the growth trajectory, share common characteristics such as a growing large population comprising skilled and unskilled labour force, copious natural resources and the largest marketplace for the rest of the world.

This edited book, *China and India: History, Culture, Cooperation and Competition*, offers a unique perspective on various important cross-country issues and their implications for the two emerging Asian superpowers—China and India. We emphasise the competing visions and beliefs the Chinese as well as Indian research scholars and academicians have in terms of the socio-cultural, political and economic relations of these two countries. The first part of the book elaborates on the historical and cultural issues along with international relations pertinent to both the countries. The rationale for inclusion of contribution of sociocultural factors to the economic transformation as well as the political and strategic relationship between these two countries is to provide a comprehensive picture of the nature of cooperation and competition that exists between them. Apart from cultural and religious exchanges, economic exchange between the two nations since ancient times has also played a significant role in their development process. The latter part of the book comprises the issues related to the economics and business across these two nations that cover a wide variety of topics such as the manufacturing sector development, corporate social responsibility norms, comparison of health sectors and so on.

The chapters in this book present a series of research-based discussions related to contemporary issues. Since policy makers in both the countries have realised that strong cooperation in various domains is prerequisite to achieve sustainability and prosperity in today's world, the chapters provide an excellent account of the past and present economic and social environment which is crucial for making endeavours mutually beneficial. We sincerely believe that this book is capable of taking the reader on a journey through history, culture, economic, social and political aspects of the exchange and cooperation between China and India from the past to the present.

Acknowledgements

First and foremost, we would like to thank Professor Arindam Banik, Director, IMI Kolkata, who has been instrumental in taking forward this publication. Without his encouragement and guidance, it would never have been possible to publish this book. We express our sincere gratitude to Professor Bakul H. Dholakia, Director General, IMI, for his continuous support and guidance.

This book would also not have seen the light of the day without the intellectual contribution on the part of the researchers at Sichuan Academy of Social Sciences, China. Their contribution has added an unparalleled dimension to this endeavour. Our sincere thanks goes to Professor Hou Shuiping, President, Sichuan Academy of Social Sciences, China, and Professor Guo Xiaoming, Vice President, Sichuan Academy of Social Sciences.

We would also like to thank RP-Sanjiv Goenka (SG) Group for their incomparable infrastructural and administrative support in the preparation of the manuscript. Our special thanks goes to Mr Sanjiv Goenka, Chairman, RP-SG Group. We would also like to thank Mr Subhasis Mitra, Executive Director and Group Company Secretary, RP-SG Group, Mr Mani Sankar Mukherji, Chief Group Advisor (Corporate Relations), RP-SG Group and Mr Sunil Bhandari, Executive Director (Corporate Services), RP-SG Group.

Finally, we thank Ms Rajashri Chatterjee for her exceptional editorial assistance at each stage of the book, right from careful reading of the manuscript to the correction of proofs as well as for her tremendous hard work and eye for detail.

Introduction

In the last two decades, among the emerging economies of Asia, India and China have recorded remarkable economic growth, experienced enormous socio-economic changes and established themselves as potential superpowers. The cultural, academic and economic exchange between the two countries started centuries ago. Since then, with the passage of time, both the countries have undergone significant transformation towards economic structure, policy design and development. Still, the two countries are much similar to each other especially in terms of a growing large population, abundant natural resources, a vast pool of employable workforce and a fast expanding economy.

There is evidence to support some linguistic exchanges between the Shang-Zhou civilisation and the ancient Vedic civilisation in 1500–1000 BC, even before the transmission of Buddhism.[1] There also exists some literature supporting the Sino–Indian interface in the Han dynasty (BC 206–AD 220). The interaction and communication between the two got further developed during the Tang (618–907), Song (960–1278) and the Yuan (1279–1368) dynasties. The great Indian epic, the *Mahabharata*, and the famous *Arthashastra* of ancient India contain references of China. The emperors, envoys, diplomats, scholars, monks, pilgrims and traders from ancient India and China have contributed enormously in bringing the two civilisations together. There is a plethora of such notable names in the ancient history. Nobel laureate Rabindranath Tagore visited China twice, in 1924 and in 1929. His constant striving for Indo–Chinese mutual understanding and collaboration in the fields of education, culture and institution building such as the creation of Cheena Bhawan (the Chinese Quarters) at his university Visva-Bharati in Santiniketan, West Bengal, is observed as one of the landmarks in the history of the cultural interface between the two nations.

The Sino-Indian relationship, however, has been undulating; it has gone through different phases during the last five decades or so, moving from deep hostility in the 1960s and 1970s to a rapprochement in the

1980s and a re-adjustment since the collapse of Soviet Union (Arif 2013, Bai Xianjing and Gao Jing 2006). The relationship improved much during the post-Cold War period. Gradually the two nations realised the need for cooperation in different domains with respect to the peace and economic prosperity at home and in Asia. Given the present scenario, the direction and depth of the relationship between the two countries is extremely important for the development of the Asian region as a whole.

In 2013, former prime minister of India Dr Manmohan Singh and Premier Li Keqiang of China declared 2014 as the Year of Friendly Exchanges between India and China and, hence, throughout 2014 various Indian festivals were organised across several cities of China. The festivals displayed Indian performing arts, exhibitions of modern Indian art and depictions of Buddhism links between the two countries. The visits of Chinese President Xi Jinping to India and that of Indian Prime Minister Narendra Modi to China have aimed at ramping up trade, investment and re-jigging lingering bordering issues, thereby cementing bilateral relations. India has also shown her willingness to join as a founding member of the new Beijing-backed Asian Infrastructure Investment Bank (AIIB).

The rise of China and India (Chindia) is likely to have enormous business implications. It will be mostly beneficial to the world, for example, advanced economies may enter the large consumer markets of the two countries through organised retailing and by investing in manufacturing (Sheth 2008). Also, China and India both are gradually becoming more integrated to the rest of the world and would reap the benefits of their endeavour.

With their fast expanding economy, the two nations are gradually becoming the manufacturing and service hubs of the world and are in need of a large amount of natural resources. In 2006, the leaders from African countries came to Beijing for a meeting, which was driven by the fact that China needed resources that Africa had in abundance whereas the latter could benefit itself by utilising the technical expertise of China. Indian and African nationals had also met, discussing mutual benefit during this period. In this way, Chindia has tried tapping the strengths of various other nations for their development. However, a closer look at the development process of the two countries reveals that they follow a different pattern. Interesting contrasts between the two growing countries received serious attention from scholars and leading research institutions across the world.

Given this background, there is a need to look into different aspects of the socio-cultural, political and economic relations of the two countries.

INTRODUCTION

The chapters of the book are based on a set of select research articles from research scholars and academicians from China as well as from India. The book aims at presenting a well-rounded perspective on various important cross-country issues and their implications for their respective economies. The book encompasses history, culture, political relations, economic perspectives and issues concerning both the countries. In order to have an in-depth understanding of the differences from various perspectives, the contribution of socio-cultural factors and the role of political and strategic relationships are incorporated. We have adopted a holistic approach in selecting the articles. The topics covered in the book are not confined to any specific area of research, rather the topics range from historical and cultural factors to the factors related to international relations and the current business strategies adopted by these two countries. The book is divided into two parts: Part I—History, Culture and International Relations and Part II—Economy and Business: Comparative Focus.

Part I of the book contains the chapters based on historical and cultural issues along with international relations concerning India and China. Chapter 1 primarily discusses the profound influence and contribution of the two ancient independent civilisations on the sustainable development of the Eurasian civilisation as a whole and explores how these cultural dissimilarities led to the functioning of these two economies in a different manner. In this attempt, a well-crafted comparative study of the influence of the Indus valley civilisation and the ancient Shu civilisation on sustainable development of economy and culture has been put forth. The chapter captures the comparable and the contrasting aspects of urban planning and social stratification structure that prevailed in the two ancient civilisations. How the cultural exchange from ancient times has gone through a transformation, thereby shaping the present relationship has also been explored in the chapter. This section also includes a chapter (Chapter 2) that shows that Shu merchants were the earliest merchants to enter India and were engaged in commercial activities from China. It has tried to trace the origin and the connotation of the two terms 'Seres' and 'Cina' in ancient India as there is a controversy over the topic and it has been debated through the ages. The chapter presents the concepts of 'Serindia' and 'Indochina' used to define the exchange and interaction between the Chinese and the Indian civilisations and delineates the role of the 'Silk Road' in western transmission of silk and communication between China, India and other Eurasian civilisations. These chapters are eloquent about the extensive cultural exchanges between Indus Valley and Shu civilisations along with the interaction the two had with other ancient civilisations.

The cultural differences between China and India are reflected in their ethical behaviour and religion, and have implications for another form of cultural exchange, that is, tourism. Tourism faces both positive and negative impact of cultural differences. Chapter 3 suggests that the two nations have to know, understand and respect each other's culture and carry out cultural exchange in order to enhance bilateral tourism cooperation. As far as the cultural aspect is concerned, Chapter 4 focuses on insights available from the life and work of Rabindranath Tagore, the Nobel Laureate poet from India, with special attention to his constant striving for Indo-Chinese mutual understanding and collaboration in the fields of education, culture and institution building. The section possibly would not have been comprehensive without a discussion from this aspect. The chapter also throws light on transcendental leadership, as explained by Tagore, to combat hours of crises at an inspirational level. On a more functional plane, the chapter offers alternate models of leadership, innovation and community development for modern organisations seriously engaged in initiatives on leadership excellence, corporate social responsibility and human development based on Tagore's philosophy and wisdom. The chapter commemorates Tagore's unique role in highlighting the historical contribution of the Chinese and Indian civilisations and in exhorting the two modern nations to revitalise that noble cause and create a rich terrain to act as a foundation for assuming leadership roles on the global platform. Tagore had extolled the Chinese culture through his lectures in China, and the Cheena Bhavan in Visva-Bharati was created to strengthen the Indo–China relationship for the future and raise the Asian voice against the aggressive capitalist forces of the West.

Chapter 5 provides the historical perspective of the spread of religious culture specifically in the 15th century. In addition to the governmental exchanges based on tributary trades, there were also two folk forces which acted as the messengers for cultural exchanges between China and India, that is, the 'western monks' and merchants. The communication between China and India and the spread of religious culture in the 15th century could be referred to as a turning point in Sino–Indian relations as they brought about significant cultural changes. The author mentions that although these exchanges, both in national and civilian dimensions, were not very successful, they injected fresh blood into the nations. Both the countries derived a variety of cultural attributes that in turn helped in enriching the patterns of manifestation and spiritual connotation of the cultures. More importantly, the lessons learnt from these early interactions provided beneficial reference for Sino-Indian exchanges in the contemporary world.

INTRODUCTION

A discourse on India's effort in recent times to improve its cultural soft power by spreading its culture and values to the world, which is of great significance to China, has been presented in Chapter 6. As the cultural industry is an important carrier of communication, the Indian government attaches much importance to the industrialisation of cultural products so that they can be made uniquely charming and easily recognised. However, China suffers from severe backwardness in terms of its cultural industry and the industry has a low impact overseas; which does not match with China's population, resources and economic development level. Hence, certain strategies have been put forth which can assist China to strengthen the production of cultural products in the nation and promote its cultural soft power.

This section gradually shifts its focus towards the international relations and political scenario in the neighbouring countries in relation to the two emerging superpowers—China and India. A nation's international relations play a significant role in driving the development process of its economy. In particular, this section incorporates three chapters attempting to discuss the significance of international relationships India and China have with Pakistan and Afghanistan presently, and its impact on the functioning of the respective countries. It has highlighted the re-orientation of Sino-Indian relationship in the context of the Bangladesh China India Myanmar-Economic Corridor (BCIM-EC) and the US 'Pivot to Asia' strategy.

First, a vivid account on the background, and the possible impact of the BCIM economic corridor as an intriguing topic of discourse in recent times has been presented. The corridor aims to solve various critical issues such as trade imbalance between China and India as well as the security problems of the area covered by the same. It will help in the advancement of China's open strategy for the southwest while benefiting the East Policy of India. Second, there is a focus on the USA implementing its 'Pivot to Asia' strategy that attempts to seize the benefits of Asia's economic growth by sowing discords and divisions among Asian countries. Chapter 8 reflects that in this background, China will try to align its relation with Pakistan to China's national strategy and the interests of Asia as a whole and this re-orientation of the China–Pakistan relationship is often interpreted as a threat by India, giving rise to certain destabilising factors to the regional security. Third, there is a narrative of the opportunities and the challenges involved in Sino–India cooperation in Afghanistan because of the country's unique geographical location and the fact that it is connected to Central Asia, West Asia and South Asia.

Part II of the manuscript records the economic and business-related issues across these two nations. Apart from cultural and religious exchanges as put forth in the previous section, economic exchange between the two nations since time immemorial has also played a significant role in their development process. The chapters in this section discuss the following important issues.

First, Chapter 10 sheds light on how China and India have responded differently to globalisation. It tries to map the discourses woven into the politics of self-representation that India and China's responses show up, which can explain to a great extent how their foundational choices have been different and have made them alter egos of one another. Globalisation has unleashed multiple flows: from West to non-West, from non-West to West and within non-Western nations themselves and Chinese success in lifting itself up by its own bootstraps in the past few decades has been inspirational to India and has also influenced its political and economic landscapes, despite the existence of border disputes and a tense political relationship between them. Next, the part includes a chapter (Chapter 11) that has delved into the regional inequality issue in the two nations over the post-liberalisation era. While China has adopted economic reforms in terms of liberalisation, pragmatisation, marketisation and corporatisation since 1978, the process of liberalisation, privatisation and globalisation commenced in India in 1991. The study mentions that trade liberalisation and liberalisation of financial sector along with excessive focus on reduction in fiscal deficit are primarily responsible for the increase in regional inequality in India over the period of globalisation. On the other hand, the factors which primarily explain the regional inequality in China are fiscal decentralisation, inflow of foreign direct investment, development and openness of financial sector. The preferential government policies and change in the allocation of factors of production have also led to regional imbalance in China. The primary focus of this chapter is to show that variation across different regions of the country changed in response to globalisation with the indication that China has been able to reap more benefit from globalisation and liberalisation as compared to India. The chapter examines the issue of divergence/convergence across regions within China and India based on select macroeconomic variables. Moreover, what role infrastructure development plays is also investigated, especially in the case of those states which fail to extract maximum benefit from globalisation. In particular, the chapter looks at whether favourable geographical location, better infrastructure development and appropriate

INTRODUCTION

implementation policies at the state level led to higher income during the post-globalisation period in China and India in the recent past.

Second, in the present scenario, a major challenge before Indian economy is to restructure the manufacturing sector of the country, while an explosive growth of Chinese economy is primarily led by a strong manufacturing base. Manufacturing plays a vital role in a nation's economy and is invariably a focal point of value creation for society, as the sector creates jobs and produces goods. Chapter 12 attempts to provide an understanding of the manufacturing strategies adopted by China that have led to explosive growth and cross compare the policies with regard to India. The chapter puts forth that the inherent strengths have assisted India to be a services destination primarily, while China has become a primarily manufacturing base on the global platform. While China seems to be making good progress towards services as apparent from R&D and banking centres that have developed in the Yangtze River Delta (YRD) region, especially; India on the other hand does not seem to be making very significant progress in manufacturing in spite of efforts being made in the last few years. Again, although China has done well with regard to skill building and promotion of business environment through special economic zones (SEZs), the quality factor has slightly been the flip side of manufactured items from China. Over the years, as in other economies of the world, there have been shifts in competencies in the Indian manufacturing industry. However, many issues need to be taken care of and there are obvious possible ways by which India and China could create a rich symbiotic ecosystem.

Third, another chapter (Chapter 13) provides an interesting evaluation of the position of India in relation to China and other emerging Asian economies in terms of the corporate social responsibility practices followed by corporates. It makes an attempt to find out the status of corporate social responsibility (CSR) activities, regulations and performance of Asian emerging countries. An analysis of the listed Indian companies at the Bombay Stock Exchange (BSE) during 2012–13 along with a comparison of CSR activities among the Asian countries on the basis of ASR reports are done in order to find out the possible implications of the newly laid down principles for CSR provisions under the new Companies Act, 2013. The study has observed that India has outperformed China and other developing economies in CSR contributions and activities in recent times.

Finally, the manuscript contains two chapters (Chapters 14 and 15) comparing various important issues across India and China. The chapters in this part describe how the health sectors of both the countries have performed over the years and how the linkage between social responsibility strategies and firm performances differ across these two countries. To understand the functioning of the health system of these two countries, Chapter 14 focusing on health explores the historical, social and political developments which have shaped the current status, while Chapter 15 reaches a number of significant conclusions based on case studies of Indian and Chinese companies in the context of CSR—a prominent topic of discourse in recent times.

Both China and India face similar challenges that put a massive burden on their health delivery system, especially in terms of meeting the demands of a rapidly growing population. The growth in income, too, has been instrumental in creating a high consumer expectation and a demand for high-quality health care service. Still, there is a widening gap between the rich and the poor and the urban and rural populations of both countries. The final chapter examines explicit CSR strategies followed by corporations in developed economies, as disclosed in annual reports, and compares it with those followed by China and India. The study explores the relationship between CSR strategies and firm performance.

The book has, thus, attempted to present the issues and perspectives of the Sino-Indian relations and cultural exchanges as well as its sociopolitical and economic evolution and development through the history. It also documents their influence on other civilisations. In the contemporary world, both the nations have realised the need for cooperation in various domains to achieve sustainability and prosperity. The book will take the reader on a journey through history, culture, economic, social and political aspects of the exchanges between China and India from the past to the present. The chapters are based on the views and opinions of respective authors. These do not represent the opinions of the editors or the organisations they are in.

Note

1. Embassy of the People's Republic of China in India http://www.indianembassy.org.cn/DynamicContent.aspx?MenuId=4&SubMenuId=0 (accessed on 11 May 2016).

References

Arif, Sheikh Mohd. 2013. 'A History of Sino-Indian Relations: From Conflict to Cooperation'. *International Journal of Political Science and Development*.
Sheth, Jagdish. 2008. *Chindia Rising: How China and India Will Benefit Your Business*. Tata McGraw-Hill.

PART I

History, Culture and International Relations

PART 1

1

Indus Civilisation and Ancient Shu Civilisation

A Comparative Study

Zou Yiqing

Introduction

The Indus valley civilisation is a native civilisation of the subcontinent of South Asia and is one of the world's most famous ancient civilisations. About 700,000 years ago, the Indus valley lying to the northwest of the Indian subcontinent had human settlements. Around 7000 BC, the Indus River valley entered the Neolithic Age. Indus valley appeared to be very prosperous with small towns. Many parts of the cities were constructed with solid mud bricks. People began to domesticate animals and cultivate crops. Around 2600 BC, the Indus valley civilisation gradually reached its peak. On the land region of 1,300,000 sq. km of the Indus River basin appeared thousands of large and small cities and villages. One of the main centres of civilisation was called Harappa. Therefore, the academic circles gave another name to the Indus valley civilisation—the Harappan civilisation.

The most notable feature of the Indus valley civilisation is the development of the urban civilisation. The construction of the cities of Mohenjo-daro and Harappa was the most outstanding representation of the urban civilisation of the region. The cities were characterised by neat and sturdy brick houses, water supply, drainage system, prosperous commercial trade and an industry of exquisite handicraft products. Around 1900 BC, the Indus valley civilisation began to decline and it disappeared at about 1750 BC.

The ancient Shu civilisation is one of the important components of the history of Chinese civilisation's diversified development pattern. The ancient Shu civilisation developed on the Sichuan basin in Southwest China with the Chengdu plain as the focus. Archaeological data shows that, in the early Pleistocene, the Sichuan basin had human activities. Around 6000 BC, the centre of the ancient Shu of the Chengdu plain region had entered the Neolithic or the New Stone Age and the formation of the early farming communities had started. Around 2000 BC, the ancient Shu region witnessed the threshold of the civilisation and the birth of the Sanxingdui civilisation. The ancient Shu civilisation with brilliant bronze culture became eye-catching. The urban civilisation reached a considerable height and there was emergence of the hierarchical system of the cities. The ancient Shu capital of Sanxingdui and the industrial and commercial centres of Chengdu are typical representations of the highly developed ancient Shu civilisation. Qin defeated and conquered Shu in 316 BC. Subsequently, the ancient Shu civilisation gradually underwent transformation by the Han culture and finally progressed into the Chinese civilisation seen by us today.

The Indus valley and the ancient Shu civilisations are two ancient civilisations that developed independently. They played an important role in the ancient Eurasian civilisation. But these two civilisations were far apart from each other. Their formation and timing were different and characteristics also varied. But they had certain characteristics in common, for example, their economies, which were based on farming, developed in ancient times and they had built the world's oldest artificial irrigation system. Numerous and glorious cities were also another important characteristic of both. They had cultural exchange and mutual influence with wide influence on other civilisations as well. A comparative study of the Indus valley and the ancient Shu civilisations will help us to deepen our understanding of the connotation of ancient civilisation and understand the profound influence of the ancient civilisations on the sustainable development of economy and culture.

Here, a comparison is carried out between these two ancient civilisations from three perspectives: the water conservancy projects, city construction and international cultural exchanges during that period. In the next sections, these are discussed in detail.

A Comparison of Water Conservancy Projects

Both Indus valley and the ancient Shu civilisations built large water conservancy projects representing the infrastructure of a civilised society and supported the development of agricultural economy and the economic prosperity of the city.

Indus River basin terrain is high in the northwest and low in the southeast because of which the river flows from north to south. The Indus River basin also has high temperature in the plains of the south because of its sub-tropical location whereas cold air blows on the north due to the presence of the Himalayan Range. The southwest monsoon winds from the Indian Ocean brings abundant rainfall annually for about 6–10 months. There is dry weather and low rainfall at other times of the year. Because of high temperature and rainfall being too concentrated, crops do not get enough water during the dry season. During the rainy season, floods occur often and farmlands are destroyed. Moreover, the arrival and the strength of the monsoon have a significant impact on the Indus River plain agriculture. Therefore, the construction of water conservancy projects and artificial irrigation and drainage system is a very important thing for the agricultural production.

Irrigation canals appeared on the Indus river plain at around 4000 BC Around 2600 BC, the peak of the Indus valley civilisation, the construction of water conservancy projects reached a higher level. Water conservancy projects were mainly for agricultural irrigation and construction of city water supply and the drainage network especially in the cities was outstanding.

Archaeological data shows that there is a lack of documentation of water conservancy projects for agricultural irrigation. Engineering practices focused on the construction of irrigation canals, high dams, reservoirs for water storage and flood control. Irrigation and water conservancy constructions guaranteed the development of agriculture which was the basis of the Indus valley civilisation. The highest achievements of Indus valley civilisation were the construction of water conservancy projects, city water supply and drainage system.

The two major cities of the Indus valley civilisation were Mohenjo-daro and Harappa. They built the world's most advanced city water supply and drainage system. City water supply used to come from two sources—(a) by constructing a drainage channel from the river, not far from the city and (b) by digging wells in the city. In Mohenjo-daro, there were many wells on the streets and in the houses. About more than 600 tube wells were found at the sites. These wells were innovative, made of bricks and were constructed for the supply of water. The shape of these wells was beneficial as it prevented deep underground side pressure (Brown 2002, 40–44). The city had a network of wells to provide clean drinking water to every street. The city also built a wide network of drains to facilitate every family. Many families built bath and toilets; drainage of which relied on the outside wall where the waste and the water passed through a chute into the streets' drains. The drainage system of every street was interlinked and the same was divided into broad and narrow branches. Drainage ditches were laid with bricks with many filtering facilities in order to prevent the inflow of dust. Drainage ditches with polished edges were built as an arc around the corner of the houses to prevent blockage. Some drains away from the streets were exposed in the open air but mostly drains were built underground on both sides of the streets. Others were not only built underground but were large enough to hold people moving around freely inside to facilitate their maintenance. The drains sloped from high to low and were finally sluiced directly into streams in the lower reaches of the river. The elaborate design and perfect thoughtful plotting of this city's drainage network system was rare in the early civilisations of the world.

Archaeologists at Mohenjo-daro found a structure known as 'the big bath' which is a bathing pool, a feature unique in ancient Indian buildings. It is a huge pool measuring 12 m in length, 7 m in width and 2.5 m in depth that was surrounded by long corridors and rooms (Bai Xianjing and Gao Jing 2006, 16–17). The pool had a daub of thick asphalt and had been built with bricks (fired carved brick). The bricks of the pool were held tight; the joints were only a few millimetres thick to prevent leakage. The big bath was built with wells and drainage ditches all around, which were the components of the city water supply and drainage system. Scholars think that the big bath was used as a public bath by the citizens. It not only reflects the superb artistry of the Harappan people regarding water conservancy construction but also provides evidence that they led a luxurious lifestyle and water was considered to be a precious element. Some other scholars think that the big bath was not only used for daily bath but it might have contained a religious connotation and have been used for holy worship in the water. This might have been the beginning of India's religion worship culture while taking a bath.

The large scale water conservancy project on the Chengdu plain is an outstanding representation of water conservancy by the ancient Shu civilisation. It is the highest achievement of governance in controlling floods.

The downstream of the Chengdu plain often suffered from floods. The Minjiang River swelled when the snow melted on the Minshan Mountain in the summer and autumn, causing massive flooding. It flooded villages and fields on the Chengdu plain. The remains at the archaeological sites of the Chengdu plain provide evidence of the cities and townships damaged or destroyed by flood and even rebuilt/scoured repeatedly (Brown 2002, Duan Yu 2001b, 30). The Chengdu plain's water conservancy project was mainly constructed for flood control and irrigation.

King Yu combated flood with the first large-scale water conservancy project in ancient Shu. It consisted of artificial channels and reservoir—river water from the Minjiang flowed towards the east into the Xunian River, the Pi River, the Jintang gorge and then southward into the Tuojiang River and Yangtze River in Luzhou city (Duan Yu 2001b, 45–47). The channels delivered river water and helped in farmland irrigation as well.

In the Xia and Shang dynasties, the Chengdu plain entered the civilised age based on agricultural development. There was emergence of the handicraft industry in the cities along with the extensive use of bronze items, which greatly promoted the development of agricultural production and irrigation system. The ancient Shu had been carrying out water conservancy work on a large scale during the Spring and Autumn and the Warring States Period. Yulei Mountain originally blocked the river and water could not flow eastward. So the plain had no access to river irrigation and agricultural development in the region was seriously affected. King Kaiming cut the Yulei Mountain, dug a river and created an artificial channel. Thus an artificial river was made. The upper reaches of the Minjiang River flowed into the river below which helped in drainage and irrigation. This was the history of how the ancient Shu people fought against flood, harnessed flood water and developed irrigation facilities to live and work in peace.

Kaiming, the king of the ancient Shu state, who moved the capital to Chengdu, was known for his flood control measures. He harnessed rivers and lakes and undertook the construction of a series of water conservancy projects in Chengdu. Archaeologists found a number of Eastern Zhou period's artificial pebbles on Fangchi street, which was the site for water conservancy project in Chengdu (Duan Yu 2001a).

Development of the irrigation system in the Chengdu plain progressed from simple to complex when the Shang and Zhou dynasties were ruling. The Kaiming dynasty's irrigation system was mainly composed of artificial rivers (Jiang), ponds, dams and channels. Engineering technology used wooden tripod dam, bamboo gabion, bamboo sediment baskets, piles engineering and masonry pebble. Irrigation system played the dual function of drainage and irrigation.

The irrigation system of the ancient Shu kingdom aimed at lesser threat from the floods and proper release of flood waters. King Kaiming's decision to cut Yulei Mountain resembled Shu governor Li Bing's idea to construct the Dujiangyan irrigation project in the time of the Qin dynasty. This project represented his rich experience and advanced technology used in the construction and there was not any ancient Shu person with such knowledge for thousands of years.

Through a comparative study between the Indus valley and the ancient Shu civilisations regarding the construction of water conservancy projects, we can find that the city water supply and construction of the drainage network system achieved high levels in the Indus valley civilisation. The ancient Shu civilisation, as the centre for construction of water conservancy projects, controlled river water from overflowing and also made great achievements in water conservancy. The Indus valley civilisation had the world's most complete city water supply and drainage system. The method of construction of cities thus followed became one of the most essential features of the urban civilisation. The ancient Shu civilisation harnessed rivers for water conservancy projects that not only controlled the Chengdu plain floods but also helped in farmland irrigation. From then on, people could control the floods and droughts on the Chengdu plain. It laid the groundwork for 'the land of abundance'.

The drainage system in the cities of the Indus valley civilisation was constructed using fired plain brick or carved brick and waterproof material such as asphalt. Bricks were produced in a sophisticated manner and at many places traces of polished bricks were found. The barrier walls of the wells were laid with fired bricks shaped in a way to give a circular shape. These techniques portrayed the excellent skills of the builders. The construction of the water conservancy projects of ancient Shu was also extraordinary. Its three functions were: releasing flood waters, flushing and irrigation. The project displayed the conception, grand precision, designing and construction capability of the builders.

A Comparison of City Construction

Urban civilisation was the most significant symbol of the Indus valley civilisation. The two outstanding representative cities of the Indus valley civilisation were Mohenjo-daro and Harappa.

Mohenjo-daro was located on the right bank of the Indus River. The city was formed around 2600 BC and was 320 km away from the Arabian Sea which lies in the south. The Mohenjo-daro site had an area of 7.68 sq. km in total with an estimate of the entire population being 35,000. The city was divided into two parts—uptown (also known as Castle) and low town. The low town was the main part of the city. It included commercial and residential areas where the merchants, craftsmen and civilians lived. Uptown was a small castle. It was built with soil on a 9.15 m high platform. The castle included a tower, a corridor of the palace, a hall with many pillars and a large bath as previously mentioned. Religious and secular rulers lived in the castle (Bai Xianjing and Gao Jing 2006, 22–23).

Mohenjo-daro as a city was nicely planned and designed. It possessed a proper layout of city streets and buildings. The city was surrounded by walls. The city looked like a rectangular grid and had big roads which ran north to south through the city. There were streets that ran from east to west intersecting one another at right angles every 200 yards. It consisted of a chessboard block. There were many alleys in the city. The streets were lined with courtyard buildings and bungalows (Brown 2002, 5). There were water supply wells and a sewerage system. The city had a large warehouse for grain storage with upper and lower ventilation ducts. The city walls and buildings of the Indus valley civilisation were mostly made of bricks (mud brick and baked brick).

Mohenjo-daro and Harappa are very similar in terms of the design of the cities. Not only that, design of other cities of the Indus valley civilisation also has a surprising similarity which showed that they belonged to the same type of culture. Archaeological data of the Indus valley civilisation shows a nice building with two floors which had a bath upstairs and a sewer passing out of the room. In contrast, there was no such bathing and drainage setup or equipment in the small houses. It showed a clear demarcation between the rich and the poor in the Indus valley civilisation and hence it had entered a stage of development of social stratification.

In the vast region of the Indus valley civilisation, the economic and cultural outlook of every city was the same or similar irrespective of whether they were near or far. Though the two cities of Mohenjo-daro and Harappa were 400 km apart, they were similar. There was also no difference in social stratification, the act of one's own free will, independence and so on. They showed some characteristics of the chiefdom society (Lin Chengjie 2004, 16).

The earliest city of the ancient Shu area came into existence on the Chengdu plain. At the end of the Neolithic Age, a number of towns were formed on the Chengdu plain. In the Bronze Age, the ancient Shu civilisation was born. Sanxingdui was the centre and Chengdu, the sub-centre for the early city system.

Sanxingdui was located on the Chengdu plain on the banks of the Yazihe River in Guanghan, Sichuan. The city was formed in 2000 BC and was the capital of the ancient Shu kingdom in the Yufu dynasty. Sanxingdui was built with tall and thick adobe walls. The city was big and populous. It had a total area of 3.6 sq. km, about 22,000 households and around 110,000 people (Duan Yu 2009). Archaeological sites show there were functional zones. In the city's central axis, there were the Shu kingdom's palace and the workshop area, with residential area on both sides.

The ancient city of Sanxingdui had high and thick walls which reflected the existence of sufficient labour resources for disposal and collection of the building materials. The palace in the city supported a huge population and was rich in natural resources, production resources and wealth of the community. It means that the complex society was formed within the vast city circle. It also shows that the way of life had been different from the prehistoric chiefdom system which was characterised by social organisation, centralisation of authority or a social control system. A centralised government organisation was formed through which various kinds of labour related to production as well as non-production specialised personnel (such as craftsmen, sculptors, architects, businessmen and so on) were managed.

When the Sanxingdui sites were excavated, a living area was unearthed with a large number of pottery, wine containers and food. Housing ruins showed that civilians lived in small wooden or mud houses whereas dignitaries lived in bucket structured big sheds with halls and lifting beams. This put forth the fact of profound class differentiation in the society. The living area consisted of criss-cross drainage channel. A large number of craft pottery products were unearthed. A stone slave with his hands bound behind his back was also found but no agricultural production tools were found. In contrast, the mass production tools and workshop site area showed that the builder groups were partitioned in accordance to the owner being honourable or humble, which depicted an early functional partitioning. In contrast to a simple tomb where funerary objects were found, a lot of gold, copper and jade was buried in the sacrificial pits. High walls and deep trenches were the symbols of class conflict. The early writings also put forth a distinction on the basis of physical and mental attributes of the labour groups. There was also evidence of the formation of the urban–rural continuum. The scale of convergence of various production resources and social wealth show that the social control system of the city was much superior to the society in general. The sites portrayed theocratic monarchy.

Large-scale population, large number of producers, centralised surplus wealth, establishment of business relations, development of long distance trade, formation of complex social stratification and classes in society and strengthening of theocratic kingship were the main characteristics of an early city. From the point of view of economic progress, the ancient city of Sanxingdui showed some significant characteristics such as the growth of different industries and centres. It displayed the characteristics of a typical urban centre of the ancient times (Duan Yu 2001a).

Early Chengdu, developed after the Sanxingdui city, was a city of considerable size and an important centre of ancient Shu culture during the Shang dynasty. Early Chengdu stretched along the Pijiang River from the arc area of the north to the south which was wide, continuous and distributed over more than 10 km (Luo Kaiyu 1989, Wang Yi 1988). Chengdu had 55,000 households and the total population of 280,000 during the Eastern Zhou period. A large wooden building of a total area of 15,000 sq. km was unearthed which had a veranda gallery. Bronze ware and jade from the Shang dynasty and the Spring and Autumn Period were also unearthed from the site. Ancient Shu words engraved on a pottery wheel of the Shang dynasty was also found here.

Sanxingdui and Chengdu form the earliest city system in the ancient Shu civilisation of the Chengdu plain, with the former lying to the north of the latter. The ancient city of Sanxingdui displayed characteristics of a strong centre of theocracy. Theocracy played an important role in the formation of city with political institutions and social organisations. The early development of Chengdu was different from Sanxingdui. The right of kings was by far the most important factor in the city formation process. Chengdu was further developed in the Shang dynasty and it eventually became an open industrial and commercial city, that is, there was freedom of trade in the ancient city (Duan Yu 2012).

When the Indus valley civilisation and the ancient Shu civilisation are compared with respect to the city construction, it is observed that they had good planning and design along with reasonable layout and a proper foundation to support a large population. The Indus valley civilisation was characterised by a chiefdom form of a society and was mainly urban, but the ancient Shu civilisation was national in character. The chiefdom system was characterised by the same kind of city construction planning and the type of culture across cities. City functioning did not distinguish among the cities and the competition among the cities became fiercer and had the potential to spark the outbreak of armed conflict easily. But in the Shu civilisation, there were functional and rank differences among cities and so they were complementary to each other, and it was difficult to have the intense conflict between them. Sanxingdui was the capital of the ancient Shu civilisation and the political centre of the ancient Shu kingdom with tall walls and neat planning and construction. However the city of Chengdu that ranked below Sanxingdui did not possess city walls and clear boundaries and focused mostly on industrial and commercial activities.

A Comparison of International Cultural Exchanges

The Indus valley civilisation and the ancient Shu civilisation displayed openness in culture. They showed complex civilisation features. Many seals from Mesopotamia were unearthed from the sites of the Indus valley civilisation. Similarly, in Mesopotamia many seals from the Indus valley civilisation were also unearthed. This fully reflects the frequent interactions in terms of trade between the two regions. In Mesopotamia, clay tablets with records of merchandise trade between Mesopotamia and ancient India in cuneiform were found at around 2350 BC. Ancient Indian sale of goods included rare wood, wood inlaid table, ivory comb, lapis, pearl, cornelian (Brown 2002, 23). High-quality gold, silver and bronze wares were found at the sites of the Indus valley civilisation. Cotton was native to Indus valley civilisation and archaeologists found many cotton mills, printing and dyeing workshops. It should have been the main trade in goods. Mesopotamia exported wool, cloth, clothing, leather products, oil and cypress to the Indus valley (Brown 2002, 24).

Besides Mesopotamia, the cities of the Indus valley civilisation also used to promote foreign trade to Iran, Central Asia, Afghanistan and China. Archaeological research shows the presence of ivories, seashells, bronze swords and so on in Southwest China, which depicts its interaction with the Indus valley civilisation (Duan Yu 2014).

The Indus valley civilisation had economic and trade exchanges with many regions but its relationship with the Mesopotamian civilisation appears more 'close'. The Indus valley civilisation showed some features similar to Mesopotamia. With respect to religious culture, the Harappan people worshipped a fertility goddess, a buxom mother goddess and the goddess of girls and so on, and seals were also found that resembled the culture in Mesopotamia (Brown 2002, 27). The people linked their families back to heavenly objects such as the sun, the moon and the stars. This reflects that there were long-term close cultural exchanges and interaction between the Indus valley civilisation and the Mesopotamian civilisation.

The ancient Shu civilisation was born and developed in southwest China. It not only maintained close ties with the Central Plains civilisation, but also carried out extensive economic and cultural exchanges with South Asia, Southeast Asia and West Asia through the Southern Silk Road.

Oracle bone inscription recorded the mutual influence of the Central Plains civilisation and the ancient Shu civilisation. The interaction between the two is also reflected by the bronze culture. In Sanxingdui, bronze statues, an ampulla and several bronze dragons resembling the Central Plains' dragon image were unearthed. The triangular, bronze dagger-axe of the Central Plains culture that originated in Sichuan was later found among the Yin dynasty ruins. A bronze, willow leaf-shaped sword spread from Sichuan to southern Shanxi provinces and Gansu provinces. The kettle and Zeng of the Shu culture was first found north of Qin and later spread to other areas.

China and Southeast Asia had frequent cultural exchanges since ancient times. China often occupied the leading position in exchange with Southeast Asia. Several cultural factors and customs of ancient Southeast Asia such as corn planting, boat-coffin burial and sarcophagus burial included in the funeral customs as well as the stone cultural relics and bronze items bear evidence of those being derived from ancient Shu. The most high-profile historic event was the migration of An Dương Vương to south and the establishment of the dynasty in northern Vietnam which helped in spreading Shu culture to Southeast Asia. During 4th century BC, Qin defeated the ancient Shu kingdom. A group of about 60,000 people led by An Dương Vương migrated to the Red River area (Vietnam) through the Southern Silk Road. An Dương Vương established the dynasty that lasted for 130 years in Jiaozhi.

There was already a road between the ancient Shu civilisation and the South Asian subcontinent. This route was the main channel of all the economic and cultural exchanges or communication, starting from Sichuan to Yunnan via Burma to India or Pakistan, and was called the

'Shu-Hindu Road'. The route was preliminarily formed in the Shang dynasty and played a big role in the Warring States era.

A large number of toothed shells were found in Sanxingdui, which is located in an inland basin. Those must have been imported from the northern area of Indian Ocean. A large quantity of ivory which had been brought from India was also unearthed from Sanxingdui sites and Chengdu Jinsha sites. India is the native place for the elephants. The ruins of the sites at Mohenjo-daro revealed that ivory manufacture was once prosperous. This reveals the connection of Sanxingdui sites with India, where many elephants were found. Even thousands of sea shells found in sacrifice pit in Sanxingdui provide evidence of being imported from the northern part of the Indian Ocean.

The most famous commodity of export in the ancient Shu civilisation was Shu cloth and Qiong bamboo sticks that were dispatched to South Asia. The ancient Indian book *Arthashastra* written in the 4th century BC mentions that the silk fabric of ancient Shu became very popular in India. It indicates that the Shu people had frequent economic and trade exchanges with India during the Warring States period. There is a good reason and data to believe that in ancient times China was called 'Cina', which was the name used for 'Chengdu' in ancient India.

Culture exchanges were reflected from the archaeological data between the ancient Shu civilisation and the early civilisations of West Asia and the near East. Archaeological data showed that Mesopotamia created a bronze statue depicting the cultural tradition at the beginning of the year 3000 BC. In Egypt, a whole body bronze statue was unearthed in 2900 BC. A bronze statue of a man was unearthed in the Indus valley civilisation in 2000 BC. In Sanxingdui, golden sceptres, golden masks, bronze statues, bronze heads, bronze masks and bronze animal masks resembling the features of the early civilisations of West Asia and the near East were unearthed.

From the extensive study of the cultural exchanges of the ancient Shu civilisation and the Indus valley civilisation, it is not difficult to infer that both the Indus valley civilisation and the ancient Shu civilisation had extensive cultural exchanges with other civilisations. They not only absorbed the cultural factors of other regions but also spread their own culture to those areas. However, the Indus valley civilisation and Western civilisation had more obvious interactions owing to various reasons like the geographical location, transmission lines and economic and trade activities. The ancient Shu civilisation had more in-depth and lasting cultural exchanges with the surrounding areas and was especially greatly influenced by the Central Plain's culture. This pattern of mutual influence has been there since the Neolithic Age. The ancient Shu civilisation gradually transformed into the Qin, Han civilisations which further culminated into the modern Chinese civilisation. The ancient Shu civilisation spread the Chinese civilisation to Southeast Asia, South Asia, Central Asia, West Asia and the Mediterranean region through the Southern Silk Road, which not only made outstanding contribution in the transmission of Chinese civilisation, but also showed the important position of the ancient Shu civilisation in the ancient Eurasian civilisation.

Although, as individual civilisations, the ancient Indus valley civilisation and Shu civilisation have disappeared in the long river of history, but their essence has not disappeared. The features of Indus valley civilisation were inherited by the Indian civilisation in its later phases while the Chinese civilisation has inherited its cultural core from the ancient Shu civilisation.

References

Brown, Dale. 2002. *Ancient India: Land of Mystery.* Trans. Li Xu. Beijing: Huaxia Publishing House.
Bai Xianjing and Gao Jing. 2006. *The Mystery of the Subcontinent in the South Asian.* Beijing: Haichao Publishing House.
Duan Yu. 2001a. *The History of Ba-Shu Culture.* Chengdu: Sichuan People's Publishing House.
———. 2001b. *The Kingdom of Ancient Shu.* Chengdu: Sichuan People's Publishing House.
———. 2014. 'The Southern Silk Road and Traffic of the Ancient China and the Western'. Academic report presented at the Taihu Forum Conference, Paris.
Lin Chengjie. 2004. *The History of India.* Beijing: The People's Publishing House.
Wang Yi. 1988. 'The Discovery and Significance of Shu Culture Ruins in Chengdu'. *Chengdu Cultural Relics* 1.

2

Unfolding the Westerly Transmission of Chinese Silk*

Duan Yu

The Connotation of 'Cina'

'Cina', the term used to mention China in ancient India, finds its earliest reference in the Sanskrit writings of the 4th century BC or even earlier. In the past, people usually thought that the word Cina refers to Qin or Chu and few people associated it with Chengdu.

Cina considered as Qin or Chu does not have any reliable material as the basis. Previously, the French Sinologist Paul Pelliot (1962) thought that Qin Shihuang established the Qin dynasty which was called Cina by India. The Qin dynasty was founded in 221 BC, but the name Cina appeared as early as in 4th century BC in India. Hence the statement by Pelliot cannot be established. Some scholars think that Cina is the name used in India for the Spring and Autumn Period of the Qin dynasty. However, in the Spring and Autumn Period, Qin had no control of Longxi and ethnic minorities in Beidi. Qin Mugong had occupied 12 states, but the occupied area was only 300 miles. Moreover, many ethnic

---

* This chapter is based on the paper which is one of the stage achievements of the Chinese National Social Science Fund Project 'the Southern Silk Road and the Eurasian Civilization' (10&ZD087).

minorities surrounded Qin from the west, north and east, blocking Qin to move to north or west. Qin did not move west into the ethnic minorities' areas. Then how did its reputation spread far and wide to the western world? Qin eventually occupied northwest China at the beginning of the 3rd century BC. However, the word Cina had already appeared in India then. Obviously, the origin of the name of Cina has nothing to do with Qin. As for the identity of Cina as Jing, it is difficult to establish because the foundation is not reliable.

The ancient Shu culture had a long-term and profound influence on Nanzhong regions during the Shang dynasty. India did commodity trading, using seashell money as a medium and other cultural exchanges in the Sanxingdui culture period. It provided the conditions that helped in spreading the name of the ancient Shu throughout India. According to the *Historical Records* and *Han Shu* records, Shu merchants arrived in Yunnan at a very early stage and then got engaged in trade in Dianyue, and sold Shu goods such as Shu silk and Qiong bamboo stick to the Hindus. Dianyue is the present Assam region in East India (Wen Jiang 1980). Hindu means India. The ancient Indian book *Arthashastra* written in 4th century BC mentioned that silk fabric of ancient Shu became the bestselling item in India. It mentions that silk and woven leather belts were Shu's specialties. *Historical Records* put forth that Zhang Qian saw Shu silk and Qiong bamboo stick in Afghanistan, which procured that through its trade with India with the help of local businessmen in the Wudi period. The *Historical Records* is consistent with *Arthashastra*. Zhang Qian saw Shu goods such as Shu silk and Qiong bamboo sticks in Central Asia as the only Chinese goods. This reflects the Shu merchants' frequent trade activities in India during the Warring States period. Data also reflects the continuity of the Sanxingdui and Indian cultural exchange during the Shang dynasty. India has a better understanding of ancient Shu than any other Chinese region due to the long-term exchanges.

The name 'Chengdu', conceived very early, has been recorded in *Shanhaijing*. Lacquer engraved with the 'Made in Cheng' (Made in Chengdu) imprint stamp was found in Zeng Jia Gou, Yingjing, Sichuan in the Spring and Autumn Period. The word 'Cheng' was used by scholars in the past to restore its ancient sound. It means that the final is Geng and the initial is Chan. However, based on the southern dialect pronunciation, its final should be Zhen and its initial should be Chan. The pronunciation is just 'Zhi'. According to the double syllable as per the western language, the pronunciation is Cina. It shows that Cina is actually the Chengdu.

Cina in Sanskrit would have got similar words in ancient Iran, Persia, Sogdia and Greece (Laufer 1964). Cina has been confirmed as the transcription or reincarnation of Chengdu. The similar words found elsewhere have been homologous with Chengdu and also portray Sanskrit Cina reincarnation. This phenomenon is also consistent with the direction of propagation of Chengdu silk from West India to Central Asia, West Asia and Mediterranean areas of Europe (Duan Yu 1994).

The Connotation of 'Seres'

According to ancient Greek and Roman literature, there was a place called 'Seres' in the Far East. Most of the western literature used Cina as the code name for Seres. The word is generally translated as Seres in Chinese, according to its pronunciation and few works directly translated to Chinese.

However, what is meant by the term Seres? It has always been controversial in academic circles at home and abroad, and different scholars have different opinions. The French Sinologist Henry Yule thought that Seres and Serica are two words that come from Greece and Rome, originating from Chinese Sericum or Sericon, meaning silk. This word was miscommunicated by Altai town. China silk was loved by the early Western European society. The Sogodiana and the Parthia merchants exported silk to the West. Silk became a cherished commodity for the Greek and the Roman women and was named according to its origin Seres. Sin and Sinai were derived from the Qin empire when emperor Qin Shi Huang united China. He also opined that the origin of the name Seres can be traced back to 221 BC though silk trade existed even earlier (Yule 1915). However, the word Sin has its source in Qin Shi Huang's Altai town speech and emperor Wudi of the Han dynasty spread that to Central Asia. But Seres with its source from the 'Sin' word system was known to the western people as early as in the 4th century BC. Obviously, both Sin and Seres probably originated in Altai and should have been derived from the Sanskrit Cina which was consistent with time and the presence of a route that had an influence on the transmission of the Chinese silk from Sichuan to India and the West. Henry Yule thought the name Seres to have come from the road westward whereas the name Cina to have originated from the sea westward, though there is no credible evidence. Pelliot insisted that Seres and Sin are from Cina. American Oriental scholar B. Laufer (1964) also agreed to this view. It should be said, at this point, that Pelliot and Laufer are right.

The names Seres and Thinai were called China in the West during the Christian era. Seres first appeared in Europe in the 4th Century BC. Thinai first appeared in a book called *Eritrea Voyage* by a merchant who wrote this book in Alexander City at the end of the 1st century AD. Seres was called Tzinitza and Tzinista in *The Scenery of the Christian World* which was written by Coase Mas, a Greek clergyman. The word is sourced from Latin (Fang Hao 1987). According to the French Sinologist Coedes (1987), the words Tzinitza or Tzinista are clearly a Greek translation of the Sanskrit Cinathana. Obviously, the etymology of Seres or Thinai and Tzinitza or Tzinista traces the source of the words to Cina which is the Sanskrit translation of Chengdu.

Eritrea Voyage is an important literature which analyses oriental geography in ancient Greece (Coedes 1987). *Eritrea Voyage* recorded about a Thinai inland city which exported raw silk, silk thread and silk to India through two different roads. The roads through the east coast of India led further east, Jinzhou, in the east of the Ganges River and finally through other areas to Seres. One of the roads, through Bactria, led to the large commercial centre at Barygaza (now Roach) while the other road along the Ganges River led to southern India. There lived the Besatai who moved from the capital of Seres to India every year. They carried a lot of reed and used to fabricate cablin (cinnamon) which was also exported to India. According to the German scholar F. von Richthofen, Besatai used to stay generally in the areas lying between Assam and Sichuan. Greek and Latin writers of ancient literature from the Far East as well as editor Gedaisi completely agree with Richthofen. This study confirmed the presence of the traffic line between China and India passing through Sichuan to Yunnan and Myanmar to India and Central Asia.

The Ancient Chinese Note written by Henry Yule and *The Travelogues* written by Arab Maihar Hale mentioned a famous city called Sindabil in China. Yule recorded that Sindabil was misunderstood as a Chinese city by the Arabs. This perhaps has been an Indian city in the name of Kandabil or Sandabur. The name of the city was not found in China and the closest pronunciation relate to the word Chengdu. *The Travels of Marco Polo* recorded *Sindifu* as the capital of Sichuan. It was the capital of Shu during the Five Dynasties period (Zhang Xingliang 2003).

None of the names of the capitals of the regimes or cities during the late Tang dynasty or during the greater portion of the time belonging to the Five Dynasties' period or the Song dynasty bear a pronunciation close to Sindabil and Sindifu. However it can be seen that the Arabs would use the name Sindabil to refer to the capital of China.

From the speech analysis it has been found that both Sindabil and Sindifu roots are exactly the same. The ancient Greek Sina and Seres has its roots as Sin. Sin was derived from ancient India's Sanskrit word Cina and the remaining syllables are suffixes. Thus, Sindabil and Sindifu etymology evolved from Sina and Seres, while Sina and Seres evolved from Cina. This evolution is due to the Chengdu production of silk and the spread of silk to the Arabs by India. Chengdu was the capital of Shu. The concept of Chengdu silk impressed Arab minds. They not only retained the name of Chengdu (Sindabil), but also used the name to refer the Chinese until the 10th century. Yule mentions that in the Arab Maihar Hale's *Travelogues* 'the city name *Sindabil* was misunderstood by Arab and the city belonged to India'. Writings reveal the relationship between three places in the history of the silk route: Chengdu (Sindabil) as the place of silk production, India (Sindhu) as the place helping in transit of silk and India and Arabia as a silk trade destination. Irrespective of how the terms were known, Seres, Cina or Sindabil refer to the region named Chengdu, which was the capital of the ancient Shu in Southwest China.

Tan Zhong (2006), a scholar, pointed out that Central Asia was called Serindia by the Europeans and the word 'Ser' was an abbreviation of Seres or Serica meaning 'silk' and 'Serindia' meant 'China and India'. This was not different from the Southeast Asian peninsula known as Indochina. The two concepts of Serindia and Indochina refer to the exchange and interaction between the Chinese and the Indian civilisations. The Europeans arriving at Serindia and Indochina (Central Asia and the peninsula in Southeast Asia) felt the enormous influence of these two countries on each other in Central Asia and hence have used these two names. The word 'India' comes from the name Sindhu. The word 'Sind' is another name of the ancient Indian river Sindhu, which is now located in Pakistan and is the birthplace of the famous Indus valley civilisation (Tan Zhong and Geng Yinzeng 2006). Seres, obviously is linked with Sindhu (Sindhu is a Persian variant of Hindu that entered into Greece, where due to error in pronunciation the word got modified into Indus from where the name India originated) that entered Central Asia from India. The Europeans already knew the name Cina as early as in the 4th century BC and the Sanskrit word Cina turned into the western word Seres when used in the European languages. Thus, the names Seres and Sindhu entered Central Asia probably through India and Pakistan and then to the West. Zhang Qian mentioned Shu merchants' trade activities in Hindu, which is actually Sindhu through transliteration. It refers to the Indus river region in Northwest India. We can know that this route was for international transit and was the western lines of the Southern Silk Road. This route is from Southwest China to India from where through Pakistan and Afghanistan it led to Central Asia and finally to Iran and the Mediterranean in West Asia. The ancient Chinese literature is consistent on this. A chapter in Weilue's *Xirongzhuan* records the Shu merchants' trading activities in Dianyue (Assam in East India). *Historical records'* Dayuanliezhuan recorded Shu merchants' trading activities in Hindu (Northwest India).

Ketai Haas lived in 4th century BC, when the name Cina had already spread widely in India. The ancient Shu merchants came to India via Yunnan and Myanmar. One of the main routes was from Assam in East India to Northwest India (Hindu). This corresponds to Ketai Haas's records that relate Seres and North India and is consistent with time, region and route of the transmission of silk of ancient Shu westward (Duan Yu 2009). It should be said that this is not a coincidence.

Westerly Transmission of Chinese Silk

Chengdu silk is a sort of brocade, which has fascinated all since ancient times. Yang Xiong of the Western Han dynasty in *Shudu Fu* once praised its bright and gorgeous look, the variety, and wrote articles praising it. Shu brocade, produced at a very early age, was developed to a more mature stage in the Shang and Zhou dynasties.

The ancient Shu region has initially developed overland traffic with India and Southeast Asia early in the Shang and Zhou dynasties. Western archaeological data also showed that Chinese silk have been transmitted to Europe in around 600 BC. Five different Chinese plain weave silk fabrics were also found at a cemetery named kerameikos (in Greek) in 500 BC. Chinese silk had spread to Egypt as early as in the 11th century BC (Scott 1993). Chinese silk had been popular in Europe in the 4th or 5th century BC. This implies the initiation of the open communication between China and these foreign countries in the early ages. According to the Chinese ancient literature, the Han dynasty opened the Silk Road in the western regions at the end of the 2nd century BC, much later than the archaeological findings reflect Chinese silk westward Europe.

Silk has its origin in China. The silk weaving had reached a considerable level as early as in the Shang and Zhou dynasties (Xia Nai 1972). Sichuan is one of the regions where Chinese silk originated. Sichuan silk weaving was considerably developed during the Shang and Zhou dynasties (Duan Yu 1996). A bronze sculpture wearing an animal head and long clothes, decorated with various patterns was unearthed from the No. 2 sacrificial pits in Sanxingdui. It showed the characteristics of Sichuan brocade and embroidery. The Chengdu silk industry had reached a high level in the Spring and Autumn and the Warring States Periods. Brocade and embroidery, the products of Chengdu of the ancient Shu, were found at Changsha of Hunan province and Jiangling of Hubei province in the Warring States periods. Zhang Qian saw the 'Shubu' in Bactria during the time of the Wudi emperor of the Han dynasty period, which is the product of silk in ancient Shu. Indian scholar and professor Haraprasad Ray pointed out that 'patta (cloth)' should have been used to express 'silk' in Indian Assamese because India had no silk at that time, therefore there was no word for silk. *Shudu Fu* by Yang Xiong of the Han dynasty recorded 'Huangrunxibu, Yitongshujin' in Shu which means that Shu's yellow silk is of the best quality. Archaeologist M.C. Joshi of India pointed out the ancient Sanskrit literature records that put forth that Hindu gods like to wear Chinese silk, especially Lord Shiva likes yellow silk. The yellow silk should have been called 'Huangrunxibu' by Yang Xiong. From the analysis of ancient Indian literature, Shiva appeared at around 500 BC, that is, during the Zhou dynasty period. The Central Plains still did not know the existence of India, but the ancient Shu had trade of silk with India via Yunnan. Ancient Indian books written in the 4th century BC mentioned that 'Cina produced silk and bond' and 'Cina produced bales of silk', which actually refers to the Chengdu production of silk and silk fabrics. Ji Xianlin (1982, 76) pointed out that silk industry was developed in Southwest China, especially Chendgu; this area abuts the border with Myanmar. The traffic routes were here. The silk was sent to Myanmar and through Myanmar into India. The source of this silk was this area only. It is not difficult to know that the westerly transmission of Chinese silk should have been or was mainly from the Shu-Hindu road in the Pre-Qin period. A large quantity of Chinese silk was unearthed at a fortress in Kabul, Afghanistan. According to research, this batch of silk had been transported to Central Asia through the Southern Silk Road. Kabul was a key point in the Southern Silk Road, so this batch of silk found here cannot be accidental.

Thus, it can be seen that this route was an important line in the westerly transmission of Chinese silk through the Southern Silk Road. The line was from Southwest China to India, India to Afghanistan through Pakistan in Central Asia, after which it was transported to the west to Iran, West Asia, the Mediterranean areas of Europe and Egypt in North Africa.

A series of historical facts show that the Shu merchants from China were the earliest to engage in commercial activities in India. Shu merchants transmitting silk over this long distance to India led to the spread of silk, and silk further became popular in the West due to the opening of the Silk Road. Chinese silk was exported to South Asia, Central Asia, West Asia and the Mediterranean areas of Europe along the sea and the grasslands in north and south China, which directly promoted the formation of the Southern Silk Road, the Northern Silk Road, the Maritime Silk Road and the Grassland Silk Road, which again fostered communication and interaction between the ancient Chinese and Eurasian civilisations.

References

Coedes, George. 1987. *Textes d'auteurs Grecs et Latins, Relatives à l'Extrême-Orient.* Trans. Geng Sheng. Beijing: Zhonghua Book Company.
Duan Yu. 1994. *Re-Study on the Origin of the Name 'Cina': The Name of Cina Originates in Chengdu, the Ancient Traffic and Culture in Southwest China.* Chengdu: Sichuan University Press.
———. 1996. 'Huang Di and Lei Zu and the Origin Time of Chinese Silk.' *Forum on Chinese Culture* (4)
———. 2009. 'The Early External Traffic in Southwest China: The Southern Silk Road in the Pre-Qin to Han Dynasty.' *Historical Research* (1).
Fang Hao. 1987. *The History of Communication between China and the West, Volume 1.* Changsha: Yuelu Publishing House.
Ji Xianlin. 1982. *A Preliminary Study on the Problem of Chinese Silk Input India, the Collections of China and India Cultural Relations.* Beijing: Sanlian Bookstore.
Laufer, B. 1964. *Chinese Iran Coding.* Trans. Lin Yunyin. Beijing: The Commercial Press.
Paul Pelliot. 1962. *The Origin of the Name 'Cina': The History of Research on the South China Sea and the Western Regions.* Trans. Feng Chengjun. Beijing: The Commercial Press.
Philippa Scott. 1993. *The Book of Silk.* London: Thames & Hudson.
Tan Zhong and Geng Yinzeng. 2006. *India and China: Exchanges and Agitates between the Two Civilizations.* Beijing: The Commercial Press.
Wen Jiang. 1980. *The Research of Dian and Yue, Chinese Literature and History, the 2nd series.*
Xia Nai. 1972. 'The History of Silkworm, Mulberry and Silk in Ancient China.' *Archaeology* (2).
Yule, Henry. 1915. *Cathay and the Way Thither.* New Edition by H.Cordier. *Preliminary Essay on the Intercourse Between China and the Western Nations previous to the Discovery of the Cape Route,Volume 1*, London.
Zhang Xingliang. 2003. *The Compilation of Communication between China and the West, Volume 2.* Beijing: Zhonghua Book Company.

3

Sino-Indian Cultural Differences and Their Impact on Tourism

Xiang Baoyun

Introduction

Both China and India are among the major cradles of ancient oriental cultures, and the people of both the countries have created splendid cultural achievements since ancient times, leaving a glorious page in the history of the development of human civilisation. However, the cultures of both countries differ significantly from each other in terms of cultural types and cultural characteristics. This great difference exerts huge influence on tourism. This article provides an analysis of how the Sino-Indian cultural differences impact tourism in both these nations. Based on the available data, the article recommends dealing with cultural differences so as to boost Sino-India tourism development on the way.

Major Sino-India Cultural Differences

Both Chinese and Indian cultures belong to the oriental culture. During the long history, both the cultures have influenced and learnt from each other (Guo Hongji 2011). However, there are great differences in terms of cultural types and cultural differences. It is possible to analyse their differences from three different perspectives. They are (a) ethical culture versus religious culture (b) unitary culture versus multi culture and (c) culture of optimism versus culture influenced by spirituality and myths about afterlife.

Ethical Culture Versus Religious Culture

It is often argued that Chinese culture is ethical centering on Confucianism and Mencius, whereas Indian culture is religious centering on Hinduism. The major components of Chinese culture include benevolence, righteousness, sense, wisdom, belief, the Doctrine of the Mean, human orientation and atheism, combined with the deep-rooted ideology of 'the big unification'. Its main characteristic is the combination of Confucius Morality and Confucian culture, and the religious elements do not take the upper hand (Yu Yifeng 2000). However, the major components of Indian culture are Hinduism doctrines of tolerance, asceticism, worship of spirits, retribution and samsara, racial system, and bodhidharma. Its outstanding characteristics are that all its religious doctrines and concepts lie in the human hearts and behaviour. Followers of this religion look for soul purification, maintenance of the racial system, promotion of non-violence and believe in cause and reincarnation. In other words, religious elements dominate to a great extent.

Unitary Culture Versus Multi-culture

Chinese culture is co-created by united Chinese Nation, which is a blend of multiple ethnics living in the Huanghe River basin and Yangtze River basin, including those ethnics that moved from the remote areas to the hinterland of China. Chinese culture is quite unaffected by foreign cultures in history and for thousands of years, the culture has been passed down from one generation to another without any interruption. Chinese culture's unity (created jointly by Chinese nation) and inheritance (a direct line of succession) along with its consistency help in outlining the culture in a much clearer and easier way. It is a typical example of unitary culture. On the contrary, historically, India is closely linked with various countries, nations and religions, making its culture like that of a colour palette. Since the 15th century BC, people such as the Australian aborigines, the Mediterranean ethnics, Armenians, Dravidians, Aryans, and Mongolians came to live in India one after another. They co-existed with Indian aborigines (Negley people) and co-created the Indian culture system. The Indian culture has been continuously invaded by foreign civilisations, such as the Aryan culture, the Islam and the British culture, forcing it to absorb different foreign elements to enrich its own culture. Therefore Indian culture is not just about the creation of various outbound ethnics with local residents, it also puts forth a marked evidence of presence of foreign civilisations— a typical example of multi-culture.

Culture of Optimism Versus Culture Influenced by Spirituality and Myths about Afterlife

The Chinese culture pays great attention to worldly happiness. Since ancient times, from the elites to common people, from daily necessities to topics of sex, health, longevity and entertainment, they all demonstrate the belief of being content with the status quo, of doing what one enjoys and avoiding what one worries about (Chen Youyi 2003). They also coincide with the ideology of 'after the rain comes the sunshine' and 'every cloud has a silver lining'. Though people understand that after death there is no spirit, that life is too short and filled with uncertainty, they still show great hopes for the future, believing that as long as they keep on going and practicing, they will embrace their good luck one day. Therefore, they pursue happiness in celebrating births, being alive and their daily life. In short, Chinese culture is a typical culture of optimism. Hinduism believes that the more one suffers, the more his soul will be superior and he will be closer to God and happier in the afterlife. So it is no wonder that in history, prince Sakyamuni gave up the crown to become a beggar for years before he ascended to the stage of Buddha; Mahavira, the founder of Jainism, abandoned his prince title to become a sadhu, being less aware of the ants creeping on his body; and Gandhi, Father of India, a strict vegetarian wearing his self-woven cloth, firmly refused to become president or other high-ranking officials. Today, there are still a lot of people who choose to adopt vegetarianism and are ready to become a sadhu. It is fair to say that Indian culture is a typical example of culture influenced strongly by spiritualism along with myths about afterlife.

Impacts of Sino-Indian Cultural Differences on Tourism

Positive Impact

Ground for Tourism Resources

Each country and each nation has its own historical evolution, during which it develops its unique cultural characteristics. It is the cultural differences that lay the ground for different tourism resources. Both China and India are renowned civilised countries of the world. During the long course of cultural evolution, both countries created a variety of world-famous tourism resources that are beyond comparison. It is useful to mention here that a world heritage site is a place such as a building, city, complex, desert, forest, island, lake, monument or mountain that is listed by the United Nations Educational, Scientific and Cultural Organization (UNESCO) as being of special cultural or physical significance.[1] According to UNESCO,[2] 1,031 sites are listed: 802 cultural, 197 natural and 32 mixed properties in 163 states parties. It appears that among the sites ranked by country, Italy is home to the greatest number of world heritage sites with 51 sites, followed by China (47), Spain (44), France (41), Germany (40), Mexico (33) and India (32). UNESCO references each world heritage site with an identification number; however, new inscriptions often include previous sites now listed as part of larger descriptions. Consequently, the identification numbers exceed 1,200 even though there are fewer on the list. Tables 3.1–3.2 reveal an interesting picture in this aspect.

Internal Driving Force

From the standpoint of culturology, a subset of tourism concerned with a country or region's culture, specifically the lifestyle of the people in those geographical areas, the history of those people, their art, architecture, religion(s) and other elements that helped shape their way of life (Hans Kung 2006, 248), it is fair to claim that cultural differences are a strong internal driving force for tourism. It is due to such huge differences and the consequent pursuit of the foreign culture that thousands of Chinese flock to India to appreciate the Ganges River, the mysterious Taj Mahal, the colourful stone grottoes and temples, the gentle yoga and the delightful Bollywood movies and music. Likewise, thousands of Indians

Table 3.1
China's World Heritage Sites

No.	Heritage Sites	No.	Heritage Sites	No.	Heritage Sites	No.	Heritage Sites
1	Tai Mountain, Shandong	13	Giant Stone Buddha at Leshan Mountain, Emei Mountains, Sichan	25	Qingcheng Mountain and Dujiangyan	37	Dengfeng Heritage Site
2	Great Wall	14	Lushan Mountain Jiangxi	26	Yungang Grottoes	38	Danxia China
3	Qin Shi Huang Tomb	15	Suzhou Garden	27	Three Parallel Rivers Yunnan	39	West Lake Hangzhou
4	Imperial Palaces of the Ming and Qing Dynasties	16	Pingyao Ancient Town Shanxi	28	Goguryeo Imperial Palaces, tombs and Nobles' Tombs	40	Heritage Site of the Yuan Dynasty Upper Capital
5	Huang Mountain Anhui	17	Lijiang Ancient Town Yunnan	29	Historical City Area Macau	41	Chengjiang Lagerstatte
6	Huanglong Valley Sichuan	18	Temple of Heaven, Beijing	30	Giant Pandas' Habitat Sichuan	42	Tianshan Xinjiang
7	Wulingyuan Scenic Spot Hunan	19	Summer Palace Beijing	31	The Shang Dynasty's Ruins in Anyang	43	Hani Terrace
8	Jiuzhaigou Valley Sichuan	20	Wuyi Mountain Fujian	32	South China Karst Region	44	Peking Man Site
9	Wudang Mountain Hubei	21	Dazu Rock Carvings Chongqing	33	Kaiping Watchtowers and Historic Villages	45	Mogao Grottoes in Dunhuang Gansu
10	Confucius Temple and Confucius Garden	22	Ancient Village Southern Anhui	34	Fujian Earth Building	46	The Grand Canal
11	Chengde Summer Resort Hebei	23	Imperial Tombs of Ming and Qing Dynasties	35	Sanqing Mountain Jiangxi	47	The Silk Road
12	Potala Palace Tibet	24	Longmen Grottoes	36	Wutai Mountian Shanxi		

Source: UNESCO World Heritage Center, July 2014

Table 3.2
India's World Heritage Sites

No.	Heritage Sites	No.	Heritage Sites	No.	Heritage Sites	No.	Heritage Sites
1	Agra Fort	9	Manas Wildlife Sanctuary	17	Sundarbans National Park	25	Champaner-Pavagadh Archaeological Park
2	Ajanta Caves	10	Churches and Convents of Goa	18	Nanda Devi and Valley of Flowers National Parks	26	Chhatrapati Shivaji Terminus (formerly Victoria Terminus)
3	Ellora Caves	11	Fatehpur Sikri	19	Buddhist Monuments at Sanchi	27	Red Fort Complex
4	Taj Mahal	12	Group of Monuments at Hampi	20	Humayun's Tomb, Delhi	28	The Jantar Mantar, Jaipur
5	Group of Monuments at Mahabalipuram	13	Khajuraho Group of Monuments	21	Qutb Minar and its Monuments, Delhi	29	Western Ghats
6	Sun Temple, Konarak	14	Elephanta Caves	22	Mountain Railways of India	30	Hill Forts of Rajasthan
7	Kaziranga National Park	15	Great Living Chola Temples	23	Mahabodhi Temple Complex at Bodh Gaya	31	Great Himalayan National Park
8	Keoladeo National Park	16	Group of Monuments at Pattadakal	24	Rock Shelters of Bhimbetka	32	Rani-ki-Vav (the Queen's Stepwell) at Patan, Gujarat

Source: UNESCO World Heritage Center, July 2014

flock to China to witness the Great Wall, the Forbidden City, emperor Qin's terracotta warriors or to take a closer look at the giant pandas and to appreciate the 5,000-year-old civilisation (Tables 3.3 and 3.4).

Negative Impact

The Choice of Tourism Destination

The lack of understanding of foreign cultures or some bias against other cultures may diminish the attraction of tourism destinations among tourists or even deter them from going there, hence influence their choice in

Table 3.3
Number of Indian Tourists to China 2006–12 (in ten thousands)

Year	Total	Business	Tourism	Visit Friends and Relatives	Others
2012	61.02	21.09	18.8	0.09	21.04
2011	60.65	23.15	17.75	0.09	19.66
2010	54.93	19.16	18.37	0.06	17.33
2009	44.89	12.94	16.62	0.05	15.29
2008	43.66	12.84	15.52	0.0045	15.26
2007	46.24	17.64	14.81	0.0065	13.72
2006	40.51	13.86	13.65	0.015	12.84

Source: Chinese Tourism Statistical Yearbook

Table 3.4
Number of Chinese Tourists to India 2006–12 (in absolute figures)

Year	Total	Business	Tourism	Visit Friends and Relatives	Others
2012	169,000	108,800	25,400	8600	26,200
2011	142,200	94,600	18,300	8500	20,500
2010	119,500	71,700	12,700	13,300	21,900
2009	100,200	50,500	41,600	4100	400
2008	98,700	16,000	82,700	0.00	0.00
2007	88,100	200	87,900	0.00	0.00
2006	62,300	100	62,000	0.00	200

Source: India Tourism Statistics (2007, 2008, 2009, 2010, 2011, 2012)

selecting destinations for the purpose of tourism. Chinese tourists often believe that India is a country teeming with religious conflicts, a strict hierarchical system, ethnic conflicts, less-developed infrastructure and poor service. On the other hand, Indian people often consider that China is a country without a unified religion and is characterised by severe supervision along with serious secularisation. Thus, they are very particular in selecting their tourist destinations. This is manifested in Table 3.5. Most Chinese tourists choose Hong Kong, Macau, Japan, South Korea, Southeast Asian countries and countries in Europe and America as their tourist destinations; while Indian tourists prefer countries and regions like Saudi Arabia, Kuwait, Thailand, Singapore, Malaysia, the USA, China, Hong Kong and the UK.

Hindrances in Communication and Culture

Cultural differences lead to different cultural backgrounds, languages, values and aesthetic standards. This may result in the difficulties in communication and cognizance, thus hindering contact between the tourists and tourism destination inhabitants. The tourists therefore lose the pleasure of experiencing the local beauties while travelling. The major factor that hinders the contact between China and India in this context is the difference in languages and cultural backgrounds.

Cultural differences bring differences in religious belief, customs, culinary habits, daily life taboos and so on. Therefore, there are different requirements for accommodation, food and services. For instance, Chinese tourists are used to eating rice and noodles as their staple food and drinking hot boiled water; while Indian tourists prefer vegetarian food with strong flavours and cold drinks. In reality, however, there are a few Indian restaurants in China's tourist cities. The sight of Indian restaurants is not commonplace outside large metropolises (Prashantham 2015). The special requirements due to cultural differences push tourist service managers and providers to their wits' end, thus increasing the difficulty in serving the tourists.

Dealing with the Cultural Differences

Both China and India are the two most populous countries in the world and the two emerging nations with a booming tourist industry. In the context of the huge potential in the tourism sector; the factors like how to deal with the cultural differences to carry out tourist cooperation

Table 3.5
Top Tourist Destination Countries and Regions for Chinese and Indian Tourists, Respectively

	1	2	3	4	5	6	7	8	9	10
China	Hong Kong	Macau	Korea	Taiwan	Malaysia	Japan	Thailand	US	Cambodia	Vietnam
India	Saudi Abrabia	Thailand	Singapore	Kuwait	Malaysia	USA	China	China Hong Kong	UK	Nigeria

Source: State Communiqué on 2011 Chinese Tourism Statistics and India Tourism Statistics (2012)

SINO-INDIAN CULTURAL DIFFERENCES AND THEIR IMPACT ON TOURISM

better, promote each other's places of interest, develop market-oriented tourism products, enhance services and tap into each other's tourist markets demand critical and careful analysis. This in turn will help tourism to become a bridge connecting the people of both the countries for better friendship and deeper political, economic and cultural cooperation, which are the issues that need further and more profound consideration.

The whole nation embraces exponential development of tourist consumption when a country's average GDP reaches $1,000–$3,000, according to the general rule of global leisure and tourism development. In America, this happened in the 1960s, in Europe it happened in the 1970s and in Japan in the 1980s. The past ten years have witnessed fast economic development both in China and India. With the ever increasing national incomes, both countries have stepped into an era of rapid tourist consumption with two huge markets for a population of 1.3 billion and 1.2 billion, respectively. For example, the numbers of outbound tourists in 2006 were 34.5236 million persons and 8.3396 million persons respectively from China and India; these figures climbed to 83.1827 million and 14.9248 million by 2012, with an annual increase of 20 per cent and 13 per cent respectively (Table 3.6). Such huge outbound tourism markets provide a broad and bright future for bilateral tourism cooperation.

As mentioned above, there are accomplishments in Sino-Indian tourism cooperation. However, the negative impact brought about by cultural differences render the number of tourists to the respective

Table 3.6
Numbers of Outbound Tourists from China and India from 2006–12 (million)

Year	China	India
2012	83.1827	14.9248
2011	70.25	13.9940
2010	57.3865	12.9880
2009	47.6563	11.0660
2008	45.8444	10.8678
2007	40.954	9.7832
2006	34.5236	8.3396

Source: State Communiqué on 2011 Chinese Tourism Statistics and India Tourism Statistics (2012)

countries in disproportion to the general trend keeping in mind the fact that in both the nations the demand for tourism is rising. For instance, the number of tourists to India from China and from India to China as proportion of their outbound tourists are only 0.2 per cent and 4 per cent, respectively. In other words, among 500 Chinese outbound tourists, only 1 chooses India as the destination; and among 25 Indian outbound tourists, only 1 goes to China. Hence with respect to the huge outbound tourism consumption markets, China and India should tackle their cultural differences in an active manner to enhance their tourism cooperation comprehensively.

Areas for Cooperation

Tourism Marketing

Cultural differences can be a hindrance to Sino-Indian tourism cooperation if neither party knows and understands each other well (Wang Xiaoying and Ni Xiangqin 2005). However, if both countries have sufficient understanding and respect each other's culture, the differences can become a significant aspect to their comprehensive cooperation. Therefore, both China and India should get to know each other better and deeply through various ways like promotion of bilateral tourism, sales promotion and exchange. There are a variety of activities available, such as tourism exhibitions, tourism explanation meetings, introduction meetings and setting up of comprehensive tourism websites for extensive publicity of the countries' places of interests, customs and religious beliefs (Qiu Yonghui 2006). In this way, it can clear away the obstacles and popularize tourism in each country.

Market Orientation

Cultural differences, the major sources attracting outbound tourists, are the fundamental reasons for different tourism consumption behaviour. Hence, the tourism industries in both countries should first understand the differences and adjust their development strategies to design the right market-oriented tourism products. For instance, as the hometown of Buddhism and yoga, India may promote 'Buddha-Tourism-Package' and 'Yoga-Experience-Package' to attract Chinese tourists; and China, as the origin of Silk Road and leisure resorts, may promote 'Silk Road Tourism Package' and 'Vacation Package' for the Indian tourists.

Enhancing Service Quality

Cultural differences result in unique features in terms of religious beliefs, traditional customs, culinary habits and daily life taboos; and likewise a difference in demand for accommodation, food and drinks and services. The tourism industries in China and India apart from fully understanding each other's cultural differences, thus, have to respect each country's differences in the aforementioned areas. They also have to adopt different manners when welcoming and receiving tourists with personalised services. For instance, there should be more Chinese restaurants providing Indian cuisines and vegetarian food; more Indian restaurants offering Chinese food, hot boiled water, more tourist guides and services in Chinese language.

Cross-cultural Awareness and Search for Business Opportunities

Communication is the best way to eliminate the obstacles resulting from cultural differences, so both countries' tourism industries should set up a flexible communications mechanism for easier and smoother cultural exchange. They should also foster cross-cultural awareness by hosting events such as Sino-Indian 'Country Year' or 'Tourism Year' to carry out various tourism and cultural activities themed on each country's culture, so that more Indian tourists come to China and vice versa. Through this cross-cultural tourism exchange both parties can look for new business opportunities, making tourism a bridge connecting the Chinese and the Indians which will in turn strengthen Sino-Indian cooperation in the arena of politics, economies and culture.

Notes

1. The list is maintained by the international World Heritage Programme, administered by the UNESCO World Heritage Committee and composed of 21 UNESCO member states which are elected by the General Assembly. For details see 'The World Heritage Committee', http://whc.unesco.org/en/committee/ (accessed on 19 January 2016).
2. As of July 2015.

References

Chen Youyi. 2003. 'Influences of Ethnic Cultural Differences on Modern Sino-India Historical Endings.' *Guangxi Social Sciences.*

Guo Hongji. 2011. 'Potential Influences of Cultural Elements on the Rising of Sino-India Economies.' *Gansu Theory Research*.

Hans Kung. 2006. *Tracing the Way: Spiritual Dimensions of the World Religions*. Continuum International Publishing Group.

Prashantham, S. 2015. 'China and India: Rivals and Friends?' *The Hindu*. http://www.thehindu.com/opinion/op-ed/prime-minister-narendra-modis-china-visit/article7231248.ece (accessed on 15 April 2015).

Qiu Yonghui. 2006. 'Sino-Indian Cultural Exchange against the Backdrop of Globalisation.' *Journal of Sichuan University (Social Science Edition)*.

Wang Xiaoying and Ni Xiangqin. 2005. 'An Analysis of the Cooperation & Development between Sino-Indian Tourism Industry.' *South Asian Studies Quarterly*.

Yu Yifeng. 2000. 'An Initial Research of the Antinomy Paradox in Cultural Differences on Tourism.' *Hubei Journal of Adult Education College*.

4

India, China and Beyond
Tagorean Insights into Culture, Leadership and Human Development for Management

Sanjoy Mukherjee

Prologue

It was the worst of times. The apocalypse had begun to cast its haunting spell all over the world. Billowing smoke, flashes of missiles, deafening sounds of bombs, cries of suffering of millions filled the earth and the sky. The Second World War was in full blast in Europe and all over.

It was the 80th and the last birthday of the poet, Rabindranath Tagore at his own 'abode of peace'—Santiniketan. The poet was a broken man with all hope lost in the spirit of humanism and glory of western culture and civilisation. On that occasion, in the darkness of anguish and disillusionment and yet groping for the last streak of light, the poet wrote the essay 'Crisis of Civilisation'—his last testament for humanity. This is how he concluded the masterpiece:

> I had once believed that the springs of civilization will issue from the heart of Europe. But today, when I am about to leave the world, that faith has deserted me. I look around and see the crumbling ruins of s proud civilization strewn like a vast heap of futility. And yet I shall not

commit the grievous sin of losing faith in man. I shall wait for the new dawn, a new chapter in his history when the holocaust will end and the air will be rendered clean with the spirit of service and sacrifice. Perhaps that dawn will come from this horizon, from the east where the sun rises. (Tagore 1996, 726)

Introduction

The 2008 global economic meltdown had a catastrophic impact on the West, especially in the USA and Europe, the aftermath of which is yet to be overcome. Though the turbulence and shock waves hit India and China, but the recovery time to normalcy was far less in these two Asian economies largely because of the strength and resilience of these two ancient cultures and civilisations. The present chapter will highlight the importance of further intercultural understanding between India and China for mutual enrichment. This will not only strengthen the bonding between the two countries but will create a rich cultural terrain that will act as the foundation for assuming economic leadership on a global platform. In this regard the chapter will primarily delve into an exploration of the insights available from the life and work of Rabindranath Tagore, the Nobel Laureate poet from India, with special attention to his constant striving for Indo-Chinese mutual understanding and collaboration in the fields of education, culture and institution building such as the creation of Cheena Bhavana (the Chinese Quarters) at his own university Visva-Bharati in Santiniketan, West Bengal. The chapter is a qualitative study based on Tagore's life and his communication and correspondences with the world. The paper will thus champion the cause of raising the voice of humanism from Asia on the basis of Tagore's contribution towards fostering Indo-China relationship in order to counter the dominant forces of aggression of Western capitalism and the resulting dominant paradigm of modern management education. It will then draw out lessons from Tagore's insights and experiences in education, which will offer an alternative paradigm to modern management and transform its contents and pedagogy for the sustenance of individuals, organisations and the planet at large.

World civilisations are replete with cultural synthesis but Sino-Indian synthesis does not have many parallels. The cultural relations between India and China can be traced back to very early times—more than 2,000 years. During these centuries of contact, the two civilisations contributed to each other's fund of goodwill and knowledge in various fields. Cultural interactions between these two great countries form a fascinating study. India and China are two great civilisations with a long history. A number of Indian monks such as Dharmarakshsha, Kasyapa Matanga and others frequently visited China. Similarly, Chinese monks such as Xuan Zang, Fa Xian, Yi Jing and others travelled to India to collect Buddhist texts.

The chapter will attempt to provide insights into Tagore's significant contributions towards social obligations. This assemblage brings together a mosaic of forward-looking ideas as well as perspectives on Indo-China's past civilisational sagacity and its intellectual circles' sensitivity as a challenge to the capitalist West and its resultant education system. The Asian voice may draw inspiration from Tagore's ideas and ideals of alternative education based on contact and consonance with the human being and the natural environment. Management education may well unlearn and humanise in the days to come in the light of Tagore's pillars of alternative education with its unique characteristics: intimate contact with nature and teachers as role models; emphasis on character rather than behaviour; fostering community living and practices; development of aesthetic quality beyond rational faculties; liberating work from monotony towards expression of joy and freedom; enhancing multiple levels of human competencies and awakening grass-roots sensitivity as well as global concerns. It will also touch upon the history of Sino-Indian cultural concord with special reference to the secular ideas of Tagore in regard to a deeper understanding of Indian and Chinese civilisations and the educated public in general.

The chapter will then throw light on the imperative of transcendental leadership, as explained by Tagore, to combat hours of crises at an inspirational level. On a more functional plane, the chapter will attempt to offer alternative models of leadership, innovation and community development for modern organisations seriously engaged in initiatives on leadership excellence, corporate social responsibility and human development based on Tagore's philosophy and wisdom.

Finally, this chapter also goes as a tribute of the authors to Rabindranath Tagore who travelled not only in China but world over with his message of universal humanism beyond all boundaries. His purpose of visit to China was to kindle the spirit of love and universal brotherhood that was to be the essence of the relationship between these two great nations. This year marks the 90th anniversary of Tagore's first and memorable visit to Shanghai.

Objectives

In view of the above, the aims and objectives of the chapter are threefold:

- Highlighting the importance of Indo-China intercultural understanding and confluence for creating a strong terrain for the emergence of an alternative and strong economic leadership, with a powerful yet different Asian voice as a challenge and response to Western capitalism
- Presenting and analysing the invaluable contribution of the Nobel Laureate Indian poet Rabindranath Tagore towards fostering of the cultural and civilisational relationship between India and China
- Drawing out lessons for modern management and leadership from the experiments and insights of Tagore towards humane and holistic principles and practices in future

Relevance of Tagore Today

A question may well be raised in the context of strengthening Indo-China relationship and understanding and generating alternative learning in modern education especially management education. What is the relevance of a poet and philosopher like Rabindranath Tagore in this present age of globalisation and technological bonanza? The following points may be highlighted in response to the question above.

- Though essentially a poet, Tagore from childhood received wisdom from the celebrated body of ancient Indian Literature—the Upanishads. The messages of the Upanishads were not born out of intellectual discourse and argumentation only but also out of direct realisation of the Self and Truth by the sages and seers of India. They were anchored in the essence of Indian ethos and culture but the light of their wisdom radiated worldwide with equal impact and relevance. One of the cardinal messages of the Shvetashvatara Upanishad Chapter II Verse 5 begins thus—*Srinvantu viswe amritasys putah* (Listen. O children of immortality world over!) The sages were addressing not just the people of India but the global audience. Rooted in the Upanishads, Tagore evolved his thoughts on education and human development with a universal appeal and christened his university Visva-Bharati where 'Visva' reaches out to the world while 'Bharati' preserves the Indian uniqueness. 'Visva-Bharati founded a unique approach to international fellowship, based on a humanism that flowed out of man's longing and capacity to live in harmony' (Das Gupta 2011, 71).

Coming specifically to the Indo-China relationship, Tagore deeply sympathised and admired the Chinese culture since his youth, something he inherited from his ancestors who had visited China. Moreover, as the Nobel Laureate economist and philosopher Amartya Sen points out, the poet was convinced that 'there was something deeply incomplete in the priorities of the Western world, a gap in the closing of which eastern thought, from India and china, had something constructive to offer' (Sen 2011, 4). Tagore was always a champion for the cause of raising the Asian voice on the basis of his principles and philosophy of humanism to combat the forces of materials and aggression from the West. In this regard, he made a powerful statement in his lecture at the Tokyo Imperial University in 1916 that challenged the roots of Western culture and civilisation.

> The lamp of ancient Greece is extinct in the land where it was first lighted, the power of Rome lies buried under the ruins of its vast empire. But the civilisation whose basis is society and spiritual ideal of man, is still a living thing in India and China.
> (Das Gupta 2009, 246)

During his lectures in China, this critique became sharp and specific. 'I cannot, however, bring myself to believe that any nation in this world can be great and yet be materialistic... Materialism is exclusive, and those who are materialistic claim their individual rights of enjoyment, of storing and possessing' (Tagore 2009, 77). His alternative Asian voice subsequent to this critique had a bold alternative to offer: 'All our true enjoyment is in the realisation of perfection. This can be reached not through augmentation but through renunciation of the material for the sake of the ideal' (Ibid., 151). All throughout his lectures in China, he was launching as if a crusade in the world of thoughts and ideas to garner our strength in Asia and build our unity.

> In Asia we must seek our strength in union, in an unwavering faith in righteousness and never in the egoistic spirit of separateness and self-assertion ... In Asia we must unite, not through some mechanical power of organisation, but through a spirit of true sympathy. The organized power of machine is ready to smite and devour us, from which we must be rescued by the living power of spirit which grows into strength, not through mere addition, but through organic assimilation. (Ibid., 51)

He had unflinching faith in the humanising potential of the voice from the East.

> Let the awakening of the east impel us consciously to discover the essential and universal meaning of our own civilisation, to remove the debris from its path, to rescue it from the bondage of stagnation that produces impurities, to make it a great channel of communication between all human races. (Das 1999, 99)

Thus, he was ever fervent in his appeal for Indo-China bonding that became more alive in reality when he created the Cheena Bhavana in his university to strengthen and nurture this bonding. The details will follow later in this chapter.

- In the 20th century, Tagore was a strong and living proponent of holistic education for an overall human development. He translated his vision into reality by founding his university in the lap of nature far from the humdrum of the metropolis of Calcutta where he himself had nightmarish experiences of attending schools in his childhood. He ran away from all the schools he tried, as he could not survive and withstand the drudgery of rote learning devoid of meaning and touch of life. Here are some of those painful reminiscences and realisations of his lifeless experiences in conventional learning that packs the brain with abundance of information only for utilitarian gains.

> [T]he child's life is brought into the education factory, lifeless, colourless, dissociated from the context of the universe, within bare white walls staring like eyeballs of the dead. We are born with that God-given gift of taking delight in the world, but such delightful activity is fettered and imprisoned, stilled by a force called discipline which kills the sensitiveness of the child mind, he mind which is always on the alert, restless and eager to receive firsthand knowledge from Mother Nature. We sit inert, like dead specimens of some museum, whilst lessons are pelted at us…our mind misses the perpetual stream of ideas which come from the heart of nature. (Tagore 2009, 87–88)

Now, if we take a look at the recent developments in the field of management education, one of the striking resemblances with Tagore is the shift from the conventional teaching towards a lively learning process where the faculty is compelled to be a learner too in every interaction with the students. Secondly the lashing effect of crony, cowboy capitalism on management education has been instrumental in perpetuating an education system which only churns out number crunching machines, advocates of careerism, materialism and consumerism. This has led to a search for alternative paradigm in management thinking and practice among conscientious academics, business leaders and consultants worldwide. The quest for meaning of work, purpose of life, spirit-based leadership, social responsibility of business, concern for nature and environment, engagement in ethics and values are increasingly finding space in the discourse of management teaching and practice. Thought leaders are trying to explore alternative sources and methods of learning from disciplines like history, literature, biographies and the ancient wisdom of the East that are beyond the corridors of structured management literature and curriculum. The life, insights and works of Tagore and his experiments on education have become increasingly relevant in this regard for management education to come out of dehumanising capitalistic influence towards a vibrant and joyful endeavour with a human face.

At this point, the chapter will turn to highlight the significant contribution of Tagore in establishing and nurturing the relationship between India and China and raise a strong, unified and humanistic Asian voice against the galloping tirade and tyranny of Western capitalism and aggressive materialism.

Tagore and Indo-China Bonding

Rabindranath Tagore shared a very special relationship with China as evident from his lectures during his China visit and also in his endeavour to integrate Chinese culture and wisdom in his educational experiment in Visva-Bharati, the unique university and centre for higher learning created by him in the Birbhum district of West Bengal. Tagore was a visionary and always forward-looking. He sought to promote the cause of India–China understanding, envisioning the ascent of India and China to a higher platform of civilisational leadership and fraternal partnership.

Tagore played a unique role in highlighting the historical contribution of Chinese and Indian civilisation and in exhorting the two modern nations, India and China, to revitalise that noble cause. Welcoming the famous Chinese painter Xu Beihong to Santiniketan, Tagore reiterated that the true rebirth of a civilisation comes not from 'a deadly pursuit of power' but 'from expression of the inner heart'. He thought that China and India had done this during ancient times when the two countries 'shared the dawn of a great renaissance' (Tan Chuang 2011, xxiii). Tagore looked forward to an era of kinship between our neighbouring lands and he reiterated the importance of Sino-Indian collaboration in the assertion of historical forces in the East that will save us from the encroaching darkness (Tagore 1996, 850). The premonition of the poet is looming large today in the form of dangers of cultural homogenisation and economic colonisation from the West in the horizon of human civilisation worldwide.

Tagore had the vision of Indo-China fraternity in modern times. He was an Indian with an international mould of thinking. Tagore's strategy was future oriented. He saw individuals as a meeting ground for several civilisations. Among the illumined Indian thinkers, he was one of the earliest who championed the cause of a mutually enriching relationship between the two ancient civilisations and cultures of India and China. He was very keen on fostering camaraderie and intercultural understanding between the two nations and their people in our present times. It became abundantly clear from his setting up of the Sino-Indian Cultural Society and later the Cheena Bhavana, the Chinese department in his university at Santiniketan.

Ji Xianlin, the veteran expert of India in China who was awarded the Padma Bhushan by the Government of India, extolled Tagore as an icon of friendship between India and China. About Tagore and his visit, he said: In 1924, the great patriotic modern Indian poet Tagore visited China. It was an earth-shaking event at that time (Wang Shuying 2006, 289). He added later: 'He [Tagore] visited China, and invited scholars and artists to India, hence enhancing mutual understanding between the two peoples. Such mutual visits sowed the seeds of friendship, and continue to blossom magnificent flowers even today' (Ji Xianlin 1966, 181).

The response from Tagore to the invitation was no less warm and inspiring. On the eve of his departure to China, he told the press: 'When the invitation from China reached me, I felt that it was an invitation to India herself, and as her humble son, I must accept it.' He further added: 'I am hoping that our visit will re-establish the cultural and spiritual connections between China and India' (Hay 1970, 145).

The millennia-old rich shared spiritual and cultural heritage between the India and China was also highlighted in the speech delivered by Liang Chi Chao, president, Universities Association, Peking at the Beijing Normal University that later appeared as the Introduction (translated by Tan Chung) in the book *Rabindranath Tagore: Talks in China*. The book was published in India in 1924, 1925 and later in 1999. The words are awe-inspiring indeed:

> Both in character and geography, India and China are like twin brothers. Before most of the civilised races became active, we two brothers had already begun to study the great problems which concern the whole of mankind. We had already accomplished much in the interests

of humanity. India was ahead of us and we, the little brother, followed behind. (Das 1999, xi)

Tagore, on his part, extolled the Chinese culture in one of his lectures: 'Your civilisation has been nurtured in its social life upon faith in the soul. You are the most long-lived race, because you had centuries of wisdom nourished by your faith in goodness, not in mere strength. This has given your great past' (Rao 2011, xi).

Zhou Enlai, the premier of the people's republic of China also spoke generously of Tagore, during his visit to Santiniketan in 1956 on the occasion of the award of Desikottam, the highest honour conferred by Visva-Bharati on a person of national or global eminence. 'The Chinese people have cherished him [Tagore] with profound sentiments. The Chinese people can never forget Tagore's warm affection for them' (Rao 2011, xii).

Tagore had cast great inspirational influence on Jawaharlal Nehru, the first prime minister of India on nurturing Indo-China relationship and their civilisational, philosophical as well as spiritual connectivity. This was the foundational inspiration of Panchsheel (the five principles of peaceful coexistence). Tagore's visit to China opened the minds and captivated the imagination of the Chinese intellectual elite, some of whom adored him for his passionate espousal of the strength of the Asian voice—the Eastern cultures and civilisations. In a world that fraught with violence and aggression, Tagore spread the message of mutual well-being and complementary interests and competencies that was existing between the two nations since millennia. Gautama Siddhartha, an Indian astronomer in the 8th century, was made the president of the board of astronomy in China, for example. A rare visionary and ever future oriented Tagore was an advocate of creating a higher platform of civilisational wisdom, shared cultural heritage and Sino-Indian intrinsic bonding for strengthening our bilateral relations far beyond mere political and economic parameters. The spirit of such bonding would be a blend of the Indian concept of *vasudhaiva kutumbakam* (the world is one family) and the Chinese vision *Shijiedatong* (world in grand harmony).

Tagore's visit to China in 1924 may have evoked mixed reactions, especially among the revolutionary and fiery Chinese youth, but on hindsight the immense significance and the positive responses generated in the visit could hardly be ignored. It was instrumental in revival of Indo-China relations at a deeper level that started waning after the Song dynasty. Tagore was the first eminent Indian thinker to be invited by the intellectual elite of China, along with such stalwarts such as John Dewey and Bertrand Russell, while the Chinese people were trying to find their own place, platform and voice in a world dominated by the aggrandising West. Tagore was a beacon of light in a dark tunnel. He revived the bond that existed between India and China in the distant past and raised a powerful alternative Asian voice in the global political and cultural scenario. Tagore had firm faith in the geo-civilisational paradigm of Sino-Indian relations; that is worthwhile for us to consider as it may open the vista for open and transparent, balanced and equitable dialogue between not only India and China, but also among all the countries in the Asia-Pacific region. Tagore's nationalism had its roots in a free-flowing and abiding spirit of internationalism that may come as a powerful message to the youth of both China and India.

India and China are presently interacting with each other not only in bilateral trade but also on issues pertaining to a global economic platform. While there are complexities in mutual relations and several zones of divergence, it is important to strengthen our bonding on areas of convergence by charting out spaces of commonality of interests. The enlightened future between the two nations may well be based on the Chinese concept of *Zhong-Yin Da Tong* or 'the great harmony between India and China' in the backdrop of the global vision of Tagore's university, *Yatraviswam Bhavati Ekanidam* or 'where the world becomes a single nest', also the motto of Visva-Bharati. This will mark a new paradigm of Indo-China equation, upholding our mutual cultural and civilisational values and opening up new arenas of effulgence of creativity and innovation for mutual progress as well as directions for the world in future.

The homogenising influence of Western capitalism has not only posed serious threat to eliminate cultural diversity that characterise different parts of the world but also shaped the philosophy and practices of education, especially mainstream management education. To cater to the demands of a global industrial monoculture, the scope of flourishing one's critical and creative potential has become so limited that this education system is churning out 'products' with two characteristics—binary logic and linear thinking. On the one hand, Tagore's voice of humanism was a formidable challenge to the foundations of aggrandising corporate capitalism, endless material pursuit and rampant consumerism, on the other, the new and innovative education system propagated by him and institutionalised in his university aimed at holistic human development and the natural expression of our full creative potential. He questioned the very premise of a robotised education system that reduces human beings to money-earning machines.

At this juncture, the chapter will identify some of the malaise that has penetrated and pervaded modern management education system and also highlight the various initiatives that are engaged in search for an alternative management paradigm that is spirit-centred, humanistic and enlightening.

The Changing Paradigm in Management Thinking and Education

It has been mentioned earlier in this chapter that there is a growing critique of mainstream management education and its dominant paradigm based on capitalism and industrial monoculture. It may be pertinent here to share some of these alternative initiatives. In 2004, Ian Mitroff, professor emeritus, USC Marshall School of Business, sent an open letter to the deans and faculty of business schools in USA where he came down bold and sharp on our existing management education and identified five areas of failure that resulted in the following aberrations among the students and faculty:

1. A mean-spirited and distorted view of human nature;
2. A narrow, outdated, and repudiated notion of ethics;
3. A narrow and highly limited definition of, and the role of, management in human affairs;
4. A overly reified conception of the 'sub-disciplines' of the field of management; and
5. A sense of learned helplessness and hopelessness among faculties, students, and workers regarding control of their careers and lives.

All this points towards some glaring pitfalls in both the process as well as the outcome of mainstream management education—dominance of our techno-economic identity over deeper and nobler aspects of human nature; failure to impart ethics education in a manner that is vibrant, engaging and relevant to the students; sharpening of instrumental reason at the cost of critical rational faculties; denigrating the power of lofty emotions in personal and organisational transformation; splitting the holistic conception of management into disconnected pigeon holes of areas and sub-disciplines; loss of meaning in work and purpose in life.

In recent times, there has been emergence of rising critique of our prevalent methods of learning among the academic circles in business and management. Such critical voice is often being raised by recognised stalwarts in this field (Bennis and O'Toole 2005; Ghoshal 2005). There is also a search for an alternative holistic paradigm of organic connectivity so that 'our heart and head does not split knowledge into dualities of thought and being, mind and body, emotion and intellect, but resonates with a wholeness and fullness that engages every part of one's being.' (Kind et al. 2005) To usher in new air and new light into an otherwise structured, fossilised and ossified management education, illumined thinkers and leaders are seeking insights from humanities' disciplines (literature, arts, films, music, theatre and so on), sports, spirituality and others to establish the missing connect between learning and life. Otherwise we keep on 'solving the wrong problem precisely' using methods that are primarily techno-economic in nature whereas the systemic and spiritual perspectives are ruthlessly pushed out of our vista of vision and concern. The serious implications of attempting pseudo-solutions to the problems of our economy and society have been aptly depicted by Ims and Zsolnai (2006) in the opening chapter 'Shallow Success and Deep Failure' of their edited book *Business within Limits*. In this book, they went ahead to present an alternative holistic and humanistic world view rooted in deep ecology and Buddhist economics. Michael Ray (1992), on his part, proposed a similar paradigm in which he advocated that vision must replace profit as the key aim of business. Chakraborty (1995) identified the main pillars of wholesome business transformation in his concept of 'Business Ashram' on the founding principles of Indian philosophy, culture and ethos. This resonates with Stephen Covey's (1992) emphasis on character beyond professional competence in his proposed shift in management metaphor from stomach to spirit.

The need to explore certain non-conventional sources and methods of learning has been highlighted by Mukherjee (2007) for a comprehensive all round development of the individual in organisation. This is aimed at developing a 'quality mind' (Chakraborty 1995) or 'quality consciousness' (Chatterjee 1998). The search for alternative sources of management learning prompted Michael Gelb (1998) to draw our attention to the principles of learning and creativity laid down by Leonardo da Vinci, the stellar figure of the Italian Renaissance. Weick (2006) propounded a new approach to learning through 'heedful relating' by cultivating the art of 'mindfulness'. There has been an increasing interest in Spirituality at Work (SAW) as is evident from the rising number of publications on spirituality and holistic management (Bell and Taylor 2004; Biberman, Whitty and Robbin 1999; Cash and Grey 2000; Fischer 1999; Mitroff and Denton 1999; Pruzan et al. 2007). The concepts of synchronicity (Jaworski 1998) and Spiritual Quotient or SQ (Zohar and Marshall 2000) are significant developments in this direction.

It is time to shift attention to Tagore and his experiments in alternative education to draw out pertinent lessons for transforming ourselves and our organisations for a better tomorrow for the individual, the society and the planet at large.

Lessons from Tagore for Modern Management

There is a unique characteristic of greatness that may be called universal relevance. This is what makes a genius like Tagore and his work and messages relevant across space and time, covering all disciplines of knowledge and action much beyond his poetry and philosophy. The discipline of management is no exception. Moreover, Tagore was instrumental and successful as an institutional leader on the grounds of universal appeal, excellence in holistic education and sustainability; as the university created by him is thriving even today attracting talents from the world over. What did he leave behind for us that may be helpful in the transformational process in management paradigm and education highlighted in the previous section?

- *Global in appeal, local in roots:* Tagore was invited to deliver lectures not only in China but in different parts of Asia and the Western world. His path-breaking ideas and experiments in learning and education were warmly received by the global audience. This was possible because of two reasons. First, Tagore's was an authentic Asian voice deeply rooted in Indian culture and ethos. Second, he was also well-versed in and respectful of the cultures of the host countries. In China, wisdom of Lao-tze would often come alive in his deliberations. But he was bold and vocal about what Asia and India, in particular, can contribute to the world. On a similar note, he inspired the Chinese people: 'Bring out your light and add it to this great festival of lamps of world culture.' (Tagore 2009, 76) In management education and practice, the necessity of leaders with a global mindset is often emphasised these days. There are three stages of developing such a global mindset as we learn from Tagore: (a) assimilation of the key tenets of one's own culture (b) penetrating the depth of other cultures and (c) identifying the zones of commonality and convergence between them for conjoint future action. Thus, Tagore provokes us to address some uneasy questions. Can there be a global mind without local anchorage or rootedness in one's own culture? Are we ignited enough to highlight what Indian culture and wisdom can offer to modern management today?

- *Holistic management philosophy and education:* Of late there has been a lot of thrust on evolving a holistic philosophy education in management. But there needs to be a radical change in the content, pedagogy and delivery of management education and corporate training. Otherwise, the number crunching mind driven by economic rationality will never be able to imbibe holistic perception. Tagore was sharp in his critique of over quantification. 'Numbers add but do not connect.' (Ibid., 147) He was also bold in his comment on the techno-economic model of progress that has given impetus to the sweeping industrial civilisation and monoculture and the needs of which are faithfully catered by mainstream management education. 'Progress towards what and for whom?' he raised such critical questions almost a century back (Tagore 1937, 5). Tagore's insights into imparting learning process in consonance with nature are of cardinal importance when it comes to developing curriculum that promotes holistic learning. It helps in sharpening our sensory faculties that receive signals and vibrations from the surroundings and lead to knowledge creation. In his talks in China he said, 'I believe that children should be surrounded with the things of nature which have their own educational value.' (Tagore 2009, 89) When he created his university he told the students that they would be given two sets of teachers—the teachers as human beings and the teachers as the trees around. The relevance of these messages of Tagore become abundantly clear today when we find corporate executives and business school students are being sent for mountaineering adventures and retreats in the heart of nature for revitalisation, renewal and re-establishing the organic connect with life.
- *Cultivating emotions and aesthetics:* One of the major issues confronting management education today is the dominance of left brain thinking and instrumental rationality whereas many of the problems in our workplace and even in educational institutions are rooted in the emotional domain of the individuals. Even though the importance of emotional quotient is accepted these days, there is still a lot of gap in the learning methods that may be adopted for cultivating emotional intelligence. Modern education equips a student to sharpen his capacity of thinking but at the dire expense of the capacity of 'feeling'. In this regard, Tagore's experiments and insights can provide directions for reviewing and changing our business school curriculum. Beyond the conventional inputs on the usual disciplines of management, it is time for academics to consider introduction of modules or courses on literature, community development field work, observation and exploration of nature, sharpening of our sensory faculties through engagement in silence for cultivation of emotional intelligence, aesthetic excellence and stimulation of right brain thinking. All finally leading to overall human development.
- *Exalted model of man:* It may be worthwhile to remember the words of wisdom from Tagore on education: 'The education of a complete life

involves trying to recognise through a correct reading of history, of science, of the arts, in the light of man's spiritual truth.' (Das Gupta 2011, 71) Thus, Tagore's ideal of education is founded on an elevated model of man as a spiritual being which is rooted in the portrayal of the human being as children of immortality (*amritasya putrah*). This has significant implications for management education and organisational learning. Without acceptance of such a state of such an exalted state of human possibility, most of the inputs on learning process get limited to the initial levels of Maslow's need hierarchy model and the motivational strategy in organisations also gets aligned and designed accordingly. Critical issues like meaning of work or purpose of life are pushed beyond the margins.

- *Management and humanities:* Another major problem faced by modern management education is the development of misplaced confidence bordering on arrogance among the students and executives that there is a single techno-economic answer to a problem which they know and no 'grey areas' are admitted or explored. This leads to an attitude of 'nothing-but-ness' which is a result of linear and binary thinking where the search for alternative answers is given a mortal blow that leads to a serious malady-remedy mismatch. Inputs on humanities (arts, literature. music, dance, theatre and films) help us break these hard shells and cocoons of the quantitative paradigm and open the horizons of the mind to multiple alternatives in a world where the colour of the reality is grey and its shape amorphous. Tagore's learning philosophy and methodology can help enhance our capacity of 'thinking out of the box' and generate multiple alternatives and solutions to a single problem as we all observe the world from our own unique and respective positions at a time where uncertainty and change constitute the fabric of reality.
- *Silence and meditation:* In some of the courses and workshops on self-development and organisational transformation processes such as meditation, mindfulness exercise and so on, are finding space in business schools and corporate houses. This has deep positive impact on evolving a self-culture that enables us to be in touch with our inner space and harness our infinite potential that gets translated into effectiveness in leadership roles, fostering team spirit, decision making, problem solving and conflict management. But this is yet to receive general acceptance from the mainstream stalwarts as they quickly equate these initiatives with religious practice and rituals. It may be pointed out that more than a century ago, Tagore had introduced collective prayers and meditation as a part of the daily activities of the students of the university. This may build and strengthen our confidence in the efficacy of these self-development processes recommended by the sages and seers of India millennia ago. The poet Tagore only continued this tradition, leaving a positive example for posterity in any field of education to imbibe, practice and enjoy the fruits of the same.

- *CSR (corporate social responsibility) and inclusive thinking:* Over the last two decades, there has been an increasing thrust on courses and programmes on CSR. The crux of CSR is the capacity of 'inclusive thinking' on part of the business leaders that will lead to 'inclusive development' of the organisation and all its stakeholders including the community. There are two pertinent lessons from Tagore that can contribute to meaningful CSR. First, there must be an all-encompassing vision in the leadership without which inclusive thinking is simply not possible. This has its roots in the vision of an enlightened larger self of the organisation beyond the premises of the enterprise and organically connected with the community and all stakeholders for mutual enrichment. This is the first lesson that can be drawn from Tagore who had the holistic vision of the flowering of the university along with the welfare and development of the community in that region. This found expression in his experiments at Sriniketan in Surul, a few kilometres from Santiniketan. Second, this also led to a humbling process of learning among the students who would be exposed to the stark realities of the underprivileged villagers and train them on economic self-reliance leading to social empowerment through participation in governance and decision-making process. The lesson for MBA students and executives is very significant in this regard. Before one engages in CSR, it is vital to go through a learning process in contact with the community so that one gets to know what their 'real needs' are and then design the CSR strategy and delivery mechanisms accordingly. Otherwise most often the 'singularly and universally valid' (!) Western models of development founded on techno-economic rationality get imposed on the indigenous milieu and the result is a gross mismatch as the 'perceived needs' of the community by the business leaders has no connection with the 'real needs' of the community life in a third world scenario. Tagore's community development initiative with the faculty and the students can instil a sense of humility and grass root sensitivity among our faculty, students and business leaders for effective and meaningful CSR interventions.
- *Concern for ethics and values:* On the occasion of the inauguration of Cheena Bhavan in 1937 he made this bold and clear. 'Through unrighteousness, man prospers, gains what appears desirable, conquers enemies, but perishes at the root' (Tagore 1937, 5). In his talks in China he further clarifies: 'The specific meaning of dharma is that principle which holds us firm together and leads us to our best welfare' (Tagore 2009, 119). All this marshals our strength to uphold ethics and values in the field of business education and practice today. Even though there has been a renewed thrust on business ethics in academic curriculum and corporate codes of conduct, 'commerce without morality'—one of the seven deadly sins identified by Mahatma Gandhi—is rampant and prevalent in business worldwide as evident from the growing number

of scams and scandals. Surprisingly enough, those who are the masterminds and perpetrators of these crimes are mostly intelligent, educated and many of them possess a business school background. One of the major gaps in management education worldwide is that historically the curriculum and courses had laid emphasis on behaviour and personality development, but there has hardly been any mention of character. Only in recent times the vital issue of character building, that is the foundation of ethics and values, has been highlighted by a few illumined thinkers and academics (Chakraborty 1995; Covey 1992) Tagore had sounded this caution in China in his critique of the wild West 'where progress is measured by the speed with which materials are multiplying. Their measure by horse power is one before which spirit power is made humble. Horse power drives, spirit power unites' (Tagore 2009, 131). According to Xu Zhimo (2005, 42) Tagore was 'afraid we would be infected by the mediocrity and evil of profiteering'. By and large, this is the class of people that are the decision makers and at the helm of affairs in businesses worldwide—the successful mediocre! Thus, it is imperative for academics and business leaders to take a note of Tagore's warning and focus on initiatives to cultivate and disseminate ethics and values at the personal and the organisational levels for a sustainable future.

Concluding Reflections: The Leadership of Tagore

Tagore remains as a glowing paragon of institutional leadership for all disciplines to emulate and draw the relevant lessons in the respective context for modern times. His university and his new as well as alternative education model had attracted great teachers from all disciplines worldwide, some of whom came and spent rest of their life in Santiniketan. Moreover, the institution stood the test of time and sustainability even 75 years after his demise. This was possible because Tagore's leadership had two dimensions flourishing in parallel:

- *Inspirational:* Rooted in the ancient wisdom of India, especially the Upanishads, and modelled on the *Tapovan* (forest of askesis) system of Indian education in the heart of nature, he had twin objectives to fulfil: (a) awakening the infinite creative potential in man and (b) offering an education system that would be an experience of joy and freedom as a formidable challenge to mechanised, robotised and monetised modern education. In essence, he was indeed a role model of transcendental leadership with abiding faith in the spiritual truth of man and spiritual unity of the universe. Long before Maslow had identified self-realisation as the highest apex level of his hierarchy of needs Pyramid, he urged his

faculty and students to strive to attain the highest truth within and radiate that light of inspiration to one and all.
- *Functional:* The functional dimension of his leadership went beyond his academic innovations to include the welfare of the community around Visva-Bharati. It was possible because of his inclusive thinking borne out of his all-encompassing vision. This was possible because he could inspire and ignite the spark within him in the faculty and the students who plunged into action for instilling economic self-reliance and social empowerment among the underprivileged villagers through participatory development. This facilitated the increasing interest of the community in their indigenous skills development, and involvement in decision making and local governance.

The genius of Tagore will remain an enigma for generations to come. A global mind with Indian roots, he cast his spell on the thinkers, intellectuals and leaders worldwide. Through all his lectures in China and the creation of Cheena Bhavan in Visva-Bharati he strengthened and nurtured the Indo-China relationship for the future and raised the Asian voice against the aggressive capitalist forces of the West. As a pioneer of a new and alternative education, he was a glowing inspiration across all disciplines including management and community development initiatives. He will forever be venerated as a transcendental leader beyond space and time.

Epilogue

The darkness of the night was fading and dawn breaking in Mount Taishan, the holy mountain of China. Xu Zhimo, the famous Chinese poet and Tagore's dear 'Susima' (his Indian name christened by Tagore himself), had a hallucinatory experience while watching the sunrise. He wrote at the end of an essay (2005, 312–13): 'This is how I remember my hallucination while watching the sunrise on Mount Taishan and also my eulogy while looking forward to Tagore's arrival in China'.

Here is a snapshot of the vision:

> This giant has his long hair down, and the long hair flies like a black flag in the wind, clattering while flirting. This giant stands on the summit of the earth, raising his head towards the East, stretching his long arms, expecting, receiving, urging, calling silently. He is worshipping, praying, shedding tears—the hot tears mixing joy and sorrow before meeting one's cynosure…

The tears will not shed in vain, and the silent prayer is not to be unanswered.
The hand of the giant pointing to the East—
What does the East possess and is revealing?
The East possesses plenty of colours of the brilliance and glories, the East possesses
The great and universal brightness—appearing, arriving, is here now...

In the light of the above, a Tagore song rings in the ears of our mind. The song appears at the end of his last essay 'Crisis of Civilisation'. The lyrics depict his vision in his search for new light for the world (Tagore 1990, 738).

There the Saviour comes,
the earth's dust and grass on all sides
are stirred up.
In heaven hail conches, victory drums on earth roll—
the moment of the great birth is near.
Night's fortress-towers are all
tumbled to dust.
On east's crest comes the call to cast out fear,
in hope of new life.
'All hail to human awakening' is now
ringing out in skies.

References

Bell, E. and Taylor, S. 2004. 'From Outward Bound to Inward Bound: The Prophetic Voices and Discourse Practices of Spiritual Management Development'. *Human Relations* 57(4): 439–466.

Bennis, W.G. and O'Toole, J. 2005. 'How Business Schools Lost Their Way'. *Harvard Business Review* 83(5): 96–104.

Biberman, J., Whitty, M. and Robbins, I. 1999. 'Lessons from Oz: Balance and Wholeness in Organizations'. *Journal of Organizational Change Management* 12(3): 243–253.

Cash, K.C. and Grey, George R. 2000. 'A Framework for Accommodating Religion and Spirituality in the Workplace'. *Academy of Management Executive* 14(3): 124–134.

Chakraborty, S.K. 1995. *Ethics in Management: Vedantic Perspectives*. New Delhi: Oxford University Press.

Chatterjee. D. 1998. *Leading Consciously: A Pilgrimage to Self-mastery*. New Delhi: Viva Books.

Covey, S.R. 1992. *Principle-centred Leadership*. London: Simon and Schuster.

Das, S.K. 1999. *Rabindranath Tagore: Talks in China*. New Delhi: Rupa & Co.

Das Gupta. 2011. 'Sino-Indian Studies at Visva-Bharati University: Story of Cheena-Bhavana, 1921–1937'. In *Tagore and China*, eds Tan Chaung, Amiya Dev, Wang

Bangwei and Wei Liming. New Delhi: SAGE Publications, and Beijing: Central Compilation and Translation Press.

Gelb, M.J. 1998. *How to Think like Leonardo da Vinci*. New York: Delacorte Press.

Ghoshal, S. 2005. 'Bad Management Theories are Destroying Good Management Practices'. *Academy of Management Learning and Education* 4(1).

Hay, S. 1970. *Asian Ideas of the East and West*: Tagore and his Critics in Japan, China and India. Cambridge, Massachusetts: Harvard University Press.

Ims, J.K. and Zsolnai, L. 2006. *Business within Limits: Deep Ecology and Buddhist Economics*. Bern: Peter Lang.

Jaworski, J. 1998. *Synchronicity: The Inner Path of Leadership*. San Francisco: Berrett-Koehler Publishers.

Ji Xianlin Wenji. 1966. *Selected Works of Ji Xianlin, Volume 5*. Nanchuang: Jiangxi Education Press.

Kind, S., Irwin, R., Graucer, K., and De Cosson, A. 2005. 'Medicine Wheel Imag(in)ings: Exploring Holistic Curriculum Perspectives'. *Art Education* 58(5): 33–38.

Mitroff, I. 2004. 'An Open Letter to the Deans and Faculties of American Business Schools'. *Journal of Business Ethics* 54(2): 184–189.

Mitroff, I. and Denton, E. 1999. *A Spiritual Audit of Corporate America: A Hard Look at Spirituality, Religion, and Values in the Workplace*. San Francisco: Jossey-Bass Publishers.

Mukherjee, S. 2007. 'Non-Conventional Entrepreneurial Learning: Spiritual Insights from India'. *Journal of Human Values* 13(1): 23–34.

Pruzan, P., Pruzan Mikkelsen, K., Miller, W. and Miller, D. 2007. *Leading with Wisdom: Spiritual-based Leadership*. New Delhi: Response Books.

Rao, N. 2011. 'Foreword to the Chinese Edition'. In *Tagore and China*, eds Tan Chaung, Amiya Dev, Wang Bangwei and Wei Liming. New Delhi: SAGE Publications, and Beijing: Central Compilation and Translation Press.

Sen, A. 2011. 'Tagore and China'. In *Tagore and China*, eds Tan Chaung, Amiya Dev, Wang Bangwei and Wei Liming. New Delhi: SAGE Publications, and Beijing: Central Compilation and Translation Press.

Ray, M.I. 1992. 'The Emerging New Paradigm in Business'. In *New Traditions in Business: Spirit and Leadership in the 21st Century*, eds Renesch, J. San Francisco: Berrett Koehler Publishers.

Tagore, R. 1937. 'China and India'. (inaugural speech of the Cheena Bhavana). In *The English Writings of Rabindranath Tagore Volume 3*, eds S.K. Das. New Delhi: Sahitya Akademi.

———. 1990. 'Sabhyatar Sankat'. (Crisis in Civilisation). In *Rabindra Rachanabali* (Collected Works of Rabindranath Tagore, Volume 13) Kolkata: West Bengal Government.

———. 1996. 'Crisis of Civilization'. In *The English Writings of Rabindranath Tagore*, Volume 3, ed. S.K. Das. New Delhi: Sahitya Akademi.

———. 2009. *Talks in China*. New Delhi: Rupa & Co.

Tan Chuang 2011. 'Introduction I'. In *Tagore and China* eds Tan Chaung, Amiya Dev, Wang Bangwei and Wei Liming. New Delhi: SAGE Publications, and Beijing: Central Compilation and Translation Press.

Wang Shuying. 2006. *Ji Xianlin lun Zhung-Yin wenhua jiaoliu* (Ji Xianlin on Sino-Indian Cultural Intercourse). Beijing: Beijing New Century Publisher.

Weick, K. 2006. 'Faith, Evidence and Action: Better Guesses in an Unknowable World'. *Organization Studies* 27(11): 1723–1736.

Xu Zhimo. 2005. *Xu Zhimo quanji* (Collected Works of Xu Zhimo). Tianjin: Tianjin People's Press.

Zohar, D. and Marshall, I. 2000. *SQ: Spiritual Intelligence, the Ultimate Intelligence*. New York: Bloomsbury Publishing.

5

China and India
Cultural and Religious Exchanges in the 15th Century

Huang Weimin

Introduction

The exchanges between China and India were originally carried on by land. In the pre-Qin period, about 3,000 years ago, the monks or the businessmen from central India coming all the way along the Silk Road in the south or north, across the desert and snow mountains in Central Asia or through the thick forest and river valley, spread Buddhist culture or were engaged in silk trade activities. This promoted exchange and dialogue between the two civilisations. In the 12th century, the progressive navigation technology linked up the Sino-Indian maritime communication channel.

In 1405 AD, the resourceful Yongle emperor Zhu Di for the first time sent the eunuch Zheng He and his fleet to the West, which opened Sino-India maritime exchanges at the government level, though it was not an exchange between two equal countries. As a powerful nation 'conquering small countries around it', China symbolically incorporated several small countries of the South Asian subcontinent into the national territory by asking them to pay tribute to the imperial court, while India was still a fragmented place called 'five Indias' or 'five Tenjidus' according to them. The exchanges between China and India at the government level in the 15th century were recorded in three books written during

Zheng He's seven voyages to the West. These were *Ying-ya Sheng-lan* (The Overall Survey of the Ocean's Shores) by Ma Huan, *Xing-cha Sheng-lan* (Description of the Starry Rafts) by Fei Xin and *Records of Western Countries* by Gong Zhen respectively. Ma Huan, Fei Xin and Gong Zhen had followed Zheng He to the West successively and based on their true experience, all of them recorded the local customs and practices of the countries that the fleet had been to. In addition, fragmented records could be found in the *True Record of Ming Dynasty* and the *History of Ming Dynasty* and some local chronicles. From such literature we roughly know that the government exchanges between China and India were primarily among Calicut, Cochin and Bengala.

Tributary Relations with Calicut, Cochin, Bengala, Gambari and Quilon

Calicut is now Kozhikode along the coast in the southwest of the Indian continent. Thanks to the superior geographical position, Calicut was known as 'the wharf for the countries of the West'. In 1403, Zhu Di ordered Yin Qing the officer to pacify Calicut, and the head Shami Dixi sent a delegation to follow Yin Qing to the imperial court where Yongle emperor issued an imperial edict to grant Shami Dixi imperial mandate and made him the king, officially establishing the relationship of paying tribute. In 1405, when Zheng He made his first voyage to the Western ocean, Calicut was his destination. A monument was built there to remember the time (this monument has been well preserved till now). In *Ying-ya Sheng-lan*, Ma Huan praised the incredibly huge scale of trade of the city for which the businessmen all over the world had visited it frequently.

Cochin is the largest city and major port at Kerala in India. Cochin and Calicut were together called Namburi (from a surname of a Brahman) during the Song dynasty, but Cochin has had a longer history of contact and exchanges with China. According to the *History of Ming Dynasty*, 'Cochin, namely, ancient Pan Pan Kingdom, paid tribute to the imperial court in Song, Liang, Sui and Tang Dynasties' (Qing Zhang Tingyu 1974, 8440). In 1407, the imperial court of the Ming dynasty conferred the title of king upon the leader of Cochin Keyili, granted him a seal, authorised to worship a mountain as 'Mountain of the Kingdom' and even wrote a long tablet inscription for it. In 1409, Keyili dispatched for the first time a delegation to pay tribute with Zheng He's fleet.

Bengala referred to Bangladesh and the Indian states of West Bengal, Bihar, Tripura and Orissa. If Calicut and Cochin were valued by China because of their important status as trade ports, then Bengala got associated with China mainly for more complicated political factors. The Ming dynasty helped Bengala calm the dispute with the neighbouring kingdom Jaunpur by means of intervention in government affairs. First, the king of Bengala Aiyasiding passed away and the imperial court of Ming made his heir Saiwuding, the new king. Bengala was invaded by the neighbouring country Jaunpur in 1420 and Saiwuding requested urgent rescue from Ming. In September 1421, on behalf of the imperial court, the diplomatist Hou Xian went to Bengala and successfully reconciled and settled the dispute. Presumably because of the political relationship, China had always given special treatment to Bengala and maintained good contact; the latter also dispatched the most diplomatic corps to the imperial court of Ming and had the longest diplomatic relationship with China.

In addition to the above three kingdoms, Jaunpur, Soli, Gambari and Quilon also had brief contact with the Ming government. Jaunpur was in Central India of 'five Indias'. While mediating the dispute between Jaunpur and Bengala, the Ming court attempted to incorporate it into the tributary system, but Jaunpur was unwilling to accept it and did not send envoys to China. Soli is in today's river mouth of Corey, which established a tributary relationship with Ming in 1403 and dispatched envoys to pay tribute to the Ming court twice; the latter considered the long journey and did not care about how much the tribute was. The exact place of Ananda was unknown and it found little record in the *History of Ming Dynasty*. Gambari, also known as Cape Comorin, in the southernmost tip of the Indian peninsula, established tributary relationship in 1409. Quilon, a bordering kingdom of Cochin, also established a tributary relationship with the Ming dynasty in 1408.In addition, the kingdoms that had exchanges with China included Malabar, Cail, Ahmedabad, Jurfattan and Delhi, which have rarely been recorded in history.

Chinese Envoys to the Kingdoms in India

China and Indian kingdoms exchanged most closely during Zheng He's seven voyages to the Western ocean. Zheng He's fleet arrived at almost all kingdoms of the eastern and western coasts of India. Besides, the government of the Ming dynasty also sent envoys to many Indian kingdoms. The details are shown in Table 5.1.

Table 5.1
Chinese Envoys to the Indian Kingdoms

时间 (Time)	国家 (Kingdoms)	使者 (Emissary)
洪武2年 (1369)	西洋琐里 (Soli)	刘叔勉 (Shumian Liu)
永乐2年 (1403)	古里 (Calicut)、柯枝 (Cochin)	尹庆 (QingYing)
永乐2年 (1404)	西洋琐里 (Soli)	闻良辅 (Liangfu Wen)
永乐2年 (1404)	西洋琐里 (Soli)	马彬 (Bing Ma)
永乐3年 (1405)	古里 (Calicut)	郑和 (He Zheng)、王景弘 (Jinhong Wang) 等
永乐6年 (1408)	古里 (Calicut)、柯枝 (Cochin)、加异勒 (Cail)、阿拨把丹 (Ahmedabad)、小葛兰 (Quilon)、南巫里 (Malabar)、甘巴里 (Cape Comorin)	郑和 (He Zheng)、王景弘 (Jinhong Wang)、费信 (Xing Fei) 等
永乐7年 (1409)	古里 (Calicut)、甘巴里 (Cape Comorin)、小葛兰 (Quilon)、柯枝 (Cochin)、榜葛剌 (Bengala)	郑和 (He Zheng)、王景弘 (Jinhong Wang)、候显 (Xian Hou)、费信 (Xing Fei)、马欢 (Huan Ma) 等
永乐10年 (1412)	底里 (Delhi)	无名使者 (no name)
永乐13年 (1415)	古里 (Calicut)、柯枝 (Cochin)、加异勒 (Cail)	郑和 (He Zheng)、王景弘 (Jinhong Wang)、马欢 (Huan Ma)、哈同 (Tong Ha) 等
永乐15年 (1417)	古里 (Calicut)、柯枝 (Cochin)、南巫里 (Malabar)、沙里湾泥 (Jurfattan)	郑和 (He Zheng)、王景弘 (Jinhong Wang)、费信 (Xing Fei) 等
永乐19年 (1421)	古里 (Calicut)、柯枝 (Cochin)、榜葛剌 (Bengala)	郑和 (He Zheng)、王景弘 (Jinhong Wang) 等
永乐20年 (1422)	沼纳朴儿 (Jaunpur) 和底里 (Delhi)	甘泉 (Quan Gan)
宣德5年 (1430)	加异勒 (Cail)、古里 (Calicut)	郑和 (He Zheng)、王景弘 (Jinhong Wang)、洪保 (Bao Hong) 等

Source: True Record of the Ming Dynasty

Indian Kingdoms Paying Tribute to China

According to *True Record of Ming Dynasty*, Calicut sent envoys to pay tribute to China more than 8 times, Cochin 6 times and Bengala up to 10 times (Table 5.2). Indian envoys usually came to China together with Zheng He's fleet. It was said that there were so many tributary kingdoms that the court full of tributary envoys 'ranked Calicut as the first place of all kingdoms' (Taibei 1962, 3120). It can be seen how important the role of Calicut was in the diplomatic relationships of the Ming dynasty with kingdoms of the Indian Ocean. In 1433, the tributary diplomatic

Table 5.2
Indian Kingdoms Paying Tribute to China

时间（Time）	国家 (Kingdoms)
永乐元年（1402）	西洋琐里 (Soli)
永乐2年（1404）	古里（Calicut）
永乐3年（1405）	古里（Calicut）
永乐5年（1407）	小葛兰（Quilon）
永乐6年（1408）	榜葛剌（Bengala）
永乐7年（1409）	古里（Calicut）榜葛剌（Bengala）
永乐8年（1410）	榜葛剌（Bengala）
永乐9年（1411）	古里（Calicut）柯枝（Cochin）榜葛剌（Bengala）加异勒（Cail）
永乐10年（1412）	榜葛剌（Bengala）
永乐12年（1414）	榜葛剌（Bengala）
永乐13年（1415）	古里（Calicut）柯枝（Cochin）甘巴里（Cape Comorin）
永乐14年（1416）	古里（Calicut）柯枝（Cochin）沙里湾泥（Jurfattan）
永乐19年（1421）	古里（Calicut）柯枝（Cochin）甘巴里（Cape Comorin）榜葛剌（Bengala）
永乐21年（1423）	古里（Calicut）柯枝（Cochin）榜葛剌（Bengala）西洋琐里(Soli)
宣德4年（1429）	榜葛剌（Bengala）
宣德8年（1433）	古里（Calicut）柯枝（Cochin）甘巴里（Cape Comorin）加异勒（Cail）
正统3年（1438）	榜葛剌（Bengala）

Source: True Record of the Ming Dynasty

corps came to China for the last time and then Zheng He passed away; as a result of which, the sailing plan of the imperial court was suspended. The corps of Calicut and Cochin were retained in China for three years until they went back to their motherland with the tribute ships of Java in 1436. They never stepped into China since then. Bengala broke off the friendly relations with China in 1436.

The Hindu Beliefs of Calicut and Cochin

Ma Huan mentioned in *Yingya Shenglan* that Bengala was a kingdom with singular religious belief and all the people were Huis. Calicut and Cochin were kingdoms with multiple religions and five hierarchies which included the Nanpi people, the Hui Hui people, the Zhedi people, the Geling people and the Papaw people. All their kings believed in Buddhism (actually Hinduism), worshipping elephants and cattle. Moreover, Quilon and Ananda also believed in 'Buddhism'. According to *History of Ming Dynasty*, in 1374, King of Ananda Kahalu dispatched a speaker Binixi to the imperial court of Ming to pay tribute such as local specialties, detoxified medicines and stone needles for acupuncture remedies. In return, Taizu of Ming granted them Buddhist clothes, cloth and silk. Among the citizens of Calicut and Cochin, those believing in Hinduism and Islam were almost equal. The king believing in Hinduism also reached an agreement with the believers of Islam: 'the king and the citizens did not eat beef and the chieftain as a Hui Hui did not eat pork. The king and the Hui Hui people pledged that "you do not eat cattle, and I do not eat pigs". The mutual taboos remain till now' (Ma Huan 1955, 43).

In *Ying-ya Sheng-lan*, Ma Huan also gave a detailed description of the religion ceremonies of 'Buddhism' in Calicut and Cochin. He wrote that the kings of Calicut and Cochin 'casted figures of Buddha with brass' and named it 'Nainaer', built Buddha halls, tiles and platforms with brass and dug a well beside the figure. Every morning, water was drawn from the well to wash the figure for people to worship. All the people of the two kingdoms worshipped elephants and cattle, liked to burn cattle dung into white ash and applied it on the forehead or the whole body. Ma Huan also referred to an allusion of local people in Calicut, worshipping cattle as follows: a sage called Musa/Moses was respected as 'true god' by local people. The sage then went to somewhere else and ordered his younger brother al-Sameri to take over his job. His brother was preposterous and casted a golden cow and declared it 'holy god', requiring all people to obey the orders of the golden cow. He also said that those who frequently applied dung of the gold cow would acquire a gold heart. Therefore, everyone considered the golden cow as the true god. When Musa came back and found that his brother had ruined the sacred law, he immediately destroyed the golden cow and was about to punish his brother. However, his brother rode an elephant and ran away. The other people looked forward to his return in vain, only to remember him while putting on cow dung.

Nevertheless, when Ma Huan witnessed the Calicut and the Cochin people worshipping elephant and cattle, washing the Buddhist figures with well water and applying cow dung to their body, he misunderstood it as 'belief in Buddhism'. They were actually based on beliefs and customs of Hinduism. It can be speculated from the belief in Hinduism of the kings of Calicut and Cochin that most of the envoys they dispatched to China were also believers of Hinduism and some of them were Hui Hui adherents.

Despite the frequent maritime exchanges between China and Calicut and Cochin, the documentary records were quite brief. There was no more information besides customs and conditions of the local people, the dates of paying tribute and categories of tributes. Only based on such fragmental historical data, it is difficult to piece together the panorama of governmental exchanges between India and China in the 15th century. We do not know whether the diplomatic corps of Calicut and Cochin who frequently visited China exerted any influence in terms of religious and cultural exchanges in addition to the local specialties and tributes they brought, and the silk and chinaware they took back. Nor could we verify whether the diplomatic corps retained in China from 1433 to 1436 conducted Hindu preaching activities. The only thing we are sure is that the brief history of Sino-Indian exchanges in the 15th century is a transition period of great significance. It is with the opening of the sea route on the Indian Ocean by voyager Zheng He that the exchanges between China and India rose to a governmental level from civil level, which also opened a new page for the later long-standing religious and cultural exchanges.

Non-governmental Exchanges between China and India in the 15th Century and the Spread of Religious Culture

In the 15th century, in addition to the governmental exchanges based on tributary trades, there were also two folk forces who acted as messengers of cultural exchange between China and India, that is, the 'western monks' and merchants. Hindu Tantrism, which had close relation with Hindu Saktism, replaced Buddhism to become the important carrier of the religious and cultural transmission between China and India.

The Missionary Activities of Hindu Tantrism by 'Western Monks'

'Western monks' were a folk Tantrism community active in the early stage of the Ming dynasty and its members were from Nepal of South Asia and Kashmir of India. As it is known to all, Indian Buddhism was mainly Tantrism. Till the 11th century, due to the invasion of Arab and Islam and their religious persecution, Tantrism gradually declined in India. At the end of the 12th century and the beginning of the 13th century, the Islamic army marched eastward, wiping out the India Nalanda monastery and Sangrgyas-yeshes-shabs. The masters of Tantrism scattered, as a result, with most of them escaping to Tibet via Kashmir and other regions and some others fleeing to Nepal. In late Yuan and early Ming dynasty, a large number of Tantrism monks left India for China via Tibet and Nepal to propagate the religion, searching for survival space for Tantrism in China. The grandmaster of western monks was Indian Tantra monk Saha Zanshili, who was from Jiaweiluowei (near Tilaurakot in South Nepal) of Central India, born in Kshatriya caste and became a monk in Suluosa temple of Kasmira kingdom (now Kashmir). Saha Zanshili, 'proficient in the five branches of knowledge in India and injunctions', came to China in 1364 and was considered highly by Zhu Yuanzhang, Taizu of Ming, who had a temple built in Zhongshan Mountain, and let him live there. When he visited Zhongshan Mountain, the emperor would call on the master and consult about religious doctrine. Saha Zanshili did missionary work in China for 18 years, with numerous followers, among whom the famous one was Zhiguang (Buddhist name was Janne Doshimi) from Shandong province. Zhiguang was a good commander of Tantrism and 'proficient in Buddhist scripture and proud of his outstanding debate ability', well honoured by Taizu of Ming, emperors Ren Zong, Xuan Zong and Ying Zong. The western monks' community led by Saha Zanshili and his follower Zhiguang preached the religion to both emperors and queens and the common people and held religious rites for them. They also built temples and statues at different places, set up mandalas, translated scriptures and wrote books to spread Hindu Tantrism, having significant influence.

In addition to the school of Saha Zanshili and Zhiguang, in the 11th year of Yongle (1413), Shilishalibudeyue came to China from East India to preach his religion. He was the prince of Zangema kingdom of East India, with the title 'Wang Ming Ban Di Da', meaning paying 'gold statues of all Buddhists and thrones' as tributes. Therefore, one of Ming's emperors, Zhudi, specially built Zhenjue Temple for enshrinement. Another Ming's emperor, named Xuan Zong till the ninth year, granted imperial edict that the temple should be in the Indian style. To support the missionary work of western monks, the imperial court of Ming even established foreign doctrine plants, including 'Xifan Plant' and 'Xitian Plant', responsible for the printing of Indian and Western scriptures.

Not all members of the 'western monks' community were from India, as it also included many Chinese and Annan monks. The religion they preached was not Chinese Buddhism well known among the Ming people, but Indian Tantrism whose pulse had a distinct characteristic of Hindu Saktism. The main duties and missions of the western monks were to do missionary work, translating and annotating Tantra and rite rules. The dominator of Ming, however, paid more attention to their roles as cultural messengers. In the early Ming, when the influence of western monks gradually increased, Taizu Zhu Yuanzhang strictly prohibited foreign religions for 'being against local custom and corrupting religions and behaviours, with great harm'. Later 'well-behaved and prudent' masters and followers of western monks—Saha Zashili and Gumalashili—changed his prejudice and he realised that western monks could not only have positive influence on Chinese monks but also shoulder the mission of propagating the national image of China.

In fact, the Indian Tantrism sangha led by Saha Zanshili and Zhiguang shouldered the mission as messengers of cultural exchange. For example, Zhiguang received instructions to go to Nepal and other regions thrice in 1384, 1388 and 1403, to preach Buddhist doctrine, for sanctification as well as exchanging information about the local conditions, customs and religious culture of the two countries. Moreover, Sangkebala from Central India, the first follower of Zhiguang used to be a primary teacher of the foreign doctrine plant of the imperial court, 'teaching over one thousand officers, learning true doctrines in Sanskrit and Sanskrit praise and execution ground inside and outside'. Sanyandashili, the follower of Sangkebala, interpreted and translated doctrine for the officials and scholars in imperial academy and taught them Buddhist words. Yalanggeyueshiliqin, the first follower of Sanyandashili also delivered a sermon in Senglusi (a central organisation of the imperial court). It made a great contribution to the spread of Hindu religious culture in China.

The Hinduism Remains of the 'Merchants' in Quanzhou and Other Places

Besides the western monks, Indian businessmen had also promoted Indian religious culture directly or indirectly. The trade between the Ming dynasty of China and the western tributary kingdoms was divided into 'tributary trade' and 'business trade'. The former was a foreign business exchange form dominated by the government, that is, the government permitted that the tributary kingdoms could bring a certain amount of business goods with the tributary trade and dealt with Chinese people in specified places. Ming dynasty set up two bureaus for foreign shipping in Guangzhou and Quanzhou to take charge of the tributary trade with the coastal kingdoms of India. At that time, the Indian envoys usually accompanied a certain number of merchants who brought spice, black pepper and gemstones to trade with Chinese people. Business trade referred to individual trade among folk people. In the early and middle periods of Ming dynasty, strict maritime prohibition was implemented and the civilian private trade activities were banned by explicit order. However, such order was never strictly executed and the civilian trade between China and the kingdoms of India had continued till late Qing dynasty. The business trade between Calicut and Ming dynasty was especially frequent. Wang Zhifu of Ming dynasty recorded about the Portuguese merchant ships from Calicut that engaged in the trade in China. Calicut was a fair of other foreign countries in the west. They came to China in March or April to sell sundries and then left for Japan and other countries. When I was there, I saw three ships granted with three hundred thousand silver and gold. The taxation bureau allowed them to trade in the city after they paid taxation (Quan Hansheng 1972, 444).

In 2011, when Liu Yinghua, who is a medical scholar from China Tibetology Research Center in Beijing, wrote this review Boyer[1] in Calicut Manuscript Library, she accidentally discovered a Chinese ancient coin in NO 2579 writing, with four characters of 'Dao Guang

Tong Bao' cast, which showed that trade and communications between China and India continued till the end of the Qing dynasty.

The Different Indian Religious Cultures Brought by Western Monks and Merchants

Though the activities of the western monks and merchants in China in the 15th century had helped in spreading Indian religious culture to varying degrees, there were significant differences between them. The Indian Tantrism spread by the western monks was closely related to Saktism of Hinduism, while the Indian merchants from Calicut and Cochin were sincere believers of Hinduism or Islam dominating the mainland of India. Since the western monks' community had been strongly supported by the imperial court of Ming dynasty over 100 years (1403–1521) and passing on scriptures and doctrines were their main duties and mission, the influence of western monks in religious culture on China could not be matched with that of the merchants.

The different routes taken by the western monks and the merchants to come to China:

Western Monks	Starting from India to Nepal over the Himalayas through the ancient paths in Tibet of China, Tantrism was introduced and Lamaism was introduced into India in reverse.
Merchants	From the harbours in India to Malay Islands to Quanzhou or Guangzhou and other ports via the Indian Ocean, which was called 'Maritime Silk Road'.

Spread of Indian Religious Culture in China in the 15th Century

From the long history of Sino-Indian contacts, the 15th century was found to be an important turning point when interactions between India and China were developed both in governmental and civilian dimensions and Tantrism and Hinduism gradually replaced Buddhism as the main contribution of the Sino-India cultural exchange. The religious and cultural exchanges and communication between China and India in the 15th century were epitomised by the following three characteristics:

The Western Monks Depending on the Imperial Court Lost the Support of the Folk

The western monks spread Indian Tantrism, preached doctrines and disciplines and held religious rites basically to meet the needs of the royal family and the rise and fall of its fortune was also in the hands of the imperial court. During the rule of the emperor believing in Indian Tantrism, the western monks were favoured and trusted, and consequently Tantrism also showed a certain degree of prosperity. However, when the emperor did not believe in Buddhism, for example, Shi Zong of Ming dynasty banned Buddhism, the monks of Tantrism were sent back to their homeland and the influence of Tantrism also vanished. Since their main mission was to serve the royal, they did not keep any contact with ordinary people and hence the spread in the folk was quite limited which failed to win the wide belief of common people. The Tantra missionary activities of the western monks were mainly limited to Nanjing and Beijing without going deep into the large areas of the mainland.

The Localisation Communication Strategy of Tantrism and Hinduism in China Was Not Successful

Chinese scholar Tang Yijie pointed out that cultural exchange and communication were a two-way selection process, where the original culture would choose the part of foreign culture which could adapt to its cultural needs to promote the development of their own culture. When foreign culture was introduced to some different traditional cultures, it would change its form to meet the requirements of the original culture in the long river of historical development, despite their conflict with each other. In the process of Buddhism being introduced into China, it found a lot in common with Chinese Confucianism and Neo-Taoism and rapidly blended with the Chinese culture; whereas localisation communication strategy of Tantrism and Hinduism in China was not successful and had limited influence on Chinese culture. The doctrines and rite rules preached by Tantrism and Hinduism, especially the thought of Saktism totally conflicted with the philosophy of 'keeping heavenly principle and perishing human desires' in Chinese traditional culture, which created great barriers for Chinese people to accept the foreign religions. Therefore, they could not shake the dominant role of Confucian culture rooted in the Ming dynasty of China.

The Unidirectional Flow of the Sino-India Cultural Exchanges in the 15th Century

In the long history of cultural exchange between China and India, China has always been the party which accepted and absorbed and the cultural exchange and transmission showed a one-way flow. The 15th century was no exception. Although Zheng He's voyages to Indian kingdoms brought Chinese Confucian classics, medical books, acupuncture, poetry, musical instruments, paintings and calligraphy, they had little influence on the kingdoms of India. As for the reasons for the one-way flow of culture, one was the exclusiveness of Indian religious culture itself; the other was that the spread of Chinese culture in India was driven by political power. When the Ming dynasty ended the navigation plan, cultural transmission was also terminated. There was never a folk team like the western monks who took upon religious cultural transmission as their duty to assume the uncompleted Chinese cultural dissemination of the Ming dynasty.

Conclusion

Although the exchange between China and India in the 15th century, both in national and folk dimensions, was not a very successful two-way choice, it had injected fresh blood more or less from a different country to the cultures of the two countries, deriving a variety of forms with cultural attributes and characteristics of the times and enriching the patterns of manifestation and spiritual connotation of the cultures of the two countries. More importantly, in the 15th century, the experience and lessons in the cultural communication and interactive practice provide beneficial enlightenment and reference for today's Sino-Indian exchange. Today, India and China have started new cooperation and exchange as members of the BRICS countries (Brazil, Russia, India, China, and South Africa) and the religious culture also draws great attention because of the national strategy of reconstructing the cultural soft power of the two countries. What features or forms will the cultural interactions and bilateral selections between China and India in the context of globalisation show? What sparks and wisdom will be produced? What power and sources will they provide for the two countries? All these topics are worth continuous and profound research.

Note

1. Boyer is a kind of leaf, which is called *corypha umbraculifera* scientifically.

References

(Ming) Ma Huan. 1955. *Collation and Annotation of Ying-ya Sheng-lan*. Beijing: Zhonghua Book Company.
(Qing) Zhang Tingyu. 1974. *History of Ming Dynasty, Collected Biographies, Foreign Countries Volume 7, Calicut*. Beijing: Zhonghua Book Company.
Quan Hansheng. 1972. *Symposium of Chinese Economic History, Book 1*. Hong Kong: The New Asia Institute of Advanced Chinese Studies.
———. 1962. 'Item September 1st of the 21st Year of Yongle'. In *True Record of the Ming Dynasty· Wuzong, Volume 263* Taibei: Photocopy of Historical Languages Research Institution of Academia Sinica.

6

China's Enlightenment by Indian Strategies of Cultural Soft Power

Jian Li

'Soft power' is a concept put forth for the first time in 1990 by Joseph S. Nye, Jr., a professor of Harvard University in the USA. According to him, 'soft power is the ability to attract and co-opt rather than coerce for own purpose. It arises from the attractiveness of its culture, political ideals, and policies' (Nye 2005, 2). A country's soft power mainly consists of culture, political values and foreign policies. Soft power is a concept whereby humans socialise with others to fulfil own interests and hence its emergence is inevitably significant to historical progress. Now, a large number of countries have taken the improvement of soft power as an important path to enhance their comprehensive strength. 'Cultural soft power' refers to the cohesion, attractiveness, influence and competitiveness revealed in a country's cultural values, cultural products and cultural life. Representing national identity and racial image, cultural soft power can generate more lasting attractiveness and influence than political and economic forces do. It is the major carrier and an important part of a country's soft power. This chapter will explore China's enlightenment and lessons from the strategies taken by India for the development of cultural soft power.

India's Resources for Development of Cultural Soft Power

A powerful culture acts as the internal drive to a nation's survival and acquisition of international competitiveness. After its development and accumulation for thousands of years, Indian culture shows strong vitality and inclusiveness, providing the blessed hotbed for India's development of cultural soft power in modern times.

Cultural Values

India's culture contains unique values, which are roughly concluded as harmony, spirituality and inclusiveness. India's culture pursues the harmonious coexistence of human and nature and guides people to the highest level of moksha through love and dharma. In India's culture, spirituality is revealed in the spiritual pursuit of liberation in religion. Spirituality gives India's culture the tendency of placing spirit over material and soul over body. For this reason, Indian people cultivate the values and lifestyle of pursuing spirit, disdaining material, pursuing inner peace and avoiding impulsiveness. Inclusiveness of India's culture means that India greatly absorbs the reasonable elements of different cultures and makes them the organic parts of own culture, while allowing the coexistence of various cultures and maintaining cultural diversity (Chen Hongbing 2008). The traditional values of India's culture demonstrate their exclusive significance to solving global issues such as deterioration of ecological environment, caused by people's excessive exploration of the nature and the spiritual vacuum resulting from the zest for materialism.

Religious Diversity

India, as the birthplace of Buddhism, once attracted nearly 300 million Buddhists around the world. Thus, India became an important bridge between India and the East Asian circle of Confucianism. India is also the homeland of Hinduism, Jainism and Sikhism, and accommodates many followers of Islam, Catholicism, Christianity, Zoroastrianism and Judaism. Taking Islam as an example, about 162 million people believe in Islam within the territory of India. To the West, Islam connects India to the Middle East. To the East, it links India to the Southeast Asian countries, such as Malaysia, Indonesia and Singapore. The religious connection improves intimacy between countries and provides a good foundation for eliminating doubts and conflicts (Paul and Nayar 2003, 59).

Popular Culture

Popular culture has also developed extraordinarily in India. Taking the film industry as an example, India produces the largest number of films in the world. The giant Indian film industry is built on Bollywood which produces the largest number of films and sells the largest number of film tickets in the world. Bollywood has very important influence on the popular culture of the entire Indian subcontinent, Middle East, Africa and Southeast Asia, and extends such influence to the whole world through South Asian emigrants. Now, India's arts including music, dance and fashion design are displayed on the world stage, while India's yoga and food have become popular around the world. All these have enhanced the status of India's culture to people around the world.

Science and Technology and Education

India has been very successful in college education and training of high-end talents. India underscores quality education and its educational departments are rarely restricted and controlled by bureaucracy. Also, schools enjoy relatively independent and diversified development and do not follow the 'one-size-fits-all' mode of management, so as to create a free environment for the training and development of creative talents. Today, India has developed into a large exporter of information technology services in the world and has even got the nickname 'World Office' due to its highly efficient, high-quality and cheap services. Apart from software, India is also the export base of accounting, medical, tax and telecommunication services. The former UN secretary-general Mr Kofi Annan once praised India as 'a model of high technology development for developing countries'.

Non-resident Indian and Their Values

The vast number of Indians living in foreign countries is an asset for India's development of cultural soft power. More than 20 million Indian people scatter around the world and build their communities. A lot of non-resident Indians have made outstanding achievements through own efforts and extraordinary performance and therefore won the respects in the countries where they live in. These non-resident Indians often use own strong influence to actively convince the governments or congresses of the countries where they live, in order to formulate the policies friendly to India and facilitate the friendly relationship between these countries and India. Also, non-resident Indians keep remitting money back to India, and that could be considered as one of the important factors behind India's rapid progress. As more and more non-resident Indians come back to start a business, they import advanced technology, management practices and cutting edge tools and techniques to India. These in turn help India's enterprises learn about the trend of international economic progress and keep pace with the world. At the same time, most of the non-resident Indians maintain their traditional values which contribute to the spread of India's culture across the globe.

India's Strategies for Development of Cultural Soft Power

Spread of India's Cultural Values

Joseph S. Nye claims that, in a modern society, a country may easily develop its soft power if it satisfies three criteria. One of the criteria is that 'the country's dominant culture has the norms similar to the global culture'. Based on this point of view, India is regarded by the Western world as 'the largest democratic country in the world' and advocates the values honoured by the western world, which actually provides a platform for its development of soft power. The diversified tradition and inclusiveness towards other cultures is the essence of India's cultural values. Under the guidance of such values, the Indian government has put forward the ideas of 'combining different civilizations' and 'bringing the world together', which match with the universal pursuit of the international community at present, facilitate the establishment of a new international order and the communication and cooperation of countries around the world and provide the useful ideas for solving the modern national and religious issues (Ren Fei 2009).

In recent years, the Indian government has strengthened the culture diplomacy and actively exported its cultural values to other countries. In 2004, the then Indian prime minister, Dr Manmohan Singh, visited Kabul, Afghanistan, and announced a scholarship for 500 Afghan students to study in India. The Indian Council for Cultural Relations (ICCR) also offered a scholarship to 1,800 foreign students. In addition, India establishes overseas cultural centres, holds Indian cultural festivals and trains people in developing countries, so as to spread its cultural values.

Expanding the Influence of Religion

Today, India is attempting to expand its soft power into the circle of Confucian civilisation in East Asia, but Buddhism is still the primary tool. In 2006, India funded the construction of a Buddhist temple in Indian style in the White Horse Temple, Luoyang, China, with an aim to present the connection of India and China through Buddhism to the world. In September 2010, a bill was adopted by the two houses of the parliament of India to officially approve the 'Nalanda Temple revitalisation programme'. Nalanda Temple is an ancient Buddhist monument in India and known as the world's first university. From the 5th century to 12th century, the temple was the most important Buddhism research centre in the world and had a capacity of accommodating up to 10,000 students. Xuan Zang and Yi Jing, the Chinese monks in Tang dynasty, studied Buddhism at the Nalanda Temple. Through this programme, 16 Asian countries including India, China, Japan, South Korea and Singapore will cooperate to redevelop Nalanda Temple into a research and religious communication centre and combine it with Buddhism and modern university, so as to attract foreign students, promote India's culture and expand India's influence (*People's Daily* 2013).

Soft Power and Cultural Industry

India pays special attention to the development of cultural industry to enhance its cultural soft power. For example, India's film industry is not only an important part of India's cultural industry, but also an important tool to spread India's cultural soft power. When the new government of Afghanistan was established, the Indian foreign minister took the opportunity of visiting Afghanistan to distribute many CDs of Hollywood films and music instead of food or clothing to the Afghan people. The Indian TV series *Kyunki Saas Bhi Kabhi Bahu Thi* (Every Mother-in-Law Was Daughter-in-Law Once) became the most popular TV series in Afghanistan with the rating of above 90 per cent and caused many Afghan people to be absent at some religious ceremonies when the series were being telecast.

As a part of its popular culture, India's music has been widely favoured in many countries, while India's apparel and food are also very successful in other countries. While enjoying India's films, TV series, food and apparel, people also feel the charm and influence of India's culture, which further spreads and promotes India's cultural soft power around the world. For this reason, the Indian government increases the investment in the advertising of India's culture. According to the annual budget of 2008, the Indian government appropriated an extra fund of ₹750 million to ICCR, a major execution department for India's foreign cultural relations, increasing ICCR's budgetary fund to ₹1.52 billion in 2008, which is a 117 per cent increase over the previous year (Ren Junjie 2008). The fund was mainly spent on spreading and promoting India's music, literature, dance, arts, food and film to the outside world.

Influence of the Non-resident Indian

Non-resident Indians are not only powerful propagandists of India's culture, but also powerful supporters for India's improvement of cultural soft power. As Yashwant Sinha, the former foreign minister of India, said, 'Overseas Indian is the important source for the Indian Government to enforce policies through the respect and influence they have won in other countries' (Mohan 2003). The Indian government attaches much importance to this resource and makes efforts to consolidate its relationship with non-resident Indians. Every year, the Indian government holds the 'Overseas Indian Day' and grants preferential treatment to overseas Indian, such as dual nationality.

China's Enlightenment from India's Strategies for Promoting Cultural Soft Power

Through an overview of India's strategies and modes for development of cultural soft power, China can be highly enlightened in its own promotion of cultural soft power.

China's Traditional Cultural Values

India puts an emphasis on the propagation of its cultural values in the development of soft power, which is also applicable to China. China's traditional culture has very rich spiritual connotations in its process of development. First, worshipping the nature; the oriental culture has the tradition of 'harmony between man and nature' and advocates the 'imitation of nature'. Also, it not only opposes the 'conflict between man and nature' and the one-sided and endless change of nature to satisfy human needs with the attitude of utilitarianism, but advocates to make human adapt to the nature as much as possible.

Second, advocating gentleness; gentleness is the ideological basis for peace in Chinese nation, while peaceful dialogue and multilateral communication are also the values widely recognised in the international society.

Third, underscoring 'moderation'; China's traditional culture underscores 'harmony without sameness' and diversification advocates 'the precious harmony' and opposes war and punitive expedition. It advocates impartiality and emphasises that 'one should treat others as one would like to be treated'. All these ideas forge the unique personality of Chinese nation and support the endless vitality of Chinese culture and nation.

How can China's traditional cultural values be further propagandised and such outstanding traditional culture converted into cultural soft power? First of all, we should strengthen the sorting and development of China's traditional culture; deal well with the relationship between traditional culture and modernisation. We should consciously realise the modernisation of national culture and combine traditional culture with the spirit of the age.

Second, we should keep the values of China's traditional culture 'benevolence, loyalty, ceremony, wisdom and honesty' in the everyday conduct of Chinese people, so as to make every Chinese show and demonstrate China's cultural soft power.

Third, we should focus on the education of teenagers about traditional culture and strengthen the education and impact of national culture on teenagers, so as to make the splendid traditional Chinese culture the spiritual support for the survival and development of the Chinese nation.

Fourth, we should strengthen the communication of China's traditional cultural values to the outside world and make the valuable Chinese culture recognised and respected throughout the world and help it in becoming a very attractive culture.

Dependence on Existing Connections to Propagandise

Clearly, India spreads its cultural soft power according to local conditions. By discovering the connections with other countries as much as possible and focusing on the expanding influence of these connections, India can constantly enhance its cultural soft power. This can be borrowed by China in the propaganda of cultural soft power.

First, China should strengthen the friendly cooperation and relationship with other countries and increase the economic and trade cooperation, cultural exchange, private visits and other activities with other countries, especially neighbouring countries. China should open up and move quickly to present Chinese culture to the world, to get closer to the world and make the whole world know more about China. Meanwhile, China should, based on actual conditions, pay attention to the current public opinion in the world and differentiate inbound propaganda from outbound propaganda. Based on the specific condition of each country, each status and each object, China should fully understand the ideas, hobbies and receptivity of foreigners and then carry out the focused cultural communication.

In terms of region, the Asia-Pacific region has a close connection with China and there is a close similarity with the native language. Many Asia-Pacific countries and China have the same or similar cultural traditions and are all deeply affected by Confucian culture. In addition, China has closer political and economic exchange and cooperation with the Asia-Pacific countries, especially those neighbouring countries. Taking the Asia-Pacific region as a starting point, China can quickly improve its reputation and influence. In terms of audience, China must take into account the differences in nationality, lineage, cultural and historical backgrounds and get closer to the ideas and habits of foreigners. Wherever there is any historical connection, China should restore and facilitate such historical connection. Whenever there is any ideological similarity, much attention should be paid to the shared values.

Combining Leading and Supporting Channels for Propaganda

When developing its cultural soft power, India attaches much importance to the driving effect of its typical cultural figures, such as Rabindranath Tagore, Mohandas K. Gandhi (Mahatma Gandhi) and Indian music and fine arts. Similarly, China must centre on creating the leading channel and rely on multiple supporting channels to develop its cultural soft power.

In recent years, China is vigorously spreading Chinese culture and focusing on the creation of China's cultural brands. On one hand, China makes use of the strong influence of the Confucius Institute. On the other hand, China is also utilising the promotional effects of important international events and exhibitions, such as Olympic Games and World Expo. Since the first Confucius Institute was established in November 2004, China had established 400 Confucius Institutes and 535 Confucius classrooms in 108 countries and regions by the end of 2012 (Confucius Institute Headquarters 2012), which have become the major carrier for promoting the teaching of Chinese language, spreading the global brands of Chinese culture and propagandising China's cultural soft power. The success of Beijing Olympic Games 2008 and Shanghai Expo 2010 has made the world know better about China and its culture, considerably improving China's cultural soft power.

Despite the fact that China is exerting conscious effort in spreading its culture across different countries in the world, the private channel of spreading Chinese culture is still very narrow and weak. Hence, China should, for the improvement of China's cultural soft power, give full play to the leading role of Confucius Institute and the government's important activities while delving into diversified communication channels and creating innovative content for communication. With regard to communication channel, China should attach importance to both official and private channels. On one hand, we should depend on the important role of Confucius Institute and other official culture communication institutions. At the same time, we should actively employ the private channels such as non-government diplomacy and public diplomacy and utilise the potential and tremendous influence of sports stars with great reputation overseas such as Yao Ming and Li Na as well as overseas Chinese and resort to the diversified communication channels and flexible ways of communication. With regard to the content of communication, we should switch from 'technology-driven' and 'service-driven' to 'audience experience-driven' and focus on the experience of audience to improve the communication effect of China's cultural soft power and trigger their recognition of Chinese culture. India's yoga is the best example for the communication driven by audience experience. Therefore, China should pay attention to the practicality and experience of content in cultural communication. Apart from Chinese language, China can also give audience different physical experiences, feelings and perception by means of Chinese martial arts, Tai Ji Quan, Taoism, music, folk dances, chess, food and apparel to make them personally experience the source and charm of Chinese culture and leave deep impressions on them.

Cultural Industry and Culture Communication

Cultural industry is an important carrier of culture communication. The Indian government attaches much importance to the industrialisation of products symbolising Indian culture and gives full play to the natural features of these products, based on its endowed cultural resources to make these uniquely charming and easily recognised. The primary issue in the development of China's cultural soft power is the severe backwardness of the cultural industry (Ouyang Youquan and Ji Hailong 2013), which does not match with China's population, resources and economic development level. The vigorous development and revitalisation of the cultural industry cannot only provide the material basis for China's cultural soft power, but also become an important measure to improve national power and enhance international competitiveness.

There are already some successful examples that show that China's cultural products have become popular overseas. Taking some TV series as examples, the *Journey to the West* produced in 1986 was widely recognised overseas, *Aspirations* was very popular in Vietnam, the *Return of The Pearl Princess* caused a sensation in South Korea and other Southeast Asian countries, *Beautiful Daughter-in-law* was most favoured in Africa and the *Legend of Zhen Huan* will be played on the US mainstream TV channels. However, China's cultural industry still has very low impact overseas on the whole. Taking films as an example, China's film industry takes up only 4 per cent of the global cultural market (Yu Fan 2013).

In order to promote the marketing of Chinese culture overseas, first it is necessary to strengthen the production of cultural products. We should not only extract nourishment from traditional Chinese culture, but also infuse it with the connotations of the age and pay attention to innovation. While complying with the market rules of globalisation, we should produce the excellent cultural products that have insightful ideas, appreciable value and close connection to everyday life. On the other hand, we should strengthen the interregional cooperation in packaging, propaganda and marketing. Also, we should widen the export and service channels of cultural products, strengthen overseas marketing and speed up the establishment of overseas marketing network for China's cultural products and services. Special attention should be paid to the creation and production of films, TV series, animations and TV broadcasting programmes as well as the establishment of international marketing network. We should give full play to the roles of important international film festivals and overseas media to assiduously promote

China's broadcasting programmes and services. By developing the overseas cultural market, we will further push forward culture consumption to enhance China's cultural soft power. At last, we should depend more on private channels, not under the government's control, to spread Chinese culture, so as to realise the communication of China's cultural soft power unconsciously and invisibly.

References

Chen Hongbing. 2008. 'On Indian Cultural Essence.' *South Asian Studies Quarterly* 1.
Confucius Institute Headquarters. 2012. *Annual Report 2012*. Available at http://www.hanban.edu.cn/report/pdf/2012.pdf (accessed in June 2013).
Mohan, C.R. 2003 (6 January). 'Indian Diaspora and "Soft Power"'. *The Hindu*. http://www.thehindu.com/thehindu/2003/01/06/stories/2003010604431100.htm (accessed in June 2014).
Nye, J.S. 2005. *Soft Power*. Beijing: The Eastern Publishing.
Ouyang Youquan and Ji Hailong. 2013. 'Cultural Root and Industrial Logics of National Soft Power.' *Social Science Front* 2: 147–152.
Paul, T.V. and Nayar, B.R. 2003. *India in the World Order: Searching for Major Power Status*, Cambridge: Cambridge University Press.
People's Daily. 2013. Global News. Available at http://www.dzwww.com/rollnews/news/201009/t20100929_6711684.htm (accessed in June 2013).
Ren Fei. 2009. 'New Trends in India's Diplomacy: To Promote Cultural Soft Power.' *South Asian Studies Quarterly* 2: 12–24.
Ren Junjie. 2008. 'On India's Soft Power.' *South Asian Studies Quarterly* 4: 77–84.
Yu Fan. 2013. *Slowdown and Future: On the International Influence of China's Movies 2011*. Available at http://www.ccdy.cn/wenhuabao/lb/201206/t20120611_308087.htm (accessed in August 2013).

7

Driving Force and Constraints of BCIM Economic Corridor

Li Jingfeng

Introduction

In 2013, China's new central leadership proposed interconnection systems—two verticals, namely the Bangladesh, China, India and Myanmar-Economic Corridor (BCIM-EC) and the Sino-Pakistan Economic Corridor and two horizontals, namely One Belt and One Road (Shu Silk Road). The aim of the BCIM-EC was to strengthen the construction of the interconnection system between China and India, which is a necessary condition to achieve economic and trade cooperation between China and India. Cultural exchanges, the history of Tea Horse Road, Southern Silk Road and Stilwell Road have all demonstrated the importance of interregional interconnection. Both China and India, in May and October 2013 affirmed that the BCIM-EC is an important aspect in the relationship between the two countries.

The fundamental assumption behind the development of the corridor was that this alliance had some unique attributes which are expected to bring significant benefits to the participating countries through deepening of economic cooperation and integration by leveraging on transport, trade and investment connectivity. There is a huge potential of the countries getting benefitted by drawing on respective comparative advantages.

The significance of economic cooperation within the BCIM region was first conceptualised by Professor Rehman Sobhan, who articulated that notwithstanding the contours of the present-day political frontiers, closer cooperation among these four countries could significantly reduce transaction costs, foster trade and investment thereby accelerating growth and poverty alleviation in the region. This idea motivated the development of the platform called the Kunming initiative, to provide an opportunity to the participating countries to assemble and discuss initiatives for greater collaboration in various areas. The first meeting of the initiative was organised in 1999 in Kunming. The vision of the initiative was to gradually steer the endeavour from an essentially civil society (track two) one, to an intergovernmental (track one) one. It was recognised that political buy-in and intergovernmental ownership would be essential to realise the vision and the objectives of the initiative. Over the years, the initiative evolved into the BCIM Forum. Successive BCIM Forums, held annually, contributed significantly in generating more awareness about the potential benefits accruing from the BCIM cooperation. The progress of sub-regional cooperation at different levels under the framework of the forum is definitely necessary. In February 2013, the BCIM Kolkata to Kunming (K2K) rally was held successfully. The two sides agreed to consult the other parties to establish a joint working group for research to strengthen the interoperability of the region and for BCIM economic corridor building initiatives (People's Republic of China Ministry of Foreign Affairs 2013).

In May 2013, with the Chinese Premier Li Keqiang's visit to India, the two countries signed the 'Joint Declaration of the People's Republic of China and India', by which China and India first formally proposed the construction of the economic corridor to strengthen the interoperability of the region, promote economic and trade cooperation and cultural exchanges. During October 22–24, 2013, former Indian Prime Minister Manmohan Singh visited China and the two countries issued a 'China–India strategic partnership vision for the future development of the Joint Declaration'. With the two countries' top-level exchanging visits during a single year, India confirmed the construction of the BCIM-EC initiative and the BCIM Joint Working Group held its first meeting on schedule, marking the initiative's entry into the implementation phase. Both sides thus approved in accordance with the consensus reached by the leaders of the two countries and the two sides set up BCIM-EC working groups. Chinese working group's visit to India in October was a positive step to promote the initiative. The two sides maintained communication and consultation with Bangladesh and Myanmar. In December, BCIM convened the first meeting of the joint working group to study the specific planning of the BCIM EC. (*People's Daily* 2013)

During December 18–19, 2013, government officials from Bangladesh, India and Burma attended the four countries' BCIM-EC Joint Working Group meeting in Kunming. Chen Lijun, Director, Institute for South Asian Studies, Yunnan Academy of Social Sciences, said that the BCIM-EC line has been clear (*21st Century Business Herald* 2013).

Implication of BCIM Economic Corridor

Marked Upgradation from 'Track Two Diplomacy' to 'Track One Diplomacy'

During 1999 to 2013, BCIM regional economic cooperation forum made some progress, but no substantive breakthrough took place because the economic cooperation forum was still in the 'track two' status. The subject involved the academia and local governments of the four countries, but no direct involvement with the central government was established in that period. In this context, BCIM-EC was the initiative on which China and India for the first time reached a consensus at the government level, which meant track two (person to person) was upgraded to 'track one' (government to government).

BCIM Economic Corridor Is Expected to Drive the Regional Economic Development of South Asia, Southeast Asia and East Asia

BCIM areas are mostly relatively backward areas, where economic development is relatively weak. The regional economic cooperation forum is mainly provincial with state-led cooperative acting as a driving force for enhancing the economic cooperation in the region and is meant for promotion of economic development of corridors and surrounding area of these corridors of these countries, and the acceleration of the process of economic integration in Asia.

'Economic Corridor' Is More Defined Than 'Regional Cooperation', with the Range Narrowed and Focused

Regional cooperation is a broader concept encompassing cooperation in the areas of education, economy, agriculture, region and commerce while economic corridor is a much narrower concept. It is ambiguous and not all-inclusive. From the geographical concept, corridor means the narrow aisle connecting the two regions, such as the Hexi Corridor and Afghanistan Wakhan Corridor. From an economic standpoint, it is the main channel of connection between two economies, so BCIM-EC has a defined range.

India, Burma and Bangladesh Economic Corridor is connected to the economies of China and India, to achieve interoperability, so that the degree of economic interdependence between the two economies increase, and more exchange and cooperation between the two are achieved, which will in turn promote common development. Scholars from Indian and Chinese institutes believe BCIM regional economic cooperation should be between the range of regional economic cooperation and sub-regional economic cooperation.

BCIM Economic Corridor Will Stimulate Central and Local Initiative

On 21 November 2013, the ninth K2K Forum related to the economic cooperation between China and India was held in Kolkata. Strengthening regional economic cooperation was the main topic of the meeting. West Bengal governor M.K. Narayanan while speaking at the opening ceremony said that the exchange visits of the prime ministers of India and China that year marked a positive development of bilateral relations and trade in India, Burma and Bangladesh corridor, and this will also significantly push economic growth along the region, especially in West Bengal and Yunnan province (*Chinanews* 2013). Member of the Assam state parliament Mr Bordoloi said: 'I hope to see India become India's northeastern border gateway to the world rather than an obstacle'; he also submitted two requests to the central government of India to reopen Stilwell highways (Baruah 2004).

Driving Force of BCIM Economic Corridor

China's Consideration

From the Chinese perspective, the BCIM regional economic cooperation being upgraded to track one from the track two was a policy that opened many possibilities and it also was China's diplomatic strategy related to the neighbouring countries. BCIM-EC would promote China's western development strategy and inland strategic development, focusing on maintaining stability in border areas and national energy security, and the achievement of Chinese dream and national rejuvenation.

The BCIM-EC had important political and security significance. Its ultimate aim was to turn China's western periphery turbulence zone into a zone with peaceful development and peaceful growth. It also had important economic significance. It could further tighten pragmatic cooperation ties, resolve Sino-Indian trade imbalance through political cooperation between the two countries helping in extensive economic cooperation between two countries and ultimately the formation of economic resonance.

Finally, the BCIM-EC is likely to facilitate the implementation of Yunnan 'going out' strategy, which implies that Yunnan wants to communicate with East and South East Asian countries for economic development. Especially in 2009, the Government of Yunnan that opens China to the Southwest connecting two oceans, the Pacific and the Indian, as well as East Asia, Southeast Asia and South Asia, felt that opening the construction bridgeheads along national borders under the BCIM-EC has become more urgent and important.

India's Consideration

From the Indian perspective, one major consideration behind this initiative is political. India held their general elections in 2014. The Indian National Congress which has been governing India for 10 years, in order to get back its lost popularity focused on diplomatic areas and thus India responded positively to the initiatives of China. On 11 February 2014, in a meeting with former Indian Prime Minister Manmohan Singh in New Delhi, Chinese Special Representative and State Councilor Yang Jiechi said once again that the Indian side will actively participate in the construction of the BCIM-EC.[1] In this way the Indian side reaffirmed its position.

Another consideration for the initiative was definitely economic. In 2013, China's foreign exchange reserves witnessed new highs, reaching

$3.82 trillion, with the projection of the scale of foreign investment from China reaching $500 billion over the next five years. The Chinese government encourages Chinese enterprises to implement the strategy of 'going out' and is willing to promote more Chinese enterprises to invest in India. Currently, India is faced with the urgent need to attract foreign investment. With China's positive response to the initiative, it will be advantageous to absorb investment from China to overcome the difficulties of its economy.[2] In addition, regarding the economic zone, the problem is not just trade; the core problem is locational shift of industries and the investment. Thus, there is a benefit of using the experience, technology, trade and agricultural advantages of China for overcoming the difficulties in India and developing the economy at the same time which in turn would promote social stability in the Northeast.

The third consideration is security. In India, the problems relating to the implementation of the interconnection and mutual communication in the northeast or local economic development lie in the slow economic development of the northeastern region of India and the weak transport infrastructure. Conducive environment for maintaining security and stability in border areas is a prerequisite.

Fourth, in terms of international relations in the region, Bangladesh and Myanmar for many years were actively involved in the 'BCIM Cooperation Forum' activities. The Chinese initiative will get a positive response to this. If India does not agree, it will fall into a passive and isolated zone, undermining the country's image in this region.

Constraints of BCIM Economic Corridor

India's Central Government Concerns

First, a major concern is the security problem in Northeast India. The BCIM regional economic cooperation was established in 1999, but was stuck in the track two level for long. It was difficult to make substantial progress due to the inaction on part of the Indian government. This is because the BCIM regional economic cooperation would be going through the northeastern part of India, where security problems exist due to illegal immigrants. The seven northeastern states of India are relatively backward and there are some other problems like the tendency of the states to separate. Although the Indian government began the implementation of the East Policy from the Rao period to develop the Northeast and make Northeast India as a gateway connecting Southeast Asia to South Asia, till now this policy has not progressed much.

There is another concern relating to the Sino-Indian relations. BCIM cooperation mechanism is not very successful, partly due to the stressed Sino-Indian relations.[3] Among them, the border issue, the issue of cross-border rivers, China–Pakistan relations, Sino-Indian trade imbalance are the factors restricting the development of the economic corridor. From an economic point of view, India is also worried that the BCIM-EC could cause a large number of Chinese products flooding into India, having a major impact on India's domestic manufacturing industry. Thus, the Indian government does not hold a positive attitude towards opening up of the retail sector for foreign direct investment. The Indian government has to protect Indian manufacturers by raising import tariffs on Chinese products. The combined action of this factor along with Indian rupee depreciation will increase the cost of imports of Chinese products, thus making them unattractive in the Indian market.

Third, fuzzy Indian economic policies are responsible for Chinese investment in India being still far lower than other Asian countries. Some Chinese companies consider that India's system with respect to land acquisition, environmental permissions, regulatory framework and complex multi-stage approval process is opaque and unresponsive, and hence is hard to deal with.

Fourth, the possible effects of India–Bangladesh relation are another concern in this regard. In addition to the historical factors, there have been illegal immigration problems between India and Bangladesh. Affected by the level of economic development, people in Northeast India tend to go to other parts of India for work and education whereas the labour-intensive jobs present in the northeastern state of Assam are sometimes occupied by the illegal immigrants from Bangladesh. Statistics show that 26 per cent of the illegal immigrants in Assam are from Bangladesh (*Rediffnews* 2014).

Fifth, another problem is related to the positioning of Northeast India. On December 5, 2013, the participants of a symposium organised by the Indian Council of World Affairs (ICWA) on BCIM agreed on the issue that North East region should not be used merely as a 'corridor', rather trade and investment hubs should be created in the region.[4]

The Policy of the Present Government

On May 26, 2014, Shri Narendra Modi became the Prime Minister of the Republic of India. There are political considerations that might impact this initiative. First, to get more support for BJP in Northeast India, it is necessary for the party to consider the interests of the people of Northeast India, by way of reducing poverty in the region and strengthening infrastructure construction and other measures. But on the other hand, the prime minister in the campaign to obtain support from Hindus tried to restrict immigration from Bangladesh and set the deadline for the expulsion of illegal immigrants from Bangladesh (*The Hindu* 2014). This may have a negative impact on such an initiative.

Burma's Political Transition and National Security Issues

As good neighbours linked by mountains, the relationship between Myanmar and China is very good. The Myanmar government also held a very positive stance on the BCIM regional economic cooperation, sending government-level officials involved in relevant meetings.

Myanmar is in a political transition, but its China policy did not suffer a major reversal. It will actively participate in the 'BCIM Economic Zones' for the consideration of national interests because the China–Myanmar friendship is deep-rooted. Therefore, the political transition in Myanmar could continue to develop but any adverse change in its China policy is not likely to occur. However, the possibility of political unrest in Myanmar may occur or exist in the political transition which may affect the construction process of the BCIM economic corridor. For example, by bordering Myanmar with China's tribal militants, the Myanmar government amnesty is not likely to crush some conflict in Myanmar between Muslims and Buddhists, and such actions will have some impact on the economic corridor process.

BCIM Is the Driving Force to Boost the Economy

Sino-Indian economic cooperation will cover a larger range of population across economic corridors in India, Burma and Bangladesh whereas the BCIM corridor will influence a small part of the Chinese economy. India economic corridor connects the two major emerging economies through a narrow aisle. So the population covered by this economic zone is only about 400 million. On the other hand, due to some issues between China and India, it is impossible to significantly extend the corridor.

Current Status

Though the foundation of the BCIM-EC has been laid long ago, the collaboration has seemed to have made little progress towards achieving its objectives even after 14 years. For more than a decade, the Indian government demonstrated little interest in the project. However,

India is now showing enthusiasm over the project linking Kolkata with Kunming in China's Yunnan province and passing through Myanmar and Bangladesh (*The Hindu* 2015). The main channel of the 2,800 km K2K (Kunming-Ruili-Bhamo-Lashio-Mandalay-Tamu-Imphal-Sylhet-Dhaka-Kolkata) corridor is now almost ready. A short stretch from Kalewa to Monywa in Myanmar needs to be improved. The current Indian government has indicated that it would place high importance on regional integration with respect to its strategies on economic diplomacy. The BCIM corridor provides a strong opportunity to improve India-China relationship and will provide a boost to its India's Act East Policy.

Conclusion

BCIM-EC covers an area consisting of areas inhabited mostly by minorities where the relationship between the local and the central government is fragile. The economic corridor will promote the development of these areas and ease some conflicts about poor. It will also be helpful for solving the security problems in this region. The BCIM-EC also will help to solve the problem of trade imbalance between China and India as well as the problem of excess production capacity in China.

A lot of political and economic factors affect the BCIM-EC. But improvement in the relationship between China and India is the basic factor. It also depends on the cooperation and substantial support of the new government of India.

If China and India cooperate actively on the BCIM-EC issue, it will usher in a period of rapid development of this region, which will help in the advancement of China's open strategy for southwest and also will benefit the East Policy for India. If the BCIM-EC faces difficulty in its advancement, China may consider bilateral cooperation, promote China-Myanmar and Bangladesh infrastructure and energy development (Chen Jidong and Zhou Ren 2006), through which it can provide the basic platform for the BCIM-EC.

Notes

1. Former Indian Prime Minister Manmohan Singh met with Yang Jiechi, People's Republic of China Embassy in India, 11 February 2014 "http://in.china-embassy.org/chn/sgxw/t1127457.htm (accessed on 20 April 2015).
2. Li Jingfeng: 'Sichuan Participation in India, Burma and Bangladesh Economic corridor Construction', managers, August 2013, p. 14.

3. Study of the problem needs to be strengthened India—India and China expert Professor Xie Gang, chief issue interview, Southeast Asia South Asian Studies, 2013 Section 2, pp. 102–105.
4. 'Seminar on BCIM-Economic Corridor', India Council of World Affairs, 5 December 2013, http://icwa.in/pdfs/Pressrelease09122013.pdf (accessed on 15 April 2015).

References

Baruah, Amit. 2004 (20 September). 'Northeast as a Trade Hub'. *The Hindu*. Available at http://www.hindu.com/2004/09/20/stories/2004092001681000.htm (accessed on 20 April 2015).

Chen Jidong and Zhou Ren. 2006. 'Energy Cooperation in India, Burma and Bangladesh Strengthening the Relations Link'. *South Asian Studies Quarterly*: 8–13.

Chinanews. 2013. 'India and the Ninth Meeting of the Curtain K2K Focus of Regional Cooperation'. November 22. Available at http://www.chinanews.com/gn/2013/11-22/5533056.shtml (accessed on 20 April 2015).

Dingjun. 2013 (25 December). 'Silk Road South Line to Start Building BCIM Economic Corridors into the National Strategy'. *21st Century Business Herald*, 7.

People's Daily. 2013 (24 October). 'China-India Strategic Cooperative Partnership Vision for the Future Development of the Joint Statement', 3.

People's Republic of China Ministry of Foreign Affairs. 2013, May 20. 'Republic of the People's Republic of China and India Joint Statement'. Available at http://www.mfa.gov.cn/mfa_chn/zyxw_602251/t1041929.shtml (accessed on 20 April 2015).

Rediffnews. 2014. 'We Are in Denial, but Bangladeshis Are Still Flooding India's Northeast'. March 21. Available at http://www.rediff.com/news/column/bangladeshis-are-still-flooding-indias-northeast/20140321.htm (accessed on 20 April 2015).

The Hindu. 2014 (26 May). 'Surge in the Northeast'. Available at http://www.thehindu.com/opinion/editorial/surge-in-the-northeast/article6046674.ece (accessed on 20 April 2015).

———. 2015 (26 June). 'China, India Fast-track BCIM Economic Corridor Project'. Available at http://www.thehindu.com/news/national/china-india-fasttrack-bcim-economic-corridor-project/article7355496.ece (accessed on 14 April 2015).

8

The US 'Pivot to Asia' and China–Pakistan Relations

Implications on China–India Relations

Chen Jixiang

Introduction

In 2012, the Barack Obama administration in the USA proclaimed that it is likely to deepen the role of USA in the Asia-Pacific region. This move was later termed as the US 'pivot' or 'rebalancing' with respect to Asia. The administration's 'Pivot to Asia' regional strategy put forth its significant areas of action as strengthening bilateral security alliances, deepening working relationships with emerging powers, engaging with regional multilateral institutions, expanding trade and investment, forging a broad-based military presence and advancing democracy and human rights. However, the strategy has aroused scepticism and distrust among various Asian nations, especially China with respect to the actual motive behind the American rebalancing and has been a debatable topic of late. It has been advocated by many to be a means by which the USA is trying to seize the benefits of Asia's economic growth by sowing discords and divisions among Asian countries. Pakistan with a special geopolitical position is considered by China as a cornerstone for safeguarding South Asia's security and thwarting the US attempt to control the heartland of Eurasia—the forefront of Central Asia. To this end, China will greatly align its relation with Pakistan to China's national strategy and the interests of Asia as a whole. In fact, the drastic change in international situation prompts China to review its relation with Pakistan from the perspective of a global strategy. Although China will continue its efforts to enhance the political trust and security cooperation between the two sides, its strategic focus has shifted from economic cooperation to promotion of regionalism in Asia, including India. Nevertheless, India's strong awareness in regional dominance and its interest in other countries' economy and security often lead to over-interpretation of China–Pakistan relations, giving rise to certain potentially destabilising factors to regional security.

The Purpose of the US 'Pivot to Asia' Strategy and Pakistan's Geopolitical Environment

The US 'Pivot to Asia' Strategy, in Essence, Is a Move to Contain the Rise of Asia as a Whole

There are various assumptions with respect to the aforementioned strategic move. Asia belongs to Asian people, not to either China or the USA. But, the military presence of the USA in Asia is often considered by many to be the root of Asia's chaos and poverty and to play a pivotal role in US dollar colonisation. Asian countries have no reason to cheer for the US 'Pivot to Asia' strategy as it raises their anxiety with respect to the notion that it aims at containing the rise of Asia.

It is generally perceived that the military presence of the USA in countries across the world serves the purpose of its economic colonisation, paving the way for its dollar colonisation. To some observers, it appears to be the strategy of the USA to deprive other countries' regimes of their national identity and make them dependent on the USA by promoting its so-called democracy and human rights, thereby turning the 'elite class' of such countries into its agents for ruling or benefits tunnelling. In implementing this strategy, the USA, militarily, generally adopts such means as containment or direct attack on its target countries, aggressively creating chaos or arming opposition forces. Politically and propaganda-wise it usually isolates target countries by leveraging its advantages in global political dominance and public opinion control, and constantly fabricates lies to drive a wedge between the government and the people of target countries. Geopolitically, it might also seem that the USA is typically trying to sow discords between a target country and its neighbours; and exhausts the political, economic and military resources of countries within the area where the target country is located, which prevents collective rise of the region enabling the USA to maintain its military deterrence over the region in the long run. In addition, economically, America lures the elite class of a target country to promote full privatisation and financial liberalisation by utilising the US-led globalisation, which enables the green dollar decoupled from gold to purchase a great deal of natural resources of the target country and control its financial system, which ultimately leads the target country to lose its control over its major resources and its financial sovereignty. Thereby, it facilitates the target country's inclusion in the dollar system by becoming an economic colony of the USA.

It is advocated at times that a politically weak country characterised by constant infighting is more likely to succumb to USA's dollar dominance, as the elite class of such a country under the pressure of US military might and domestic unrest would lead to think that the US dollar is the only reliable choice. The USA promotes to the rest of the world its so-called democracy, human rights and freedom, among other values and funds the academic and media community with the aim to not to help create more democratic, richer and stronger countries; but to hook target countries to accept their domination, as a result, undermining its rivals and ultimately gaining control over the target countries to consolidate US global hegemony. Every single turmoil or decline in Asia from the collapse of the Soviet Union and the dramatic fall of Russia's industrial strength to wars and massacres in the Middle East, the unrests and poverty of Central Asia, the protracted tensions in Northeast Asia, the poverty of North Korea and even the regional chaos and tensions over the South China sea may be attributable to US military presence in Asia.

The US 'Pivot to Asia', is considered by the proponents of the Asian containment policy to restrain the rise of emerging Asian countries as a whole that might seem a move solely against China from the surface, in its substance is an ominous policy aiming at conquering major emerging economies in Asia. Seen historically and from future trends, the rise of Japan is merely a small episode in the long journey of human history, while the rise of Asia, a collective rise led by China and India, represents the long-run trend, surely leading to far-reaching changes in world order. Judging from the current developments, the rapid rise of Chinese economy has not only created historic opportunities for quick growth for other Asian countries, but has also facilitated the integration of the economic strengths of East Asia, leading to the eastward shift of the world economic centre. The shaping of this landscape is a dynamic impetus for economic growth in Asia, Africa, Europe, Russia and South America, as well as an important assurance for a multi-polar world. Given its desire to pursue global dominance and its efforts in maintaining dollar colonisation, the USA cannot tolerate the rise of Euro, which is seen by the USA as a thorn in its side, let alone the rise of Asia. For this reason, the USA has been adopting this divide-and-conquer strategy to curb the leading economies, contain Asia in every aspect, alienate Sino-Indian relationship, and encircle China, in an attempt to stall the engines driving the rapid growth of Asian economy. Given the difficulty of crushing China from within after exhausting all measures, the USA resorts to sowing dissension and taking advantage of the strategic shortsightedness of some of China's neighbouring countries to craft regional chaos, forcing China to increase its military presence at its borders and preventing the collective rise of Asian countries, with a view to avoiding the weakening of US military presence in Asia.

Pakistan's Geopolitical Environment

Pakistan is an important geo-strategic fulcrum to the US strategy of rebalancing towards Asia-Pacific. Located in the northwest of the South Asian subcontinent, facing the Indian Ocean and the Arabian Sea to its south and bordering India, China, Afghanistan and Iran in its east, north and west, respectively, Pakistan is an energy pass with world significance. It is an important estuary at the heart of Asia as well as a major geo-strategic point of penetration for USA to implement its 'control the land through the sea' strategy to penetrate the heartland of Eurasia continent (the World Island). Some thinkers on the issue assume that the prime goal of US pivot is to check China, turn off the engine of Asian economy and prevent the rise of Asia as a whole. The fulfilment of this goal necessitates the collaboration and support from US strategies for South Asia, West Asia and Central Asia. The strategic focus of the USA in South, West and Central Asia regions, as with its Western Pacific strategy, is to create chaos, squeezing the time and space required for China's development. With the support of its military bases in Diego Garcia and the Gulf, the USA has been stirring up internal strife in Pakistan among terrorism, separatism and religious extremism forces, which may threaten the Pakistani regime and the security of India and West China at any time, tumbling China's westward strategy, forming a double-pronged deployment to flank India from the south and north sides and preventing the market integration across Europe and Asia. Further, as Central Asia is a bridge connecting the Eurasia continent and a junction leading towards four directions, once Pakistan is broken by the USA; the historical grudges, ethnic contradictions and religious conflicts between the five Central Asian countries, that is, Kazakhstan, Uzbekistan, Kyrgyzstan, Turkmenistan and Tajikistan, would only be fuelled (Chen Lianbi 2001). If this is the case, Central Asia is likely to face long-term chaos and turmoil with flows of trade, resources and energy sources within the Eurasian continent interrupted and more rampant terrorist and religious extremist activities from which China, India and Russia would all suffer.

The China–Pakistan Economic Corridor, as a key part of China's efforts to accelerate the integration of Asian economy and promote the collective rise of Asia by implementing the 'One Belt and One Road' strategy, is a new approach of China to build a harmonious Asia and an innovation in China's global strategy. Although China's 'One Belt and One Road' strategy is aimed at mutual benefits and win-win results among European and Asian countries or regions of interest, its implementation will enable Asian countries to step up their respective economic and social development by taking advantage of China's rise, which in turn will quicken the pace of the rise of Asia as a whole. However, this strategy is considered by the USA as an adversity to its global hegemony. As noted in an article, the success of China's 'Maritime Silk Road' initiative will contribute significantly to regional stability, security and peace (Chaturvedy 2014). Though conducive to the peace, stability and development of Asia, this strategy is not necessarily conducive to US global hegemony. Fearing that the rise of Asia as a whole will leave a doubt about the legitimacy of its military presence in Asia, the USA besides ramping up its offshore balancing efforts at Western Pacific has also been trying to create chaos in Central Asia and the Middle East, preventing the integration of Asian and Eurasian market. With Pakistan's geographical position as a gateway to the sea for West China (Xinjiang Uygur Autonomous Region) and Central Asia, the China–Pakistan Economic Corridor can bind West China market closely together with that of South Asia, the Middle East, Central Asia, Africa and even Europe. As with the Bangladesh, China, India, Myanmar-Economic Corridor (BCIM-EC), the China–Pakistan Economic Corridor also serves as an important junction of the Land Silk Road economic belt and the Maritime Silk Road economic belt, that is, a strategic passage for land-sea interactions and a critical juncture for Asia's economic integration. According to the Rimland theory proposed by Nicholas Spykman, the Godfather of Containment, it is the peripheral regions of the Eurasian continent that are the major battlefields of confrontations between major powers and historical keys opening the way to the future (Spykman 1965). It is thus clear that, Pakistan, with its vital geo-strategic position, might become an important pawn on the chessboard of US global strategy. The politically and economically vulnerable ecology of Pakistan is quite favourable for the USA to seize such an important strategic pivot. The political disorder and weak economic foundation of Pakistan may be used by the USA to influence Pakistan. Given Pakistan's geographical position as an important strategic passage connecting the Indian Ocean and Central Asia, the USA is trying to control Pakistan and access to Central Asia, in an effort to take control of the heartland of Eurasia continent, contain China, India and Russia and maintain its high-handed posture towards Iran. The US war against terrorism has led to proliferation of terrorism, political disorder and economic slump in Pakistan. Despite that, Pakistan has paid high costs for US war against terrorism in Afghanistan. The USA still wields its sticks on Pakistan time and again. Particularly, the USA has carried out cross-border bombing operations with drones in the name of anti-terrorism disregarding Pakistani sovereignty, which has caused a great deal of civilian casualties and created social rifts hard to heal Pakistan. The USA may support one faction or an armed organisation in Pakistan to overthrow or hijack the incumbent regime in order to control or destabilise Pakistan. Once losing influence over Pakistan, China would not only face enormous geopolitical pressure and see its westward strategy deterred but would also see its oil and gas pipelines controlled by the USA. China cannot afford to let the fate of its economic development to be held in the hands of another country.

China's Reorientation of Its Relationship with Pakistan

China is reorienting its relationship with Pakistan prompted by changes in world political and economic landscape, the USA rebalancing towards Asia and the adjustment of China's national strategy.

Enhancing Security Cooperation with Pakistan

At present, Pakistan faces multiple problems and troubles, internally and externally, including pervasive extremist thoughts, domestic security vulnerabilities, lack of authority, setbacks in economic development and aftershocks of chaos after the partial withdrawal of combat forces by the USA out of its neighbour Afghanistan. Although obvious strategic conflicts exist between the USA and China, the latter, as the most reliable friend of Pakistan, should not confront head-on with the former with regard to Pakistan and must try to stabilise the relationship with the USA. Nevertheless, China should also adjust its Pakistani strategy as soon as possible to further enhance military and security cooperation with Pakistan, and help fully arm the country and its military forces so as to ensure its political stability and healthy economic development. While establishing the China–Pakistan Economic Corridor, stepping up the construction of industrial parks in Pakistan and promoting cultural exchanges with Pakistan, China should also make efforts in supporting Pakistan to ease its tensions with neighbouring Afghanistan, Iran and India, helping Pakistan create an external environment favourable to its domestic stability. It is suggested that China actively support Pakistan and Iran to develop a comprehensive strategic partnership, strongly support enhanced security cooperation between Pakistan and Iran and establish a China–Pakistan–Iran free trade zone as soon as possible. China should also generously support economic and trade cooperation between India and Pakistan in an all-round way, which will be conducive to accelerate the economic integration between China and South Asian Association for Regional Cooperation (SAARC). In addition, China should partner with Russia to restrict the USA from creating any turmoil in Pakistan, Iran and Central Asia, ensuring that the Eurasia Land Bridge is not obstructed. As a matter of fact, in terms of relations between Pakistan and its neighbouring countries, pragmatic handling of its relationship with India is of importance to its security, economy and social development. For this reason, a pragmatic approach to Pakistan–India relations, to a large extent, should be an important consideration for China in deepening its relationship with Pakistan, as well as a dimension of adjusting China–Pakistan relations.

China–Pakistan Economic Cooperation

It is an important geographical pillar for the establishment of an Africa–Persian Gulf–Xinjiang energy corridor and the implementation of China's strategy in Indian Ocean to strengthen economic and trade cooperation with Pakistan, promote Pakistan's economic development, facilitate Sino-Pakistan economic integration and cement the ties between China and Pakistan. The establishment of China–Pakistan Economic Corridor as a bond for comprehensive and deepened economic and trade cooperation between the two countries is a targeted 'win-win' strategy, facilitating continued and stable development of the Pakistan economy. Though China and Pakistan are highly complementary economically and have huge potential for cooperation, the potential of economic and trade cooperation between the two countries has not been fully tapped due to Pakistan's security situation. Pakistan boasts of a population of approximately 200 million, abundant resources and enormous economic potential. However, poor domestic security environment, political instability and shortage of energy supply, among other factors, have led to stalled economic development, substantial flight of foreign capital, rising unemployment rate and miserable life of Pakistanis. In such a condition, Pakistan desperately needs large amount of investment from China to help improve its infrastructure, boost its manufacturing sector, increase employment and raise the living standard of its people. As Chinese economy is also facing strong pressure for industrial restructuring after years of evolvement, China may choose Pakistan as a preferred destination for economic restructuring and industrial transfer factoring in Pakistan's economic position, its industrial level and China's relationship with Pakistan. The China–Pakistan Economic Corridor plan not only covers the construction of infrastructure including railways, highways, aviation routes, oil and gas pipelines, irrigation and drainage facilities, Information Communication Technology (ICT) infrastructure and so on; but also covers cooperation in energy and resource development, industrial park construction, establishment of free trade zones, and cultural and educational exchanges. Comprehensive Sino-Pakistan cooperation in economic and trade fields can promote healthy development of Pakistan's economy, enhance its industrial strength and improve people's livelihood, which in turn would contribute to Pakistan's internal stability and enhanced mutual political trust and security cooperation between the two sides.

Cultural, Social and Educational Exchanges

Facilitating exchanges through cooperation in a range of fields including language, culture, tourism, education, science and technology, sports, among others, can help consolidate the social basis of China–Pakistan relations and is beneficial to the continuation of friendly China–Pakistan relationship from one generation to another. The two countries have a deep and wide range of shared interests and strong friendship among the people, but the lack of civic exchanges between the two countries is a very important practical issue facing China–Pakistan relationship. Influenced by language, Pakistani students born in middle class families or above often are enthusiastic about romantic fictions, detective stories and biographical novels from Britain and the USA, embrace English movies and TV shows and appreciate Western lifestyle. In contrast, Chinese language has minimal influence in Pakistan and it is not until 2005 that China set up its first Confucian institute, the Confucius Institute Islamabad, in Islamabad, Pakistan. By 2013, there were barely 40 outlets for Chinese teaching and learning stationed by the Confucius Institute in Pakistani universities, high schools and language training institutions, with less than 8,000 registered participants and a limited coverage. Chinese language teaching only started to enter the Pakistani national education system in 2013 when the government of Sindh province announced that it would, beginning from 2013, open compulsory Chinese language courses in programmes for classes at or above the sixth grade in all schools and educational institutions across the province. English is in a much stronger position over Chinese in the struggle for influence over Pakistan between China and the USA, and there is a lack of people-to-people exchanges among Chinese and Pakistanis, which is very unfavourable to China and also to the generation-to-generation pass-down of Sino-Pakistan friendship. Pakistan has apparently realised this, as explicitly noted by Pakistan's former prime minister, Yousuf Raza Gilani, when he met a goodwill delegation from Xinjiang, China, on February 16, 2012. He said 'Pakistan expressed its hope to further strengthen cultural and educational exchanges with China and cement the social basis for Pakistan–China relationship'.

The Effects of the Reorientation of China–Pakistan Relationship on China–India Relations

In such a crucial period of time, featuring unprecedented, far-reaching changes in world situation, collective rise of emerging powers, overall downturn of major western powers (Yuan Peng 2012) and a big shakeout of world political and economic landscape, China's geo-strategic measures, including increasing military and security cooperation with Pakistan and establishment of a China–Pakistan–Iran free trade zone, are likely to be misinterpreted by some Indians as threats to India, straining China–India ties. In effect, China is adjusting its relationship with

Pakistan and strengthening cooperation with Pakistan and Iran, primarily aiming at checking the US 'rebalancing strategy' that is considered to be creating chaos in Asia, is a strategic move to consolidate regional peace and promoting Asian regionalism. It is essentially beneficial to India, rather than detrimental to Indian interests.

China–India Relations as Perceived by India

China and India in the 21st century share a common fate in political and economic fields in the international community. The early 21st century saw the biggest change in the world political and economic landscape, that is, the increasingly greater representation and influence of emerging economies in global governance. In terms of Gross Domestic Product (GDP) measured at constant price, the gap between the 11 emerging economies (Argentina, Brazil, China, India, Indonesia, South Korea, Mexico, Russia, Saudi Arabia, South Africa and Turkey) and G7 (Group of 7) has narrowed from $9.88 trillion in 1990 to $2.5 trillion in 2013. According to 2013 forecasts by Standard Chartered, the GDPs of emerging economies by 2030 will account for 63 per cent of the world GDP. The contribution to world economic growth by emerging economies has been outpacing developed countries since 2010. According to World Bank estimates, China contributed 4.6 per cent of the world's GDP growth in 2013, which was 14.5 per cent in 2009 and 20 per cent in 2012, two percentages points higher than that of the USA emerging economies. China and India have become the core engines of world economic growth, bringing deep changes to world geopolitical and economic landscape. However, incumbent powers, including major European powers, the USA and Japan, who traditionally led the evolution of world political and economic landscape, may try to generally disintegrate the connection and cooperation between emerging economies and constrain them from their efforts to establish a fairer and more reasonable international political and economic order by picking off leading emerging economies represented by China and India one by one. In fact, the rising China and India are leading forces that are likely to change existing international political and economic order, and at the same time, naturally the major targets of suppression for the vested interest holders of the current international political and economic order.

Some Indians believe that in order to maintain its predominance in global political economy, the USA is making every effort to push ahead the Trans-Pacific Partnership (TPP) and Transatlantic Trade and

Investment Partnership (TTIP) with the intention to exclude emerging powers, including China, India, Brazil, Russia and South Africa, from global trade frameworks, on the basis of which it would try to form a political, economic, military and diplomatic alliance or quasi-alliance to contain the development momentum of emerging economies. On March 17, 2014, an article pointed out that the TPP and TTIP are new rules of engagement considered by developed countries to update the long-established ones. Against such new rules that exclude China and India, the two countries must closely cooperate as there are overlapping regional and global interests between the two sides (*The Hindu* 2014). Thus, the two countries must think out of the box of traditional diplomatic mindset to build a new type of win-win relations between major powers.

The win–win situation with China is beneficial for India to actualise its aspiration to become a major power. Jawaharlal Nehru, the first prime minister of independent India, once explicitly noted in his book *The Discovery of India*, that 'with its current position, India simply cannot play a secondary role in the world. India should either be vigorous or disappear from the scene' (Nehru 1999, 56). Geopolitically, surrounded by sea on three sides, India's major security risks come from offshore, so its rise will be impossible without control over the sea power of the Indian Ocean. Against the backdrop of India's rising economic strength and increasing national power and the clearer trend of a multi-polar world, one important aspect of India's strategy to seek a great power status is to expand its naval supremacy in the Indian Ocean. However, the sea power of the Indian Ocean is currently firmly controlled by the USA, who tries to have major influence on the subcontinent from both land and sea through a range of military activities or military deployment in Afghanistan, Saudi Arabia, Israel, Iraq, Diego Garcia, Australia and Singapore, among other areas. The increasingly looming strategic posture of the USA towards the Indian subcontinent constitutes a heavy psychological shadow to Indian leaders who places the security of the Indian Ocean at first (Zhang Wenmu 2010).

China and India benefit from cooperation and lose in rivalry. Though Asia is seeing China and India simultaneously on the rise, the progress of Asia's back to the centre of world power will be even more treacherous once any one of the two countries is used by foreign powers. China and India, to a large extent, share the same fate with Asia, which benefits from stronger China and India, but suffers from the colonial exploitation by the West if China and India are weak. Indian leaders have well realised this. Atal Bihari Vajpayee, in his speech at Peking University in June 2003, noted that if China and India join hands, the

21st century will be a century of Asia. He also added that this will be impossible if the two countries go into intense confrontation. Despite India's dream to become an 'impressive great power', externally bordering neighbours in war and domestically faced with lack of government authority and constant conflicts between ethnic groups, religions, political sections; India is certainly unable to bear the pressures from foreign powers on its own. If China's rising momentum is cut short, then India may get disintegrated on the chessboard of western geopolitics. Besides, as the economic interdependence between the two countries becomes increasingly deeper, China is not only India's biggest trade partner, but also an observer of the SAARC dominated by India, as well as a major trade partner of six out of eight members of this organisation excluding Afghanistan and Bhutan. In this context, many Indian scholars have had a rather cool and sober understanding of China's rise. Raviprasad Narayanan, an expert on Chinese affairs at the Institute for Defence Studies and Analyses (IDSA), noted that China's rise is characterised by a peaceful and flexible pattern that is pragmatism driven, prioritizes economic development, focuses on regionalism and practices opening-up policy (Chen Yongjie 2007). Practically, a focus on regionalism, especially on good neighbourliness, is an important geopolitical strategy contributing to China's rise. Indian scholars have long got insights into this and have realised that China's rise is a historical opportunity for India to develop its economy and strengthen its national power. Thus, their views on China–Pakistan relations are more pragmatic. India expects a stable Pakistan to maintain the peace progress of two sides and the stability of the South Asian region, securing more time and space of development for India. Besides, China's regionalism does not exclude India and continued close relationship between China and Pakistan is of great significance to the stability of Pakistan and South Asia. Therefore, a peaceful and friendly relationship between China, India and Pakistan is a positive contributor to accelerating India's rise and actualising its aspiration to become a great power.

China's Foreign Policy and India's Stance toward Sino-Pakistan Relationship

China is a major factor influencing India's foreign policy. Factoring in the geographical position, history, economy and global ranking, among others; of the two countries, China's existence, development and its foreign policy will inevitably have direct or indirect implications on India's foreign policy and its policymaking. With the economic globalisation after the Cold War, China has been adjusting its foreign policy and gradually, its new foreign and trade policies are all centred on economic development. On the premise of the judgment that the interdependence between countries will surely increase, such concepts as 'diversification', 'win-win cooperation' and 'lukewarm politics and warm economy' have been introduced into Chinese foreign and trade policies. Obviously, China at this development stage does not want any unnecessary dispute to interrupt its economic development, so it can stay undistracted from developing and upgrading its economy and promoting modernisation. So far, such efforts have contributed to fruitful results in China's economic diplomacy, helped the establishment of multi-layer and multi-field international platforms for economic and trade cooperation and greatly promoted the modernisation of Chinese military force, and enhanced its hard power to safeguard core national interests. China's foreign policy prioritising economy and its economic success have affected India to some extent. India's attitude toward China's adjustment of its relationship with Pakistan will become more pragmatic over time. Though the India–Pakistan relationship remains tense, India's exports to Pakistan increased by approximately 15 per cent to $1.6 billion and its imports from Pakistan grew by 30 per cent to $488 million in FY 2012–13 when India's exports to the rest of the world decreased by 4 per cent. It is particularly worth noting that, in May 2014, Narendra Modi, the new Indian Prime Minister invited his Pakistani counterpart Nawaz Sharif to attend his inauguration ceremony, which was the first time that a prime minister of one side invited the counterpart from the other side to attend the inauguration since the independence of Pakistan. This move by Modi, in a certain sense, has shown India's pragmatism towards China's adjustment to its ties with Pakistan and China's foreign policy.

Nevertheless, India's attitude towards China–Pakistan relations remains ambiguous and entangled. India's foreign policy, though determined by diverse forces, is still strongly influenced by its military establishment. Since its economic reform in 1991, India's foreign policy has been affected by two intertwined views: one is from the military side who believes that military force is the strongest assurance to peace and security, India must develop reliable second nuclear strike capability and a full range of conventional military power and stay on high alert toward China and Pakistan; the other view is primarily from liberals who believe that economic power rather than military power should be the primary goal of India, as economic interdependence has made it impossible for violent confrontations to be profitable. Thus, they argue that India should strengthen economic and trade ties with China and India. Due to the country's political structure, the intermingling of two different views in Indian foreign policy will surely be persistent. As a result, India's foreign policy may find it hard to stick to the goal of economy priority expected by liberals and the persistent border issues will increase India's suspicions towards China–Pakistan relations. Further, the influence of countries beyond this region will also impede the positive interactions within the China–Pakistan–India multi-lateral mechanism.

India is highly dependent on other countries in the fields of economy and security. Economically, India is dependent on China and the USA, who are the largest and second largest trade partners of India, respectively; but security-wise, it is primarily dependent on Russia, France and the USA. With the US 'Pivot to Asia' strategy, India has the inclination to rely more on the USA and balance China, which can be seen from its military establishment. This inclination will considerably affect the multi-lateral economic and trade cooperation between China, Pakistan and India, as well as affect India's attitude towards China–Pakistan relationship. Given the variables above, India may be caught up in a prolonged state of entanglement with respect to China's adjustment in China–Pakistan relations.

Conclusion

The reorientation of China–Pakistan relationship does not necessarily mean a threat, but an opportunity for India. While India will still see China as a major threat to its national security before they go beyond economic partnership and become friendly neighbours, China is increasing its economic exchanges with India with a view to achieving geopolitical balance in Asia and boosting domestic economic development. The economic and trade cooperation between China and India aims at win-win results. However, it seems that China benefits more from its trade with India, with China's trade surplus with India totalling $39.09 billion in 2012, an 8.0 per cent increase or 56.8 per cent of the total trade value between the two countries.[1]

Actually, such surplus was primarily due to India's need to step up its construction of infrastructure by importing a large quantity of cheap yet good quality machinery and equipment. As a matter of fact, China and India have created fruitful results in exchanges and cooperation in such fields as economy and trade, education, science and technology, culture and tourism. Various sectors and industries of both countries have benefited substantially from the significant development of China–India ties. At present, the concepts of reciprocity and mutual benefit and win-win cooperation have gradually found their way ever deeper into the hearts of the people of the two nations, but huge trade gap, competition on energy sources, territorial disputes and security issues, among other factors, plus the relations of South Asia with countries in other regions, will remain the major causes of misunderstanding and suspicions between the two countries. Those factors, once triggered by a certain event and exploited by certain external forces, might put the China–Indian relationship in a difficult situation. However, the backbone of China's ties with India, that is, maintaining the stability and peace of South Asian regions, will not easily be changed. Further, the establishment of the China–Pakistan Economic Corridor also provides India with an important historical opportunity for both energy cooperation with China and the facilitation of economic integration in South Asia. Thus, the realignment of China–Pakistan relations cannot possibly be interpreted by India as a threat.

Note

1. Source: Statistical estimates published by Directorate General of Commercial Intelligence and Statistics and Department of Commerce of India in 2013.

References

Chaturvedy, R.R. 2014. 'Reviving the Maritime Silk Route'. *The Hindu*, April 11.
Chen Lianbi. 2001. 'Issues Concerning the Ethnic Relations between Five Central Asian Countries'. *Eastern Europe and Central Asia Research* 3: 34.
Chen Yongjie. 2007. 'How Indian Scholars View China's Rise'. *21st Century Business Herald*, September 13.
Nehru, J. 1999. *The Discovery of India*. Teen Murti House.
The Hindu. 2014. 'India-China Strategic Economic Dialogue to Discuss Counter Strategies to the TPP'. *The Hindu*. Available at http://china.cankaoxiaoxi.com/2014/0319/362591.shtml (accessed in May 2014).
Spykman, N.J. 1965. *The Geography of the Peace*. Trans. Liu Yuzhi. The Commercial Press.
Yuan Peng. 2012. 'Thoughts on Big Time and Grand Strategy—and the 10 Relationships China's Diplomacy Need to Deal with in the New Era'. *Contemporary World & Socialism* (4): 11.
Zhang Wenmu. 2010. 'Great Power Politics in Central Areas of World Geopolitical System—and the Strategic Complementary Role of India-China Security Cooperation'. *Pacific Journal, Issue* (3): 24.

9

China and India Cooperation in Afghanistan

Xie Jing

Introduction

Afghanistan has a unique geographical location. Due to its special geographical location, it is connected to Central Asia, West Asia and South Asia. It is a landlocked country, one of China's neighbouring countries and an important channel leading to Central Asia. It is part of the ancient Silk Road which is also connected to South Asia and hence is on the crossroads of civilisations. In the 19th century, it was the centre for Russia and England for controlling Central Asia. In the 1980s, before the end of the Cold War, the USA and the Soviet Union fought the last battle. It was at the end of 2001 that the USA launched the war on terror. Afghanistan has always been the hot spot of the regional conflicts and instability. As a result, problems in Afghanistan have not been purely national, but have become a regional and even global hot topic to ponder. Therefore, Afghanistan can be compared to a mirror which not only reflects the current interests in South-central Asia and the major world powers, but also the strength of the major powers. The year 2014 was a turning point in the history of Afghanistan. It has been 13 years that the USA has launched the war in Afghanistan.

The USA planned to withdraw its force in 2014; the Afghan presidential elections were also held that summer. Afghanistan elected a new president that year after the withdrawal. During that period, it caused a new balance of power in the region; at present, with the extremist groups in Iraq and the rise of the unsafe situation in Afghanistan, Afghanistan's future may be out of control and is full of uncertainty. After the withdrawal, China and India, as the region's emerging powers, stand directly in the first line. These two countries are also considered as Afghanistan's major stakeholders.

China's Interests in Afghanistan

In recent years, China has constantly strengthened its partnership with Afghanistan. First, China has a huge economic investment in and influence on Afghanistan since Afghanistan has rich mineral resources. China Metallurgical Group has 30 years of mining experience in Aynak copper mine in Logar province in south of Cartouche. This copper mine is one of the world's largest. China Metallurgical Group's total investment in infrastructure projects and mining is expected to reach $4.4 billion, and simultaneously develop a 400 MW thermal power plant. It will help in solving the corresponding coal and water issues. China National Petroleum Corporation (CNPC) has successfully bid for three oil fields in Amu Darya basin in Northern Afghanistan. This oil field is expected to earn $7 billion in the future. In addition to the resource development, Sino-Afghan trade also extends to radio communications. According to Phoenix Weekly, China ranks first in foreign investment; investment projects are also a part of the Sino-Afghan economic cooperation. Chinese investment projects focus on improving economic conditions in Afghanistan, such as the Parwan irrigation projects. As Chinese have investments in Afghanistan, the situation in Afghanistan also has an impact on the safety of the Chinese citizens in Afghanistan. Moreover, Afghanistan is closely related to China's current Silk Road economic belt building. Afghanistan, Pakistan and India are countries of the 'Silk Road Economic Zone' which depend on the solution to the Afghan problem. If the peace process is successful in Afghanistan, the three countries' economic cooperation with Central Asia will also be improved and on the contrary, they all will plunge into a state of loose or ambiguous situation which will dampen the construction of the economic zone (*Xinhua* 2013b).

Second, China has some interests in Afghanistan. Afghanistan is a neighbour of China on the western side. If Afghanistan's situation goes out of control in future, religious extremists after years of war in Afghanistan will spread to the neighbouring countries as well, such as ETIM members in Xinjiang. Before the war in Afghanistan, they would often join the Afghan 'jihad'. With their training from Al-Qaeda, they got the support from Islamic extremist organisations in Afghanistan. It was expected that if the situation in Afghanistan went out of control in 2014, with the deterioration of the security situation, the East Turkistan members would take advantage of the chaotic situation to get more resources and cause terrorist attacks spillover (Pantucci 2013). In 2014, foreign minister Wang Yi said in a press conference with Afghan foreign minister Osmani: 'Peace and stability in Afghanistan is related to the security of Western China, and more related to the peace and development of the entire region (*Xinhua* 2013a).'

Third, according to the UN Office on Drugs and Crime Data in 2013, Afghanistan drug production was even more than the total output value of many other countries and regions in the world. Actually, the Afghan drug problem is not confined to the country only but its influence has also spread across the neighbouring countries. The drug is not the only problem; what is more important is that it is followed by violence, smuggling and serious criminal activities. So China's western frontier is also facing the threat of drug trafficking from Afghanistan. In February 2014, Xi Jinping attended the Winter Olympics in Sochi, Russia, where he met the Afghan President Hamid Karzai. Xi Jinping said that China is willing to extend its assistance to Afghanistan's peaceful reconstruction and willing to strengthen cooperation by combating the 'three forces' and transnational crime (Zhao Yanrong 2014).

India's Interests in Afghanistan

India is one of the major four countries which are involved in the reconstruction of Afghanistan. It has a long-term influence on Afghanistan. India and Afghanistan share a base in security cooperation. In 2005, Indian police forces were stationed in Afghanistan to protect the Indian citizens in Afghanistan. The leaders of both the nations frequently visited the other country. They signed a 'strategic partnership agreement' in 2011. India said it would enhance security cooperation with Afghanistan, donate some arms, facilities and planned to train 20,000–30,000 Afghan National Army members, including 500 officers. Due to the close tie between these two sides, it was possible to make training more effective.

In terms of economic cooperation, India had a positive attitude towards economic investment in Afghanistan (of about $2 billion). In 2012, a summit was held in New Delhi by India and Afghanistan, which aimed at attracting foreign investment to Afghanistan. This was very important for Afghanistan. In the mining sector, in 2011, a state-run

Indian steel company bid for iron mines in Hajigak for constructing power plants. In the field of infrastructure, India rebuilt the Salma Dam power plant which is of much significance. This project benefitted all the people of Afghanistan. India and Afghanistan also cooperated to build the highway in order to get connected to Iran and they also proposed railway construction projects. On a particular note, the investment on mineral and infrastructure are often intertwined with a strong strategic significance to ultimately promote regional trade, transport and the region's energy channels.

India attached equal importance to healthcare and education. India was willing to help Afghanistan build hospitals and schools for women. This assistance was of much importance for Afghanistan. In addition, the Indian government's decision to allow Afghan students to study in India strengthened the historical and cultural ties with Afghanistan (Zhang Chunyan and Zhu Yufan 2013).

India's cooperation with Afghanistan is based on economic benefits, security issues, regional balance and strategic considerations. For a long time, Pakistan had an important influence on Afghanistan. Specifically, the Kashmir issue has a long-term effect on the bilateral relations of India–Pakistan. So India, through contact with Afghanistan, can offset part of Pakistan's influence on Afghanistan and expand its influence in Central Asia in the future to gain strategic advantage.

Sino-India Cooperation in Reconstruction of Afghanistan

Being Afghanistan's neighbouring countries, China and India stand directly in the first line after the withdrawal of the US army from Afghanistan. Since China and India have strong economic relations, it would not be difficult for these two countries to cooperate with each other in reconstructing Afghanistan. Also this cooperation would reflect the strength of regional powers necessary to weaken the influence of the Western world on this region.

From the analysis, both China and India have played an important role in rebuilding the nation Afghanistan keeping their own interests in mind. The common interests of China and India with respect to the regional cooperation with Afghanistan lie in the fact that both the sides need to have a safe and stable situation in Afghanistan, and they do not want Afghanistan to become a shelter for terrorist organisations in the future. India believes that in the process of reconstruction of Afghanistan, its security is an absolute necessity. If Afghanistan is unstable, any investment and endeavour in Afghanistan will be futile.

Second, both China and India want to cooperate with other countries in this region. At present, apart from the aid to Afghanistan and guarantee of its own security, India's Afghanistan policies do not aim at offsetting any other countries' influence in the region completely. A former Indian diplomat said that India helped in stabilising Afghanistan and integrating it to the regional cooperation for its own interests. In addition, India also has a strong desire of combating terror attacks as happened in Afghanistan, against India. At the same time, some experts pointed out that, for India the policy of Central Asia should not seek hegemony in this region, but the current policy of Central Asia should build partnerships with the power structure in the region.

In 2014, while meeting the Afghan President Hamid Karzai in Sochi, Xi Jinping stressed that China will continue to firmly support Afghan to safeguard national independence, sovereignty and territorial integrity, and support the 'dominated people of Afghanistan' in the process of reconciliation. China supports Afghanistan in the integration for regional economic cooperation (Liu Xiao Ming 2014).

Finally, at the macro level, due to historical reasons, Sino-Indian relations have some sensitive problems such as the unresolved border disputes from a geopolitical standpoint. However, this is not absolutely against cooperation. China and India are now paying more attention to the development of their economies. They are both committed to the development of the domestic economy. The competition and confrontation is not the main melody in the future development of the bilateral relations. So from the analysis, it is clear that as far as Afghanistan's future is concerned, China and India will not see themselves in a zero-sum game, rather it would involve wide interests in each other as well as cooperation with each other.

Benefits from Sino-Indian Cooperation in Afghanistan

First of all, from the point of view of the economic interests, both China and India should find points of cooperation to ensure the stability of the investment environment, and to protect investment and the citizens in Afghanistan. Afghanistan is rich in natural resources and as emerging developing countries, China and India need resources to support the domestic economic development. India and China may compete with each other in terms of their investments in Afghanistan and that may be a source of conflict between these two countries. However, for now, a more serious problem is primarily the concern about Afghanistan's security. If Afghanistan's security situation deteriorates, both the countries would lose interests in investing in Afghanistan which in turn would hamper the economic progress in China and India. Therefore, these two countries should try to strengthen the security concerns in Afghanistan, as far as possible and maintain stable investment environment for the sake of better economic prospect of China and India.

At the same time, the two countries can benefit each other by building infrastructure, for example, the construction of the road, which can achieve a win-win situation, ensuring that all can be benefitted from Afghanistan's resources. Second, in addition to the economic interests, the Sino-Indian cooperation on the non-traditional security factors is also a necessity. Both China and India now face the threat of such factors. Because of war, Afghanistan has suffered serious problems of drugs and refugees for a long time. Education and healthcare system are also quite backward. This provides an opportunity for Sino-Indian cooperation in Afghanistan. Drug trafficking has put the safety of China's western frontier at risk. For both India and China, there is a risk of terrorism 'spillover effect'. Therefore, through the cooperation in the field of non-traditional security, China and India can win the trust of local people in Afghanistan, which is very important and is the foundation of economic investment in Afghanistan. At the same time, through cooperation, China and India also can improve the degree of mutual trust (Hornung 2012).

From the point of view of cultural exchange in Afghanistan, India and China have a certain cooperation space. In the 4th century BC, the Chinese silk was introduced to India and in the 2nd century BC, China's silk was transmitted from India to Afghanistan. China, India, and Afghanistan are the countries situated on the Silk Road of the ancient times which had a history of intersection. So the two countries can use their cultural and historical link hand in hand to restore Afghanistan's archaeological career, to revitalise the country's tourism industry, to increase the employment of the local people, to strengthen the cooperation and communication between the two countries, and also use the geopolitical civilisation instead of the geostrategic thinking.

In addition, as a regional power, both China and India can play an important role of the coordinator for regional stability to shoulder responsibility through bilateral cooperation, promoting multi-lateral forum. Facts have proved that the problem cannot be solved by force. Regional dialogue is the key and SAARC (South Asian Association for Regional Cooperation) and Shanghai Cooperation Organization (SCO) should use more power and play a bigger role to promote discussion about Afghanistan after 2014. The SCO has received serious attention to solve the problems of Afghanistan. China, Russia and four Central Asian states, are the members of SCO. India and Pakistan signed the memorandum of obligations on 24 June 2016, at Tashkent, thereby starting the formal process of joining the SCO as a full member. Afghanistan is also an SCO observer country. This also provides a platform for China and India to be cooperative with each other in Afghanistan. The five aspects considered by SCO to solve the problem of Afghanistan are as follows:

- First, a complete realisation to solve the problem of Afghanistan is of utmost importance for maintaining regional stability, world peace, prospects and the healthy development of the SCO because each member country's national security interest is at stake.
- Second, provide support to the members of the organisation and other international organisations and countries which are involved in providing the economic aid to Afghanistan.
- Third, the United Nations should play a leading role in the process of solving the problem of Afghanistan. Other international organisations and national federation shall be under the leadership of the United Nations and involved in promoting stability and economic reconstruction of Afghanistan.
- Fourth, that military means alone cannot solve the problem of Afghanistan; a political solution is fundamentally necessary towards peace in Afghanistan.
- Fifth, SCO thinks the Afghan reconciliation process should be dominated by the people of Afghanistan. So, SCO may act as a good platform for solving Afghanistan's problems in the future.

Now, China and India can use the regional influence jointly presiding over a series of meetings to discuss the regional order and provide the platform to stakeholder countries thinking over the future of Afghanistan. For example, China and India successfully held international conferences in 2013; the first China–India–Afghanistan dialogue was held in Beijing. Again, the 12th meeting of foreign ministers of Russia, India and China was held at New Delhi in November 2013 where the ministers reached an important consensus. The ministers think that the three countries share many common interests in Afghanistan and also play an important role for peace and stability in Asia and Europe. China, India and Russia are indispensable partners of each other in the process of Afghanistan reconstruction.

Finally, the positive attitude of India and China towards Afghanistan has also encouraged other countries to take part in the process of reconstructing Afghanistan. Especially, the participation of Pakistan is very important in this context. Geographical factors have played an important role in this issue for a long time. Pakistan has tried to increase the impact on Afghanistan. A rise in instability may lead to more influence of Taliban in Afghanistan. Especially Durand line, the international boundary between Pakistan and Afghanistan, is a great threat for India. For a stable Afghanistan, participation of Pakistan is indispensable.

China can make use of the friendly relations with Pakistan. China should let Pakistan play a proactive role in the process of reconstructing Afghanistan. It would strengthen the mutual trust among China, India and Pakistan, which in turn would make the region more stable (Li Tao 2013).

Challenges before Sino-India Cooperation in Afghanistan

China–India cooperation in Afghanistan is still facing many challenges and uncertainty. Although there are many opportunities for cooperation between the two countries in Afghanistan, there are certain issues and concerns that need to be resolved. First, after the withdrawal of US force, the security situation in Afghanistan is uncertain. Recently, with the re-emergence of Islamic extremists in Iraq, the danger of Islamic extremism has been revealed. The US government, military, and some main important think tank reports pointed out that the future of Afghanistan is faced with severe challenges. The reports did not even rule out the possibility of the worst situation. The United Nations Office on Drugs and Crime statistics, in 2014, put forth that the Afghan drug cultivation reached all-time highs, up to 224,000 hectares, compared with 2013; up by 7 per cent.[1] So instability of Afghanistan can have a strong negative impact on China and India participating in the reconstruction of Afghanistan in the future.

Secondly, Afghanistan is affected by the influence of outside forces. Since the USA launched the war against terrorism in Afghanistan, competition has been kept between multinationals outside Afghanistan. After the US withdrawal, there will be more fierce competition between the stakeholder countries outside Afghanistan. On 31 September 2014, the

USA and Afghanistan signed a bilateral security agreement. The USA continues to provide legal basis in Afghanistan. As a result, the USA will remain in the core interests.

Third, on September 21, 2014, the Independent Election Commission of Afghanistan announced the former finance minister Ashraf Ghani as the President of Afghanistan. So the policy of new government such as domestic political reconciliation will affect the future of Afghanistan. Finally, the Sino-Indian cooperation in Afghanistan will also be challenged by other factors including the future relationships between great powers, such as the Sino-Indian relations, China–Pakistan relations and India–Pakistan relations.

Conclusion

Thus, it is clear that there is a noticeable convergence of interests of China and India in Afghanistan (Shisheng Hu et al. 2014). Both the countries feel that the rehabilitation of Afghanistan should be Afghan-led. Afghanistan possesses significant economic potential which remain unharnessed to a great extent due to its milieu dominated by insurgents. China and India are among the principal prospective investors and consumers of Afghan resources and Afghanistan's economy needs to export its natural wealth for prosperity. Both the Chinese and Indian governments and investors have displayed interests in Afghanistan in terms of the prospects in mining, hydrocarbons, infrastructure development and other sectors. The two countries should therefore work with Afghanistan to develop strategies for progress. Though China and India have both supported and trained the Afghan National Security Force (ANSF), they need to contribute significantly in future in this regard for Afghanistan's security issues. Again, China and India might not at times agree on all security-related concerns. However, the exit of the USA and NATO (North Atlantic Treaty Organization) troops from Afghanistan provides room for strategic collaboration between India and China. But both the nations are apprehensive of the security issues and domestic stability in Afghanistan as they do not want Afghanistan to turn into a shelter to the Islamic terror groups, following the withdrawal of the troops. Hence there lies some uncertainty regarding how the two countries would be able to capitalise on the opportunities and cooperate in Afghanistan with the NATO and Western interests drawing down. Nonetheless, these two emerging Asian superpowers would be among the regional players who are able to resolve Afghanistan's problems thereby assisting the country to move towards a prosperous and stable future.

Note

1. The Afghan opium survey by the United Nations Office on Drugs and Crime (UNODC) say that a record-breaking 224,000 hectares was cultivated in 2014, which was a 7 per cent rise on 2013's figure. Available at https://www.theguardian.com/news/datablog/2014/nov/12/opium-harvest-afghanistan-record-levels-after-troop-withdrawal (accessed on 12 November 2014).

References

Hornung, Jeffrey W. 2012. 'Why China Should Do More in Afghanistan'. *The Diplomat*. Available at http://thediplomat.com/2012/08/why-china-should-do-more-in-afghanistan/ (accessed on 1 August 2012).
Hu Shisheng, Sawhney, R.K. and Pantucci, R. 2014. 'A Roadmap for Sino-Indian Cooperation in Afghanistan'. Available at http://www.vifindia.org/article/2014/july/01/a-roadmap-for-sino-indian-cooperation-in-afghanistan (accessed on 25 April 2015).
Li Tao. 2013. 'The Situation in Afghanistan after the American Withdrawal and the Role of China and India'. *South Asia Research Quarterly*.
news.qq.com. 2014. 'Afghanistan's new President's Visit to China and China Will Provide $2 billion of aid'. Available at http://news.qq.com/a/20141029/028818.htm (accessed on 29 October 2014).
Liu Xiao Ming. 2014. 'Xi Jinping Met with Afghan President Hamid Karzai'. *Xinhuanet*. Available at http://news.xinhuanet.com/2014-02/08/c_119234704.htm (accessed on 8 February 2014).
Pantucci, Raffaello. 2013. 'China's Afghanistan Challenge'. *The Diplomat*. Available at http://thediplomat.com/2013/04/chinas-afghanistan-challenge/ China's Afghanistan Challenge (accessed on 5 April 2013).
Xinhua. 2013a. 'China, Afghanistan Agree to Strengthen Ties'. Available at http://en.people.cn/90883/8411495.html (accessed on 26 September 2013).
———. 2013b. 'What Will You Bring Economic Belt "Silk Road"'. Available at http://news.xinhuanet.com/globe/2013-10/05/c_132773983.htm (accessed on 5 October 2013).
Zhang Chunyan and Zhu Yufan. 2013. 'The Afghan Strategic Partnership of India: Progress, Effect and Prospect'. *South Asia Research Quarterly*.
Zhao Yanrong. 2014. 'Xi Meets Karzai in Sochi'. *China Daily*. Available at http://europe.chinadaily.com.cn/china/2014-02/09/content_17273016.htm (accessed on 9 February 2014).

PART II

Economy and Business: Comparative Focus

PART II

Economy and Business: Comparative Focus

10

Multiple Paths to Globalisation

The India–China Story

Sriparna Basu

Introduction

As a complex and multi-dimensional process, globalisation has always invoked mixed responses. Over the past two decades, globalisation has been looked at from two distinct vantage points. One perspective is that globalisation began a lot earlier than it is usually thought of and took unsuspected routes; we are accustomed to think, for example, of capitalism and free market philosophy as Western inventions, later transplanted in or imposed on Asia and other parts of the world. But historical research has traced the founding principles of free market economics earlier to *Tao Te Ching*, the work of Chinese philosopher Lao Tze.[1] From this perspective, globalisation is a reformulation of previously existing economic and social patterns (Bayly 2004; Chanda 2007). The other perception about globalisation is that, it is a product of technological revolution and the global restructuring of capital in a post-national world order involving the flow of goods, services, people and cultural habits (Appadurai 1996; Castells 1991; Lash and Urry 1994). Within this latter perspective, there is a bifurcation of views. Some regard globalisation as a ruse for global capitalism and neo-imperialism of the West driving the logic of capital and market on all regions and spheres of life and an imposition of homogeneous standards that stamp out local cultures and ways of life (Bourdieu and Wacquant 1999; Harvey 1989; Jameson 1991; Mander and Goldsmith 1996; Soja 1989; Steger 2005; Stiglitz 2002). For others, it is the irrevocable continuance of modernisation giving rise to economic, political and cultural alternatives as well as diversity (Friedman 1999; Fukuyama 1992). Each approach thus, takes the wind out of the other in critical ways—while the revolutionising logic of globalisation is counterbalanced by globalisation's depiction as an ongoing phenomenon since ancient times, the social and economic determinism that critics have read into it is challenged by the view of globalisation functioning to democratise choices. What emerges from this point counterpoint, therefore, is a clear indication that globalisation cannot just be characterised as one. While economic globalisation in the post-World Trade Organization (WTO) and -General Agreement on Tariffs and Trade (GATT) regime is fairly recent, globalisation in the context of political and philosophical borrowings is an age-old phenomenon. Second, despite the anxiety evinced by critics about nation states undergoing loss of authority under globalisation, a similar argument could be made that it could present multiple options or ways to globalise; and modern states can exercise the power and autonomy to manage and co-opt globalisation in their own ways. As argued by Panitch (1994, 64), globalisation can take place 'in (sic), through, and under the aegis of states; it is encoded by them and in important respects authored by them'. This rewriting of globalisation is certainly the case with China and India, the two biggest emerging economies of Asia.

China and India have shared similar moments in history in terms of their encounter with invasive colonial powers. In the past, both countries have been revered and then reviled in Western historiography; both had undergone major political shifts in the 20th century having emerged as independent nation states after a long struggle for political and economic sovereignty and there is considerable interplay between their idioms of self-representation and notions of progress. This essay argues that the paths taken by China and India are indeed grounded in and produced by their own modernities. But the cultural/civilisational influence that modern China has exerted on modern India has not received much attention and deserves scrutiny.

I organise the discussion around three key areas: I begin with a review of the representation of China and India in Western historiography; then I explore the historical memories that tend to surface in India and China's self-representations as they made their transition to modern statehood;

and finally I show how, beginning in the late 1970s in China and the early 1990s in India, a return to development models based on integrating into the global economic system saw China exhibiting the capability to industrialise rapidly, which had an under-recognised impact on India as it fed into impulses that resulted in a break from the Nehruvian principles of self-reliance and autarky which characterised the early years of modern India.

The Rise and the Fall

Wallerstein and Braudel argued convincingly that the unfolding moment for modern history was in a world economic system that had emerged in Asia and shifted to Europe only after 1800 (Wallerstein 1974; Braudel 1982). Before the emergence of Europe as a strong contender for trade and commerce in the 17th and 18th centuries, China and India led the show as global economic powers (Frank 1998). According to economic historian Angus Madison, both China and India contributed to over 50 per cent of the world GDP in 1600. Confucian classics were heralded for their rationality by the forerunners of the French revolution such as Voltaire, Rousseau and Diderot (Needham 1969, 90) and China was known in Europe as having adopted a rational model of governance to which could be attributed its economic prosperity (Fuchs 2006). India, during the Mughal Empire was well known for its crafts. It had the reputation of having sophisticated markets, credit and capital. According to Braudel, India for centuries had been 'subject to a money economy, partly through her links with the Mediterranean world' and 'Cambay (Gujarat) could only survive, it was said, by stretching out its arm to Aden and the other to Malacca' (Braudel 1982, 528).The Indian textile industry was the most advanced in the world; 'calicos', or printed fabrics, produced in India swept markets in England, France and Holland (Tarlo 1996). In terms of trade, India was second only to China as a trade and economic superpower in Asia, with Southeast Asia a relative backwater.

By the early 19th century however, the perception of China and India as advanced civilisations held in early modern Europe had swung to the other extreme to render them without significant past or future. For Hegel (2004, 29), Asian societies, particularly India but also China, were 'static': they lacked the dynamism and progress observable in European history.[2] This was also the outlook of India's British rulers:

their presence was necessary for progress and civilisation of India.[3] As a radical thinker, Marx felt considerable sympathy for colonialism's victims. Nevertheless, he postulated an 'Asiatic mode of production', which was unique among modes of production in a sense which is not subject to change, but could carry on indefinitely unless broken down by an external force such as colonialism. This amounts to a restatement of Hegel in economic language. It follows that colonialism is necessary to put derailed Asian societies back on the tracks of history: 'whatever may have been the crimes of England she was the unconscious tool of history in bringing about a revolution' (Marx 1853).

Even as late as in 1989, John K. Fairbank, a pre-eminent historian on China of the 20th century, when commenting on the First Opium War in China (1839–42), which led to China's defeat by the British Navy and the beginning of semi-colonial dominance of important parts of China; repeats the hegemonic paradigm of vigour of the West versus the passivity of the East when he says:

> In demanding diplomatic equality and commercial opportunity, Britain represented all the Western states, which would sooner or later have demanded the same things if Britain had not.... Yet probably some kind of Sino-foreign war would have come, given the irresistible vigour of Western expansion and immovable inertia of Chinese institutions (Fairbank and Reischauer 1989, 277; quoted in Martinez-Robles 2008).

Rewriting History: The Birth of the Nation

Interestingly, Hegel and Marx's misleading images of a static India that was 'outside history' were also adopted by Indian nationalists in their bid to carve out an independent and self-reliant Indian position, but they were put through a revaluation. According to Gandhi, 'India remains immovable and that is her glory' (Gandhi 2008, 73). Similarly, Nehru in the wake of Gandhi also stated the 'unsubdued and unconquered' spirit of India. (Nehru 1946, 563). If Western historiography had depicted India as degenerated from a glorious past, in a counter move Indian nationalist thought gave the notion an 'essentialist twist' by offering the notion of India as essentially the same despite going through travails and turbulences, colonial invasion being one of them (Breckenridge and Van Der Veer 1993, 11). The inertia that India is accused of is instead posited as equanimity and tolerance and a self-correcting capability that has enabled India to conserve her inner strength.

In this reinterpretation, India's unchanging character and lack of participation in the historical process is a mark of her ancient spirituality that outweighs the material vigour of the West. Gandhi portrays an idyllic India in *Hind Swaraj* that is supposed to have consisted of self-sufficient and self-contained villages, without trade and political exchanges with each other or centres of power (Gandhi 1909). Nehru has also followed Gandhi closely in this construction of the core of India lying in its autonomous and organised idyllic village communities that offered an alternative to the colonial rule. This inward strategy/orientation adopted by savants of Indian nationalism may well have paved the way for making autarky and socialism as central elements in the agenda for economic planning and political strategy instituted under Nehru in the mid-1950s. So in a sense, a cultural nationalist position of self-valorising autonomy became interchangeable with autarky as a form of economic nationalism that upheld economic self-independence as a way of consciously rejecting external relationships perceived as unholy influence. The inward nature of India's economic strategy in the initial phases is much commented upon in literature (Jalan 1991, 13; Nayar 1997; Srinivasan and Tendulkar 2003). The emphasis was on creating a state-owned and managed indigenous manufacturing base with an inward attention, to bring about self-reliance and future sustainability. Thus, the state was to be the final adjudicator of economic power limiting the scope of private capital, which harks back to the quasi-Marxist notion of private greed adopted by Indian nationalist thinking albeit with a twist that the ultimate pride of India lay in its spiritual rather than material progress feted by the Western nations. This 'inward strategy' thus plays out the curious amalgamation of Eurocentric images of Indian history and the nationalist fixation on Indian spirituality as a self-defining stance which neglects India's past as a great trading power.

China's nationalist narrative also partook of a reconstruction of China's past by positing China as a great and powerful nation throughout most of its history. The Chinese nationalist view reasserted China's far reaching geographical influence by inventorying China's tributary states that were subservient to the Chinese empire. Chinese textbooks of 1954 bore a map of conquest illustrating the traditional geographic influence of China and the territorial losses suffered at the hands of Western and Japanese imperialist forces during the period between Opium War in 1839 and until it was reborn as a sovereign power in 1949 (Garver 2001, 14–15). This was intended to fortify the logic of Mao's cultural revolution and garner popular support for its efforts to recreate history by wiping out a humiliating past.

India and China's historical trajectories can be seen to converge in the early stages of their nation building: both emerged as independent republics after a long drawn out struggle for political and economic freedom; both were weighed in by underdevelopment and large populations and an agrarian economic set-up where majority of the population resided. China's initial economic and industrial strategy much like India's in the early 1950s was fuelled by an anti-Western and anti-imperialist ideology and was based on the adoption of a heavy industry-oriented development strategy (Lin, Cai and Li 1996, 203). Both India and China drew their inspiration in this regard from the Soviet Union and its socialist ideology. Nehru was influenced by the economic achievements of the Soviet Union through a similar strategy (Nayar 1997, 29). For the Chinese leadership, Soviet Union's capacity for nation building in the 1930s provided a convincing contrast to the Great Depression in Western market economies. Moreover after China's involvement in the Korean War in 1950, resulting in embargo and isolation from the Western nations, propelled it to build its capacity for producing capital goods and military materials (Lin, Cai and Li 1996, 204). An autarkic closure was chosen by both countries as a means of achieving economic sovereignty where the state became the primary agent for development in a break from the mainstream international economic system.

In a Globalising World

It is significant that both China and India liberalised their economies under duress. China's historic break with the Soviet type planned economy and transition to an open market-oriented system is often attributed to disastrous outcomes of the former, associated with the Mao Zedong regime from 1949–76 when China slipped into socio-political and economic crisis.[4] In the Indian scenario, the origins of its closed door policy lay in India's long-standing goal of self-reliance; the foreign exchange crisis of 1966 further added to this tendency towards control and insulation and mistrust of all flows of funds from abroad. The ensuing outcome was reduced exports, loss of international competitiveness, degradation in quality and a high cost structure (Banik and Bhaumik 2006, 86–88). Finally, it took a severe balance-of-payments crisis in 1991 which saw foreign exchange reserves dwindling to a mere two weeks' worth of imports to break the policy inertia and make room for reforms. When Deng Xiaoping assumed power in 1978 after Mao's death, he made a series of sweeping administrative reforms parallel to changes in economic policy, such as recruiting experts into the party based on their technical expertise rather than ideological ardour. Bureaucracy's stranglehold over the system was undercut by abolishing life time tenure for senior members and party cadres were required to get polytechnic or college education within a mandated period of three to five years (Khanna 2008, 41–42). Thus, enterprise and performance were given precedence over mere party affiliation, which bred a new generation of skilled workers and a culture of performance. For Manmohan Singh, the man credited with opening up the Indian economy, matters were more complicated. Singh's historic 1991 budget met with a cold reception within the ruling Congress party and a sizeable proportion of members of parliament were outraged at the suggestion of slashing subsidies for fertilisers, among other measures, which they perceived as spelling doom for them at the polls (Jose 2011). It is not that the need for a policy shift did not become evident for the Indian policy makers through the 1980s, but what expedited the final systemic shift were the visible success of China and the fall of the Soviet Union which had provided the basis for Indian planning (Bhagwati and Panagariya 2012, 34).

The Game of Shadows

While it is true that the cultural/civilisational impact of the West has critically influenced modern Indian institutions and identity politics, such influences in India are deeply contested and fraught with anxiety. Ashis Nandy has very aptly given a name to this syndrome of the other within the self—he has described the West as the intimate enemy that is lodged within the Indian self (my emphasis). If Western influence (globalisation being one of them), whether repudiated or welcomed, is a continuous subject of vigorous debate in India, there is surprisingly less debate on another cultural influence that has steadily grown over the years—the influence of China. While intimacy with the West can be riddled with anxiety as the economic and cultural gap with it is seen as being too great to bridge; China on the other hand was in India's shoes not too long ago and its emergence as a world power attests to the declining hegemony of the West. China's growing military and manufacturing might have gained wide acceptance as an inspirational benchmark to aspire for.

In the early stages of the Sino-Indian relationship, Nehru made the initial attempts to reach out to China; India was the second country to recognise the People's Republic of China on December 30, 1949. Nehru's vision of an Asian federation, of which India and China were to become two poles, emphasised that Asian countries with a common cultural past should work together. The popular slogan of 'Hindi Chini bhai-bhai' (India and China are brothers) owes its inception to the prevailing sentiments towards China during this period. Natwar Singh, a close associate of the Nehru-Gandhi family, recounts the conversation that took place between Nehru and Bulganin during the former's visit to the Soviet Union in 1955: on Bulganin's proposal to second the USA's offer of admitting India as the sixth member of the Security Council, Nehru turned it down and wanted the offer to go to China instead (Singh 2014, 121). Nehru interpreted the offer as a move against China. Half a century later, when the US-India nuclear agreement was signed in 2005, the coalition government headed by Manmohan Singh lost its majority in parliament since the CPI(M) (Communist Party of India [Marxist]), a major partner, construed the deal as an anti-China manoeuvre by America and India; consequently it withdrew support from the government. Significantly, the CPI(M) came into existence by splitting from the pro-Soviet CPI (Communist Party of India) in 1964 because of its ideological closeness with China. This exercise repeated itself again when a further breakaway faction from the CPI(M), the Naxalites, with pro-Maoist leanings, adopted as their rallying cry 'China's Chairman is our Chairman'.

The rising soft power of China has influenced India's political and economic landscape in crucial ways. India's crushing defeat by China in the 1962 war delivered a significant learning to the former to build a strong military base, in a clear departure from the earlier pacifist approach of Nehru towards developing military power (Guha 2008, 310–12). The defeat signalled a sea change in Indian defence thinking and ground preparation strategies with defence spending rising rapidly so that by the early 1970s, it accounted for 40 per cent of the central budget and over 3 per cent of Gross National Product (GNP) (Garver 2001, 63). Similarly in 1964, when China acquired its nuclear capability it acted as an inspiration to India to have its own by 1974. Not surprisingly, as China parted ways with Maoism and state-directed capitalism in 1979, the tremors could also be felt in India. In his 'dream budget' of 1997, finance minister P.

Chidambaram defended his reform agenda by citing Deng Xiaoping: 'Development is the only hard truth' (Chidambaram 1997, 24).[5]

Beating the West at Its Game?

China's economic reforms have proved to be a two-way street. While China has redefined the economic and political landscape by dominating low-cost manufacturing of the world (Zakaria 2008, 91), it has also been marked by the world in turn. But what stands out in China's case is the way globalisation is aggressively sought and co-opted to close the gap with the developed economies and even perhaps to exceed them. Bahl succinctly captured this power play in his narrative:

> It's quite usual for the world to be in awe of China's stupendous economic expansion, thought to be stronger than the fabled American growth decades of 1820–70. Which country has grown at 9 percent every year for thirty years? Which country has increased its per capita income by eleven times in such a short period, pulling 400 million people out of abysmal poverty? Which country holds the largest horde of cold cash, a full $2.5 trillion? Which country spends $1 billion every year to develop world class infrastructure? (Bahl 2010)

The narrative that sees globalisation as the West beating down the trade doors of non-Western nations and imposing a one-way hegemony on them may therefore itself be a hegemonic one. In reality, multiple globalisations are possible and strong nation states have considerable leeway in choosing their mode of globalisation, using it to facilitate their development. On the contrary, opting out of globalisation may trigger crisis conditions and is not sustainable for long. Moreover, globalisation can be a flow within non-Western nations and the West does not have to be an essential pole to complete this circuit. Thus, the Chinese success in lifting itself up by its own bootstraps has been inspirational enough in India, across the ideological spectrum from left to right, despite the existence of border disputes and a tense political relationship between them. Globalisation has unleashed multiple flows: from West to non-West, from non-West to West and within non-Western nations themselves. This is indeed the force field within which 21st century societies must function. This does not imply the end of choice, either for the West or for non-Western societies, rather it is the multiplicity of choices that now nations have to contend with.

Notes

1. See *The Tao of the West: Western transformations of Taoist Thought* in which British philosopher John James Clarke has traced the founding principles of free market economics to the *Tao Te Ching*, the work of Chinese philosopher Lao Tze. Similarly, Adam Smith, who's *Inquiry into the Nature and Causes of Wealth of Nations* is generally credited with establishing free market principles, was inspired by the work of French physiocrat Francois Quesnay, who believed that governments should not interfere in the operation of natural economic laws. Quesnay was responsible for coining the term laissez-faire and was extraordinarily impressed by reports emanating from European travellers in late Ming and early Quing China. The latter found a money economy, flourishing trade and commerce due to the enjoyment of economic freedom, relatively large-scale mercantile and industrial enterprises, many of the latter under private ownership.
2. A similar assertion can be found in J.G. Herder's *Ideas for the Philosophy of the History of Humanity*: The [Chinese] empire is an embalmed mummy painted with hieroglyphics and wrapped in silk; its internal life is like that of animals in hibernation (Herder 1787, XIV: 13, cited in Gobel 1995).
3. See in this context, Thomas Babington Macaulay's impassioned speech in British parliament in 1933 saying that the role of the British colonizers in India was to 'give good government to a people to whom we cannot give a free government'.
4. These are best exemplified by two Maoist programmes: the "Great Leap Forward" (1959–60) undertaken to develop China's economy through a massive deployment of people followed by the "Cultural Revolution" (1966–76) which sought to eliminate subversion from within the ranks of the Communist Party. The unrealistic goals of the first plunged the country into a grave man-made famine killing nearly 30 million Chinese (Meng et al. 2015); under the second programme hundred million Chinese were persecuted and ten million people killed (Khanna 2008, 41; MacFarquhar and Schoenhals 2006; Treiman and Deng 1997).
5. See Budget 1997–98 speech of Shri P. Chidambaram, minister of finance, 28th February 1997. Available at http://indiabudget.nic.in/bspeech/bs199798.pdf (accessed on 27 May 2016).

References

Appadurai, A. 1996. *Modernity at Large: Cultural Dimensions of Globalization*. Minneapolis: University of Minnesota Press.
Bahl, R. 2010. *Super Power? The Amazing Race between China's Hare and India's Tortoise*. India: Penguin.
Banik, A., and Bhaumik, P. 2006. *Foreign Capital Inflows to China, India and the Caribbean: Trends, Assessments and Determinants*. UK: Palgrave Macmillan.

Bayly, C. 2004. *The Birth of the Modern World 1780? 1914. Global Connections and Comparisons.* Oxford: Blackwell.

Bhagwati, J., and Panagariya, A. 2012. *India's Tryst with Destiny.* India: Collins Business.

Bourdieu, P., and Wacquant, L. 1999. 'On the Cunning of Imperialist Reason'. *Theory, Culture & Society* 16(1): 41–58.

Braudel, F. 1982. *The Perspective of the World: Civilization & Capitalism, 15th–18th Century Volume 3.* Berkeley: University of California Press.

Breckenridge, C.A., and Van Der Veer, P. (eds) 1993. *Orientalism and the Postcolonial Predicament.* University of Pennsylvania Press: Philadelphia.

Castells, M. 1991. *The Informational City: Information Technology, Economic Restructuring, and the Urban-Regional Process.* Oxford: Blackwell.

Chanda, N. 2007. *Bound Together: How Traders, Preachers, Adventurers, and Warriors Shaped Globalization.* USA: Caravan.

Fairbank, J.K., and Reischauer, E.O. 1989. *China: Tradition and Transformation.* Boston: Houghton Mifflin.

Frank, A.G. 1998. *Re-Orient: Global Economy in the Asian Age.* Los Angeles: University of California Press.

Friedman, T. 1999. *The Lexus and the Olive Tree.* New York: Farrar, Straus, Giroux.

Fuchs, T. 2006. 'The European China: Receptions from Leibnitz to Kant'. Trans. Martin SchÖnfeld. *Journal of Chinese Philosophy* 33(1): 35–49.

Fukuyama, F. 1992. *The End of History and the Last Man.* New York: Avon.

Gandhi, M.K. 1909. *Hind Swaraj: Or, Indian Home Rule.* Trans. Mahadev Desai. Ahmedabad: Navajivan.

———. 2008. *Mahatma Gandhi: The Essential Writings.* USA: Oxford University Press.

Garver, J.W. 2001. *Protracted Contest: Sino-Indian Rivalry in the Twentieth Century.* New Delhi: Oxford University Press.

Gobel, R.J. 1995. 'China as an Embalmed Mummy: Herder's Orientalist Poetics'. *South Atlantic Review* 60(1): 111–129.

Guha, R. 2008. *India after Gandhi: The History of the World's Largest Democracy.* India: Picador.

Harvey D. 1989. The Condition of Postmodernity, Oxford: Blackwell.

Hegel, G.W. 2004. *Philosophy of History.* New York: Barnes and Noble.

Jalan, B. 1991. *India's Economic Crisis: The Way Ahead.* New Delhi: Oxford University Press.

Jameson, F. 1991. *Postmodernism, or the Cultural Logic of Late Capitalism.* Durham, N.C.: Duke University Press.

Jose, V.K. 2011. 'Falling Man: Manmohan Singh at the Centre of the Storm'. *The Caravan*, October issue: 1–8.

Khanna, T. 2008. *Billions of Entrepreneurs: How China and India are Reshaping their Futures and Yours.* New Delhi: PenguinViking.

Lash, S., and Urry, J. 1994. *Economies of Signs and Space.* London: SAGE Publications.

Lin, J.Y., Cai, F. and Li, Z. 1996. 'The Lessons of China's Transition to a Market Economy'. *Cato Journal* 16(1): 201–231.

MacFarquhar, R., and Schoenhals, M. 2006. *Mao's Last Revolution.* USA: Harvard University Press.

Mander, J., and Goldsmith E. (eds) 1996. *The Case against the Global Economy.* San Francisco: Sierra Club.

Martinez-Robles, D. 2008. 'The Western Representation of Modern China: Orientalism, Culturalism and Historiographical Criticism'. *Journal of the UOC's Humanities*

Department and Languages and Cultures Department (8). Available at http://digithum.uoc.edu (accessed on 27 May 2016).

Marx, K. 1853. 'The British Rule in India'. In *Selected Works*, eds Karl Marx and Frederick Engels, 345–351. Moscow: Foreign Languages Publishing House.

Meng, Xin, Qian, N., and Yared, P. 2015. 'The Institutional Causes of China's Great Famine, 1959–1961'. *Review of Economic Studies* 82: 1568–1611.

Nayar, B.R. 1997. 'Nationalist Planning for Autarky and State Hegemony: Development Strategy Under Nehru'. *Indian Economic Review* 32(1): 13–38.

Needham, J. 1969. *Within the Four Seas: The Dialogue of East and West*. London: Allen & Unwin.

Nehru, J. 1946. *The Discovery of India*. New Delhi: Oxford University Press.

Panitch, L. 1994. 'Globalization and the State'. *Socialist Register* 60–93.

Singh, N. 2014. *One Life Is Not Enough: An Autobiography*. New Delhi: Rupa.

Soja, E.W. 1989. *Postmodern Geographies: The Reassertion of Space in Critical Social Theory*. London: Verso.

Srinivasan, T.N. and Tendulkar, S. 2003. *Reintegrating India with the World Economy*. Washington, DC: Institute for International Economics.

Steger, M.B. 2005. 'From Market Globalism to Imperial Globalism: Ideology and American Power after 9/11'. *Globalizations* 2(1): 31–46.

Stiglitz, J.E. 2002. *Globalization and Its Discontents*. New York: Norton.

Tarlo, E. 1996. *Clothing Matters: Dress and Identity in India*. Chicago, IL: University of Chicago Press.

Treiman, J.D., and Deng, Z. 1997. 'The Impact of the Cultural Revolution on Trends in Educational Attainment in the People's Republic of China'. *American Journal of Sociology* 103(2): 391–428.

Wallerstein, I.M. 1974–1989. *The Modern World System I–III*, Orlando, FL: Academic Press.

11

Regional Inequality over the Post-globalisation Era

A Study on India and China

Arindam Banik and Arnab K. Deb

Introduction

After the Second World War, developing countries chose a strategy of import substitution as a means of industrialisation. However, in the past two decades, many countries have changed their development strategy and inclined towards global economic integration by trade liberalisation. Since trade liberalisation shifted production activity to low-wage countries, the restructuring of business activity through promoting innovation took place in the developing countries. Depending on the factor intensities of the industries, industrial dynamics has been greatly impacted by the removal of trade barriers. Along with it, the reorientation of the factors of production from the import-competing sector to the export-oriented sector took place as a consequence. Participation of these countries in international trade led to gains in aggregate welfare or average real incomes through various channels. It generated efficiency gains from specialisation and exchange based on comparative advantage. It also led to higher welfare and productivity due to the availability of larger varieties of final and intermediate goods.

It has been more than four decades since Hirschman and Rothschild (1973) drew attention to the changing tolerance for inequality in the process of economic development. They argued that the 'tunnel effect'[1] may be short lived and challenged the prevalent wisdom of Kuznets (1955) and Kaldor (1957). Kuznets and Kaldor offer different views of the inequality–growth relation. In the Kuznets view, inequality increases as a result of the initial stages of growth, while in the Kaldor scenario, inequality is needed to generate growth. According to Kuznets, the relationship between economic growth and inequality can be represented as an inverted-U curve. In the nascent stage of development an economy moves from an informal rural sector to an industrialised sector. During this phase of development, the industrial sector grows at the expense of the agrarian rural sector and there is a transition process of greater inequality. This Kuznets explanation of an inverted-U curve rests on 'dual economy' dynamics (Turnovsky 2013). Kaldor provided a more direct explanation for the same. Since the rich have a higher propensity to save as compared with the poor, redistribution in favour of the rich would lead to greater savings and thus resources for investment and growth.

As Deaton (2013) notes, inequality is a part and parcel of development. As some members of the population become successful in making the 'Great Escape' from poverty and deprivation, others may be left behind. In the years, since the Hirschman-Rothschild challenge and the conventional wisdom handed down by Kuznets and Kaldor, there has been progress in our understanding of the relationship between growth and inequality. The belief that economic growth generally alleviates poverty and reduces income inequality is now widely held and supported empirically by many studies. The last 40 years have also witnessed the growth through the process of trade liberalisation in the emerging economies such as India and China. However, its implication for income distribution in these countries has been a topic of intense debate among researchers.

The international trade theory, under fairly plausible conditions, predicts that the owners of the factor(s) of production a country is relatively abundant in are winners from trade liberalisation and losers are the owners of the scarce factor(s). Most developing countries are actually relatively abundant in unskilled labour. Accordingly, the trade liberalisation should benefit the unskilled workers and this in turn leads to the reduction in poverty in these countries. However, a lack of intersectoral mobility of factors, including labour is a major factor in dampening the poverty-reducing effect of trade liberalisation. It is such because if the reallocation of factors of production does not take place, the gain from specialisation cannot be fully realised. In addition, wage equality across sectors—another prime requirement for benefiting the unskilled workers from trade liberalisation—does not take place in the absence of intersectoral factor mobility. As a result, unskilled workers not being able to be absorbed in the sectors that flourish due to trade liberalisation, experience a decline in their incomes (and even an adverse change in their employment status in the presence of other labour market rigidities).

To gauge the extent to which a country can reap the benefit of a liberalisation process followed by globalisation, it is imperative to study the regional performance of the country, since a country's welfare greatly depends on how its states or provinces generate income during the post-globalisation period. It is obvious that states/provinces try to attune their production structure to international demands. However, if some states/provinces are not able to do so, it may lead to regional income disparity which in turn gives rise to unequal income distribution at the national level. Hence, an important question arises: To what extent is a state or province able to reshape its production structure in order to have the benefit of globalisation to the fullest? For geographically large emerging economies such as India and China having disparate regions, it is especially very essential to understand whether opening up to world trade has equalising impact across different regions of the country. Against this backdrop, this essay attempts to provide a comparative discussion on the recent trends in regional inequality and possible reasons for it across the two largest emerging nations, India and China.

Economic Reforms in India: Liberalisation, Privatisation and Globalisation

In 1991, India faced a major balance-of-payment crisis that had been simmering since the mid-1980s, and this called for rigorous policy reforms in the areas of domestic investment, trade, foreign investment, and the public and financial sectors. These were with a clear objective of enhancing the efficiency in the functioning of the Indian economy and making it the fastest-growing economy and globally competitive. The pace of policy change accelerated during the early 1990s when the explicit adoption of neoliberal reform programmes marked the beginning of a period of intensive economic liberalisation and changed attitudes towards state intervention in the economy. The focus of economic policies during this period shifted away from state intervention for more equitable distribution towards liberalisation, privatisation and globalisation (Pal and Ghosh 2007). This period of economic transition has had a tremendous impact on the overall economic development of almost all major sectors of the economy, and its effects over the last two decades can hardly be overlooked. Besides, it also marks the commencement of the real integration of the Indian economy into the global economy. In context to India, globalisation implies opening up the economy to foreign direct investment (FDI) by providing facilities to foreign companies to invest in different fields of economic activity in India, removing constraints and obstacles to the entry of multinational companies in India, allowing Indian companies to enter into foreign collaborations, encouraging them to set up joint ventures abroad, carrying out massive import liberalisation programmes by switching over from quantitative restrictions to tariffs and import duties; therefore, globalisation has been identified with the policy reforms of 1991 in India.

The debate on the economic policy and reform began in India in the 1980s, and continues today. Prior to the extensive introduction in 1991 of the new economic policy, as it came to be known, there was widespread apprehension that liberalisation and excessive reliance on market forces would lead to increases in regional, rural–urban and vertical inequalities in India (Pal and Ghosh 2007).

Economic Reforms in China: Liberalisation, Pragmatisation, Marketisation and Corporatisation

A salient feature of world history today is China's participation in the process of world economic globalisation. The rationale for this integration is to promote competition in the economy with the expectation that competition would bail out the inefficient state-owned enterprises (SOEs) and make them more competitive. In December 1978, Deng Xiaoping— leading the Communist Party of China (CPC)—clearly understood the importance of globalisation and initiated economic reform with an objective of transforming Chinese economy from a planned to a market economy. Accordingly, since 1978 China has adopted a market-oriented economic reform policy of liberalisation, pragmatisation, marketisation and corporatisation (Li 1997; Perkins 1988, 1994). Consequently, real annual economic growth of the country has averaged at about 8 per cent, and productivity has remained at about 3 per cent (Borenszten and Ostry 1996; Chow and Li 2002).

The first set of economic reforms concentrated primarily on agriculture, but China began to open cautiously to the world. The major reforms in the 1980s included industrial reform, revitalisation of national banks, price reform and fiscal reform. The government established five special economic zones—three in Guangdong Province—in 1980. Other economic zones followed as the reforms expanded. The slow transition from centrally planned economy continued. Economic overheating in the form of supply bottlenecks and high inflation was common in the late 1980s (Li 1994). Financial reform began with the 1993 Austerity Plan that redirected investment to Western provinces. The 1995 banking reform restructured the banking sector, while the 1997 SOE reform aimed to reduce state intervention in production. The move to open trade culminated in China's admission to the World Trade Organization (WTO), after much negotiation, in December 2001. China's accession to the WTO in 2001 was a momentous decision made by the top leadership. It was a big gamble for the Chinese enterprises; because prior to the accession, they were extremely weak in every measure compared to global firms (Nolan 2001, 2004).

The renewed investment boom driven by the influx of FDI after the WTO accession made China 'the factory of the world'. The coastal region, where most of the population lives, has attracted most of the foreign investment. China's 'Western Development Strategy' began in 2000 to attract development in the inland regions. Realised values of FDI in China reached $500 billion by the end of 2003. FDI totalled less than $19 billion during the 1980s. Wider market access and cheap labour made China the best production site of the Multinational Corporations (MNCs) that relocated core economic activities to China. These are the market leaders and became more competitive by dominating China's high-tech sectors and international trade. With industrial policies invalidated by the WTO agreements, China maintained extensive intervention in the state sector not for the purpose of making them more competitive but for making them bigger in size and enormously profitable through monopoly or oligopoly. Essentially, it has become *the assembly plant of the world*; an extension of the global supply chain. This dominant view, now-a-days is that China has benefited hugely from globalisation and this is clearly evident in its high Gross Domestic Product (GDP) growth. Chinese companies are getting bigger and stronger. As a result, China is rapidly industrialising itself into an economic superpower.

Regional Inequality in India and Its Causes over Post-reform Years

In India, the decadal average growth rates for the 1960s and the 1970s were around 3.4 per cent, implying per capita growth rates of about 1 per cent. The growth rates in national output since the mid-1980s and in particular since 1993 have been appreciably higher on average than in the 1960s and the 1970s. The growth rate in net national product per capita was 4.8 per cent per annum between 1993–94 and 1999–2000 (Marjit and Kar 2008). It is widely believed that India has experienced a major structural break in its growth performance after economic reforms of 1991. The average growth in the previous decade has been at an impressive 7.8 per cent per annum.

During the crisis years of 2008–09 and 2009–10, when the global financial crisis hit the world economy, Indian economy had shown a great resilience and the average growth rate of the economy was more than 6 per cent per annum. However, one major criticism of the post-reform growth process is an increase in regional inequality. Benefits from growth at the national level have not been spread equally across different regions of the country and gave rise to differences in the levels of per capita income between the richer and poorer regions. Topalova (2005) argues that tariff reduction on importable commodities has not been effective in reducing the incidence and depth of poverty across districts in India with the concentration of import-competing activities.

The neoclassical growth theory predicts that a region's growth rate tends to be inversely related to the initial levels of income, as in a closed economy, marginal returns to capital in a more developed region will decline, leading to convergence. In the new economic geographic and international trade literature, Elizondo and Krugman (1996) also argue that regional disparity in a federal economy may decline with economy globalisation because increasing international competition erodes the monopoly power of the highly concentrated production and trade centres. However, contrary to these theoretical predictions, empirical studies in the context of the Indian economy have found that regional inequality is on the increase, in particular since 1991 when liberalisation and deregulation policies were carried out.

In order to understand the extent of prevalent inequality across different regions of India, we need to look at select variables that articulate regional disparity. Table 11.1 represents the Gini coefficient and variation in gross state domestic product (GSDP) over different sub-periods

Table 11.1
Disparity in Per Capita GSDP: Weighted and Unweighted Indices

Year	Ratio of Minimum To Maximum per Capita GSDP (in Per Cent)	CV (Weighted by Population)	CV Unweighted	Gini Coefficient (Weighted by Population)
1993–94	30.527	34.549	38.33	0.1917
1996–97	27.586	36.781	NA	0.2071
1999–2000	28.899	37.417	35.09	0.2173
2001–02	21.556	35.610	NA	0.2078
2002–03	21.608	36.686	NA	0.2771
2003–04	22.705	36.230	NA	0.2290
2004–05	20.105	(a) 38.44 (b) 38.90	(a) 29.81 (b) 34.15	0.2409

Source: Kundu and Varghese (2010)

during the post-liberalisation years. Both the indicators show an increasing trend implying the presence of regional inequality. The post reform period is particularly important as this period has experienced enhanced economic efficiency, reduction of subsidy, and greater accountability under the strategy of globalisation that has impacted and revamped the programmes and schemes for infrastructural development and in turn has favoured the relatively developed regions. As a result, a close scrutiny over this period reveals that, except for a year or two in the mid-1990s, inequality has been on the increase during the post-reform period.

Likewise, the other catch-all economic indicator—per capita consumption expenditure—also shows a clear increasing trend as is the case with income. At the all-India level, the coefficient of variation (CV) has increased from 17.6 per cent in 1993–94 to 24.4 per cent in 2004–05 (Figure 11.1). Similar pattern is observed in the case of rural areas and smaller urban centres and across the states. One would infer that regional imbalance has gone up during the 1990s and in the following five years—the period which has seen the first and the second phase of structural reform.

In order to identify a set of lagging states during the post-liberalisation period, it would be important to probe into the state-level scenario in a disaggregated manner by considering the performance of each state separately. Ahmad and Narain (2008) classify the Indian states

Figure 11.1
Inter-state Inequality in Per Capita Consumption Expenditure

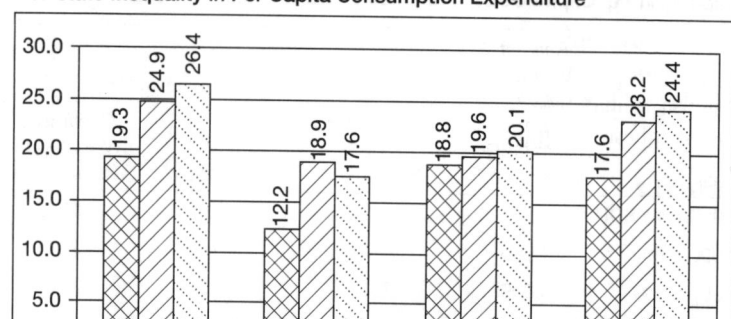

Source: Kundu and Varghese (2010)

into 'high-', 'medium-' and 'low'-income categories. The Northeastern states belong to a special category, thereby enjoying special grants from the Finance Commission as well as other preferential treatment, and constitute a separate category. This chapter shows that most of the states that had low levels of per capita income recorded low-income growth, not only in the 1980s but also in the 1990s. The low-income category states and the northeastern states were noted to have registered growth rates of 2.5 per cent and 2.8 per cent, respectively, during the 1980s, which was much below the national average. These went down further to 2.3 and 2.5 per cent, respectively, during the 1990s (Kundu and Verghese 2010).

Considering the growth performance of individual states, it is evident that low-income states such as Assam, Bihar (including Jharkhand), Madhya Pradesh (including Chhattisgarh), Orissa and Uttar Pradesh (including Uttarakhand) have experienced very low average growth rates during the 1980s. In the 1990s, the growth rates of these states have become even lower. Low growth rates accompanied by the instability in growth rates (assessed through their CV over time) pose a more serious problem for these states. In addition, unlike the middle- or high-income states, these states have also exhibited a decline in the absolute figure of per capita income or no growth in at least two years during the 1990s. Several other studies using other economic indicators at the state level confirm the increasing trend in inequality during the last two decades of the past century, thus confirming the thesis of accentuation of regional imbalance. Based on the level of per capita state domestic product (SDP) and the growth therein, a set of eight states (including three newly formed states) can be identified as belonging to the lagging region category. These states are Bihar, Jharkhand, Orissa, Madhya Pradesh, Chhattisgarh, Uttar Pradesh, Uttarakhand, and Assam (Kundu and Varghese, 2010; also see Table 11.2).

Table 11.2
Per Capita SDP and Growth in SDP for Select States

States	Growth in SDP			Per Capita SDP		
	1997–99	2003–05	2007–09	1997–99	2003–05	2007–09
Andhra Pradesh	5.12	9.25	9.10	10,160	13,996	18,001
Assam	1.32	4.90	6.36	6,585	7,602	8,640
Bihar	2.47	5.48	14.11	3,539	3,992	5,332
Chhattisgarh	2.90	10.26	8.10	8,256	10,412	12,701
Gujarat	3.44	12.36	10.89	15,613	20,349	26,447
Haryana	4.88	9.07	9.69	14,742	20,260	25,110
Himachal Pradesh	6.74	8.06	8.42	11,625	15,590	19,162
Jammu & Kashmir	5.11	5.52	5.90	8,601	9,608	10,696
Jharkhand	9.75	4.49	8.08	8,448	9,297	10,967
Karnataka	8.32	8.95	8.44	11,715	14,518	18,529
Kerala	5.83	8.46	10.00	10,961	15,339	20,104
Madhya Pradesh	7.36	6.83	4.94	8,759	9,374	10,204
Maharashtra	6.23	8.79	9.01	16,494	20,319	25,190
Orissa	6.87	11.23	8.23	6,466	8,290	10,309
Punjab	4.74	5.17	6.70	16,320	18,900	21,603
Rajasthan	5.82	11.24	8.76	9,708	11,021	12,862
Tamil Nadu	6.35	9.78	6.75	13,243	16,663	21,090
Uttar Pradesh	2.73	4.77	10.71	6,452	7,090	8,573
Uttaranchal	1.43	15.28	7.52	8,356	12,844	16,827
West Bengal	7.16	6.27	7.72	9,827	12,540	14,929
Mean	5.23	8.31	8.47	10,293	12,900	15,864
SD	2.28	2.91	2.04	3,566	4,814	6,223
CV	0.436	0.350	0.240	0.347	0.373	0.392
Weighted CV	0.409	0.325	0.244	0.383	0.422	0.441

Source: Kundu and Varghese (2010)

The earlier discussion shows a perceptible increase in inter- and intra-regional inequality in India during the reform period. However, this inequality is evident not only in terms of income but also in terms of health and access to education (see Pal and Ghosh 2007 for details). However, in this chapter our focus is primarily on the increasing income inequality across different regions of the Indian economy during the period of globalisation. It should be noted that globalisation is an outcome of liberalisation of several sectors in the Indian economy. Accordingly, in this section we attempt to discuss the extent to which liberalisation process followed by globalisation is responsible for the regional income inequality during this period.

One important component of the liberalisation process of 1991 was trade liberalisation that is essentially inequitable in nature since it distributes income in favour of the export sector and against the import-competing sector. Unless the gains from trade are redistributed, trade liberalisation will always change income distribution, which may imply higher inequality. In India, a similar phenomenon was observed. Several empirical studies found a strong link between trade openness and increased regional inequality. Aghion, Burgess, Redding and Zilibotti (2004) show that the trade liberalisation process of 1991 fostered growth only in the most productive industries located in the already advantaged states (Karnataka, Andhra Pradesh and Tamil Nadu), thereby tending to increase regional inequality.

Daumol (2010) examined the link between trade openness and increased regional inequality. Using the data for the period of 1980–2003, he showed that greater global integration of India in international trade has gone together with rising regional inequality. The study argues that the opening of the country to the foreign markets in the decade of the 1990s has generated the agglomeration process in South India that is the border region with the lowest cost access to the foreign markets. Historically, this southern region has always had vast seaports and has welcomed foreign traders and travellers. In the present days, industries located in the coastal South India can satisfy both the international market and the internal market. After the opening up of the economy to the world market in 1991, these regions have been advantaged relative to the interior landlocked regions. Moreover, more efficient sub-national government and superior quality of local education made this region even more attractive to foreign and Indian firms (Guha 2007).

Another channel through which trade liberalisation led to regional inequality is the economic growth. Recent studies on trade openness and growth, such as Calderon, Loayza and Schmidt-Hebbel (2004), show that growth effect is almost nil for the countries with low levels of per capita income and positive for countries with good level of development. Following this line of argument, trade openness was beneficial for more developed Indian states and detrimental for the other ones; this phenomenon in turn led to regional inequalities.

Another important avenue through which globalisation led to increased regional inequality is the liberalisation of the financial sector of the country. As Pal and Ghosh (2007) argue, "The most adverse effect of financial liberalisation on inequality came from policies which eased the 'priority sector' lending norms for nationalized banks." Until the 1980s, nationalised banks had obligations to fulfil the priority sector lending targets. But post-liberalisation, the priority sector's definition was widened to include many more activities, and the emphasis in banking shifted instead towards maintaining the capital adequacy level prescribed by the Basle accord. As a result, most banks now avoid lending to small farmers and small-scale industries, as they are perceived to be less creditworthy customers. This has had dramatic effects on the viability and cultivation of small enterprises that are the largest employers in the country, and has therefore indirectly impacted income distribution and poverty reduction. Moreover, the inflow of FDI in India has only marginally improved the gross domestic capital formation, but its incidence has been confined to some very small pockets, both geographically and sectorally. This has increased interstate and intersectoral inequalities in the country.

Another factor which can be held responsible for increased inequality in India during the reform period is too much emphasis on the reduction of the fiscal deficit. Direct and indirect tax rates declined in India because of the pressures from powerful lobbies. At the same time government's failure to reduce current expenditure implied that reduction in the fiscal deficit was primarily carried out by reducing capital expenditure and rural expenditure generally, as well as by selling PSUs to generate one-time revenue. Public investment in key infrastructural areas and social welfare schemes reduced because of reduction in capital expenditure. In a country like India, where the level of infrastructure development is poor, public investment in infrastructure is critical, not only for its direct developmental effects but also because it brings in private investment through its crowding in effects.

Regional Inequality in China and Its Causes over Post-reform Years

Since the 1870s, there have been three waves of globalisation in the world. Globalisation encompasses declining barriers to trade, migration, capital flows, FDI and technological transfers. The first wave of global integration, 1870–1914, was triggered by a combination of decreasing transportation costs, such as the switch from sail to steamships, and reductions in tariff barriers, pioneered by the Anglo-French agreement. From 1945 to 1980, there was the second wave of globalisation in the world. During this period, barriers of trading manufactured goods between developed countries had been eliminated, but as for developing countries, the only barrier being lowered was the barrier of trading primary commodities. The third wave of globalisation, which emerged around the year of 1980, was distinctive. During this period, emerging economies including China started getting access to global market.

A common feature of many developed and developing nations is persistent inequality across regions. This fact is in sharp contradiction with the standard neoclassical theory that predicts that regional inequalities should be eliminated through factor mobility, trade or arbitrage in a well-functioning economy (Henderson and Thisse 2004). China presents a unique and important opportunity to study regional inequality over the post-reform years. Along with the appearance of the third wave of globalisation, China's breaking into the global market is reflected through several economic changes. FDI inflow increased by about 90 times, from $0.92 billion in 1983 to $83.5 billion in 2007; the volume of foreign trade increased by 247 times, from 57 billion Yuan in 1980 to 14,097 billion Yuan in 2006; the average tariff rate has fallen substantially over the years (Yue, 2010). Consequently, the GDP in China and the per capita income soared and the country experienced rapid economic growth with an average growth rate of 9 per cent. During the last three decades, China experienced rapid, almost miraculous growth with per capita GDP in 2011 reaching 35 times of the 1978 level. However, the economic growth of this magnitude came at the expense of rising inequality in the country. As per the World Bank estimates, China's income Gini coefficient far exceeds that of South Asian countries such as India, Bangladesh and Pakistan. Income differences in China are large both inter- and intra-regionally, with inter-regional differences increasing over time (Fujita and Hu, 2001; Kanbur and Zhang, 1999).

All the three measures of inequality CV, Theil index and Gini coefficient reveal a similar trajectory of interprovincial inequality for the period from 1978 to 2006 (Figure 11.2). We can observe a fluctuation in interprovincial inequality in the late 1970s, a decline during the 1980s and a rise during the 1990s. Although it remained relatively stable or increased only slightly during 1999 through 2004, it shows a decline during 2004 through 2006. The net result is, interprovincial inequality in 2006 was about 22 per cent higher, 9 per cent higher and 8 per cent lower, than the 1978 level, according to the Theil index, Gini coefficient and CV, respectively (Fan and Sun, 2008). Therefore, the economic reforms that began in the late 1970s enhanced the development of several eastern region provinces that had previously been laggards.

Decomposition of the Theil index into its interregional (between-region) and intraregional (within-region) components reveals that component-wise contributions varied over time (Figure 11.3). Intraregional inequality was considerably higher than interregional inequality during 1978 through 1993. At the same time, the overall trend of interprovincial inequality was determined by intraregional inequality. However, between 1990 and 2004, interregional inequality increased sharply and continuously, whereas intraregional inequality first declined and then remained quite stable. In 1993,

Figure 11.2
Interprovincial Inequality in Per Capita GDP, 1978–2006

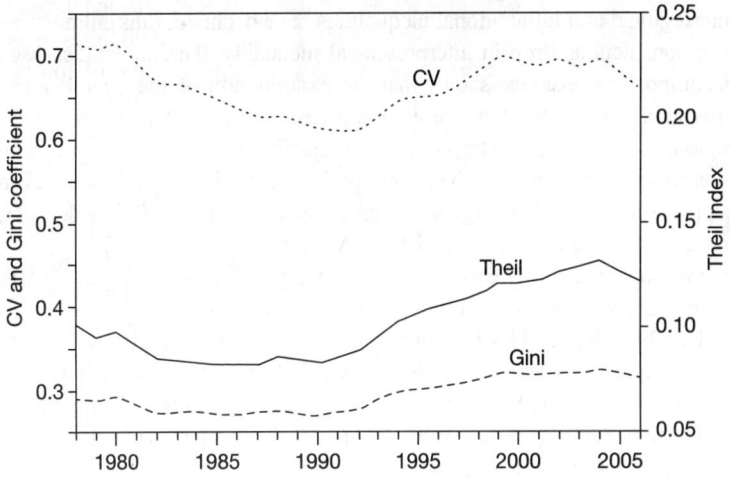

Source: Fan and Sun (2008)

Figure 11.3
Decomposition of Interprovincial Inequality, 1978–2006

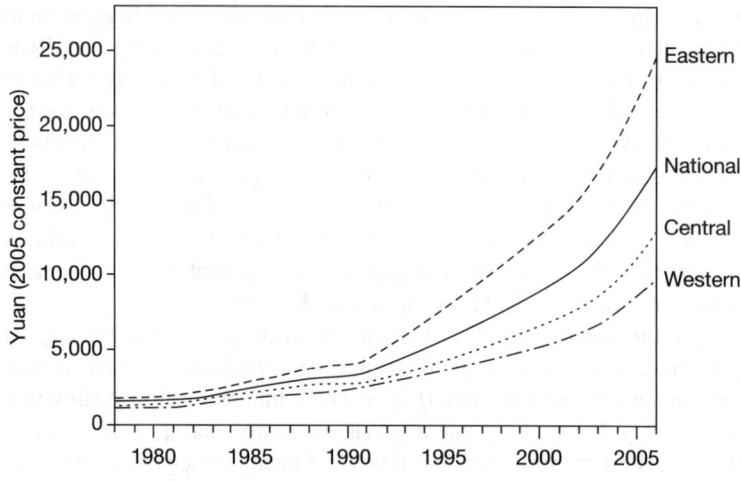

Source: Fan and Sun (2008)

interregional inequality surpassed intraregional inequality, and since then has replaced the latter as the main determinant of change in interprovincial inequality. Specifically, since the early 1990s, when interregional inequality rose, interprovincial inequality also followed suit. Finally, since 2004 both interregional and intraregional inequalities have declined, thus culminating in a conspicuous drop in interprovincial inequality. The above-discussed decomposition exercise shows that the examination of the overall interprovincial inequality alone masks important changes between and within regions. The decline of interprovincial inequality during the 1980s might be interpreted as evidence for the reform policy's equilibrating effect and even support for regional convergence, as predicted by the inverted-U model (e.g., Yang 1994; Duncan and Tian 1999). As shown in Figure 11.3, however, interregional inequality was on its way to a rapid increase in the late 1980s, which subsequently pushed interprovincial inequality towards a steep rise in the 1990s. Figure 11.4 illustrates the eastern region's accelerated growth in per capita GDP since the 1990s; such that the gap between it and the central and western regions continued to enlarge throughout the remainder of the study period (see also Table 11.1). Clearly, this gap accounted for the increase in interregional inequality since the early 1990s (Figure 11.3). The decline of intraregional inequality during the 1980s, shown in Figure 11.3, also masks specific changes within regions. In Figure 11.5, intraregional

Figure 11.4
Per Capita GDP of China and Its Three Regions, 1978–2006

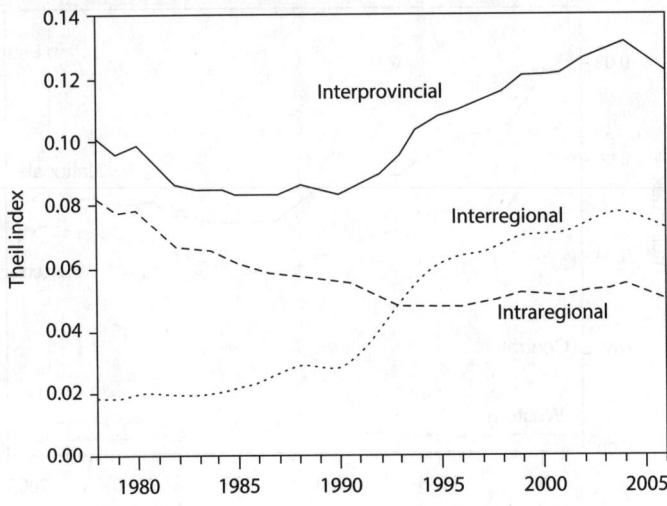

Source: Fan and Sun (2008)

inequality is further decomposed into respective contributions by the three regions. Throughout the period from 1978 to 2006, intraregional inequality in the eastern region was considerably higher than in the other two regions and remained the main determinant of the trend in overall intraregional inequality. Intraregional inequality in the eastern region was high in 1978, but declined thereafter until 1993; it then increased through 2004 and again declined thereafter. In the central region, intraregional inequality was small and exhibited an overall decline. Intraregional inequality in the western region was even smaller and remained largely unchanged over the entire study period. In summary, interprovincial inequality within the eastern region was mainly responsible for the trajectory of overall intraregional inequality.

Since increasing inequality over the post-liberalisation years has been a concern for the Chinese economy, this topic has drawn serious attention of the empirical researchers. In the literature, various factors have been forwarded to explain China's regional disparity. Tsui (1991) examines the effect of China's fiscal decentralisation on regional disparity, and he finds a positive relationship between decentralisation and worsening regional inequality before 1985. Lee (1994) investigates the relationship between FDI and regional development gaps. He

Figure 11.5
Decomposition of Intraregional Inequality, 1978–2006

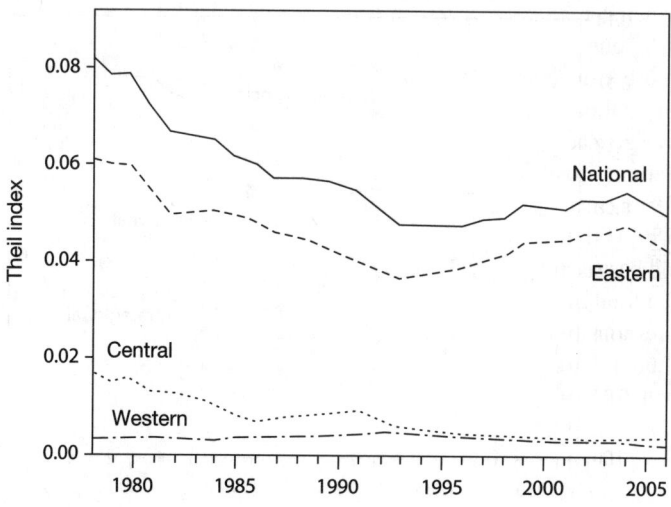

Source: Fan and Sun (2008)

concludes that the differences in the amount of FDI inflows contribute to China's regional disparity. Moreover, many studies also suggest that geographical factors and regional preferential policies are two important factors that contribute to economic boom in the coastal regions (e.g., Fleisher and Chen 1997; Démurger et al. 2001). In addition, there is also evidence that local protectionism may also play an important role in explaining China's regional disparity during the reform era (Young 2000).

Another important factor which has been found influential in explaining the regional disparity in China is the financial-sector development. The important role of the financial sector in the process of economic development has long been recognised in the literature (e.g., Bencivenga and Smith 1991; Greenwood and Jovanovic 1990; King and Levine 1993a, 1993b; Levine 1997; Merton and Bodie 1995; McKinnon 1973; Shaw 1973). A well-functioning financial system will stimulate economic growth by providing a number of important functions such as clearing and settling of payments, pooling of saving, facilitating the allocation of resources across space and time, pooling risk and reducing information costs (Merton and Bodie 1995).

More recent studies (Cai, Wang and Du 2002; Chang 2002, Chen and Fleisher 1996; Fleisher and Chen 1997; Yang 2002) show that there is growing regional imbalance. For example, Bhalla, Yao and Zhang (2003) found that inter-regional inequality is more serious than the rural-urban inequality. Yao and Zhang (2001) identified openness and transportation to be the two important factors in regional imbalance. Lin, Wang and Zao (2004) examined regional inequality in relation to labour migration across provinces, and showed that regional inequality has widened significantly between 1985 and 2000 from a coastal land income ratio of 1.31 to 1.65, while the urban-rural income ratio for the same period has risen from 1.82 to 2.42. Increase in inter-provincial migration from a total of 11.83 million in 1985-90 to 27.53 million in 1995-2000 was responsible for the growing regional inequality. These changes in the labour market could be potential reasons for imbalance in provincial growth.

Not only the changes in the labour market but changes in the allocation of other factor inputs also led to imbalance in regional income in China. After a large migration of educated workers to the coastal regions after reform, expenditure on both technology and education were largely state driven. Growth divergence between coastal provinces and inner provinces in China can be associated with the type and performance of factor inputs, as seen from the disparity in different investment resources and human capital. All investment activities were state owned before economic reform in 1978, but different types of financial resources and different forms of enterprises have emerged since 1978. Based on their originality, investments in fixed assets in China are divided into state appropriation, national bank loans, utilised FDI, self-raised funds and others. Based on their usage destination, investments in fixed assets are classified under state ownership, non-state ownership and foreign ownership. Coastal provinces have the geographical advantage and will attract more productive financial resources than inner provinces. Individual-owned enterprises equally will prevail more in coastal provinces than in inner provinces (Liu and Li 2006).

Conclusion

India and China are reasonably considered as two super powers in the world of business today. Both the countries adopted market-oriented reforms in order to integrate into the global economy. In 1978, China adopted market-oriented economic reform policy of liberalisation, pragmatisation, marketisation and corporatisation. The process of economic reforms in the Indian economy was triggered by severe foreign exchange crisis of 1991. The focus of economic policies in India during this period shifted away from state intervention for more equitable distribution towards liberalisation, privatisation and globalisation.

A paradigm shift from a centrally planned economy to a market-driven economy definitely boosted the growth performances of these countries. Nevertheless, a close scrutiny of regional income distribution in both these countries clearly reveals that success in achieving a higher growth path came at the heavy expense of strong regional inequality. While in the context of the Indian economy the degree of inequality is on the increase, the Chinese economy experiences a decline in the same over the period of globalisation. Exploring the factors behind this inequality we find that trade liberalisation and liberalisation of the financial sector—two phenomena that converted the Indian economy into a global economy—are primarily responsible for continuous increase in regional inequality. Furthermore, excessive focus on reduction in fiscal deficit through curbing the capital expenditure also causes the regional inequality to rise over the period of globalisation. On the other hand, the factors which primarily explain the existing regional inequality in China are fiscal decentralisation, inflow of FDI and development and openness of the financial sector. Along with these, preferential government policies and change in the allocation of factors of production also led to regional imbalance in China.

Note

1. The willingness of certain segments of the population to remain behind, accepting relative deprivation while others get ahead, in the hope that the advancement would later become more widespread.

References

Aghion, P., Burgess, R., Redding, S.J. and Zilibotti, F. 2008 (September). 'The Unequal Effects of Liberalization: Evidence from Dismantling the License Raj in India'. *American Economic Review*, American Economic Association 98(4): 1397–1412.

Ahmad, A. and Narain, A. 2008. 'Towards Understanding Development in Lagging Regions of India'. Paper presented at the Conference on Growth and Development in the Lagging Regions of India, Administrative Staff College of India, Hyderabad.

Bhalla, A.S., Yao, S. and Zhang, Z. 2003. 'Causes of Inequalities in China, 1952 to 1999'. *Journal of International Development* 15(8): 939–955. doi: 10.1002/jid.1033

Bhattacharya, B.B. and Sakthivel, S. 2004, March. 'Regional Growth and Disparity in India: Comparison of Pre- and Post-Reform Decades'. *Economic and Political Weekly* 39(10): 1071–7107.

Borensztein, E. and Ostry, D.J. 1996. 'Accounting for China's Economic Performance'. *American Economic Review* 86(2): 224–228.

Cai, F., Wang, D. and Yang, D. 2002. 'Regional Disparity and Economic Growth in China: The Impact of Labor Market Distortions'. *China Economic Review* 13(2–3): 197–212.

César C.R. Duncan and Schmidt-Hebbel, K. 2004. 'The Role of Credibility in the Cyclical Properties of Macroeconomic Policies in Emerging Economies'. *Review of World Economics* 140(4): 613–633.

Chang, G.H. 2002. 'The Cause and Cure of China's Widening Income Disparity'. *China Economic Review* 13(4): 335–340.

Chen, J. and Fleisher, B.M. 1996. 'Regional Income Inequality and Economic Growth in China'. *Journal of Comparative Economics* 22(2): 141–164.

Chow, G.C. and Li, K.-W. 2002. 'China's Economic Growth: 1952–2010'. *Economic Development and Cultural Change* 51 (October): 247–256.

Daumal, M. 2013. 'The Impact of Trade Openness on Regional Inequality: The Cases of India and Brazil'. Economics Papers from University Paris Dauphine 123456789/4295. Paris: Dauphine University.

Deaton, A. 2013. *The Great Escape: Health, Wealth, and the Origins of Inequality*. Princeton, NJ: Princeton University Press.

Démurger, S., Sachs, J.D., Woo, W.T., Bao, S., Chang, G. and Mellinger, A. 2001. 'Geography, Economic Policy and Regional Development in China'. *Asian Economic Papers* 1(1): 146–197.

Fan, C.C. and Sun, M. 2008. 'Regional Inequality in China, 1978–2006'. *Eurasian Geography and Economics* 49(1): 1–18.

Fleisher, B.M. and Chen, J. 1997. 'The Coast-Noncoast Income Gap, Productivity, and Regional Economic Policy in China'. *Journal of Comparative Economics* 25(2): 220–236.

Fujita, M. and Hu, D. 2001. 'Regional Disparity in China 1985–1994: The Effects of Globalization and Economic Liberalization'. *The Annals of Regional Science* 35(1): 3–37.

Guha, R. 2007. 'The Better Half'. *Outlook India Magazine*. http://www.outlookindia.com/magazine/story/the-better-half/235079 (accessed on 16 July 2007).

Henderson, J.V. and Thisse, J.F. (eds) 2004. 'Handbook of Regional and Urban Economics', Handbook of Regional and Urban Economics 4(4).

Hirschman, A.O. and Rothschild, M. 1973. 'The Changing Tolerance for Income Inequality in the Course of Economic Development'. *The Quarterly Journal of Economics* 87(4): 544–566.

Kaldor, N. 1957. 'A Model of Economic Growth'. *Economic Journal* 67(268): 591–624.

Kanbur, R. and Zhang, X. 1999. 'Which Regional Inequality? The Evolution of Rural–Urban and Inland-Coastal Inequality in China from 1983 to 1995'. *Journal of Comparative Economics* 27(4): 686–701.

Kar, S. and Marjit, S. 2001, July. 'Informal Sector in General Equilibrium: Welfare Effects of Trade Policy Reforms'. *International Review of Economics & Finance* 10(3): 289–300.

Krugman, P. and Elizondo, R.L. 1996, April. 'Trade Policy and the Third World Metropolis'. *Journal of Development Economics* 49(1): 137–150.

Kundu, A. and Varghese, K. 2010. 'Regional Inequality and Inclusive Growth in India under Globalization-Identification of Lagging States for Strategic Intervention'. Working Paper Series. New Delhi: Oxfam India. http://policy-practice.oxfam.org.uk/publications/regional-inequality-and-inclusive-growth-in-india-under-globalization-identific-346636 (accessed on 28 April 2015).

Kuznets, S. 1955. 'Economic Growth and Income Inequality'. *American Economic Review* 45(1): 1–28.

Lee, J. 1994. 'Regional Differences in the Impact of the Open Door Policy on Income Growth in China'. *Journal of Economic Development* 19(1): 215–234.

Yue, Li. 2010, March. 'Globalization and Inequality in China'. *Northeast Asian Studies* Section 18(19 merger issue): 1–13.

Lin, J.Y., Wang, G. and Zao, Y. 2004, April. 'Regional Inequality and Labor Transfer in China'. *Economic Development and Cultural Change* 52(3): 587–603.

Liu, T. and Li, K-W. 2006. 'Disparity in Factor Contributions between Coastal and Inner Provinces in Post-Reform China'. *China Economic Review* 17(4): 449–470.

Nolan, P. 2001. *China and the Global Economy: National Champions, Industrial Policy and the Big Business Revolution.* Houndsmill: Palgrave.

———. 2004. *Transforming China: Globalization, Transition and Development.* London: Anthem.

Pal, P. and Ghosh, J. 2007. 'Inequality in India: A survey of Recent Trends'. Working Paper Nos. 45, United Nations, Department of Economics and Social Affairs, New York, USA.

———. 1994. 'Completing China's Move to the Market'. *The Journal of Economic Perspectives* 8(2): 23–246.

Perkins, D.H. 1988. 'Reforming China's Economic System'. *Journal of Economic Literature* 26(2): 601–645.

Topalova, P. 2007. 'Trade Liberalization, Poverty and Inequality: Evidence from Indian Districts'. In *Globalization and Poverty*, ed. Ann Harrison (pp. 291–336). National Bureau of Economic Research, Inc. USA: University of Chicago Press.

Tsui, K. 1991. 'China's Regional Inequality, 1952–1985'. *Journal of Comparative Economics* 15(1): 1–21.

Turnovsky, S. 2013. 'The Relationship between Economic Growth and Inequality'. *New Zealand Economic Papers* 47(2): 2–28.

Yang, D.T. 2002. 'What Has Caused Regional Inequality In China?' *China Economic Review* 13(4): 331–334.

Yao, S. and Zhang, Z. 2001. 'On Regional Inequality and Diverging Clubs: A Case Study of Contemporary China'. *Journal of Comparative Economics* 29(3): 466–484.

Young, A. 2000, November. 'The Razor's Edge: Distortions and Incremental Reform in the People Republic of China'. *Quarterly Journal of Economics*, CXV, 1091–1135.

12

Manufacturing Policies and Strategies across China and India
A Comparative Analysis
Prageet Aeron and B.A. Metri

Introduction

In the early 21st century, any company looking to manufacture anything had one clear choice available in terms of destination and that was China. Advantages were many, such as artificially low currency rate with respect to the basket of global currency, low wage rates, skilled manpower and favourable government policies to cite a few. Statistically, if we look at the percentage share of Gross Domestic Product (GDP) from industry versus services for China from 1994 to 2012, we see that manufacturing has always hovered above 45 per cent (32 per cent as per value added in 2012), and it is only recently that the service sector has started to reach the level contributed by manufacturing (Figure 12.1a). In terms of the overall contribution to the world economy, China contributes about 9 per cent of the world's GDP and around 8 per cent towards the growth of the GDP across the world (Figure 12.1b). In terms of the value of manufacturing measured in dollars; China alone contributes around 22 per cent of the world's manufacturing as per 2012 figures.[1] If we look at the corresponding figures for India, we see a fundamentally different picture. India contributes about 2.5 per cent of the overall

Figure 12.1a
Percentage Share of GDP from Industry and Service[2]

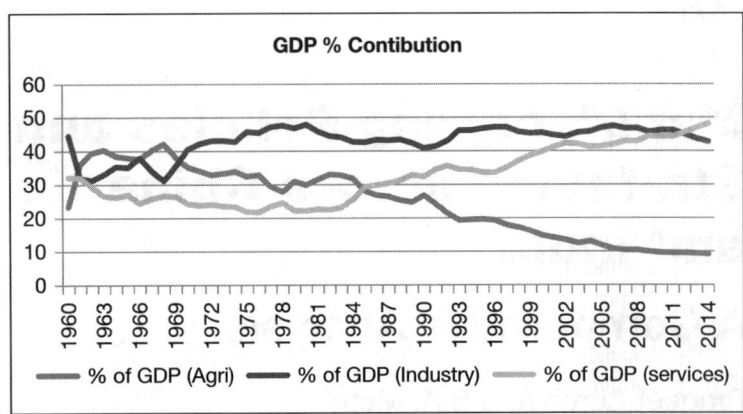

Source: Manufacturers Alliance for Productivity and Innovation, USA

Figure 12.1b
Share of China in World GDP[3]

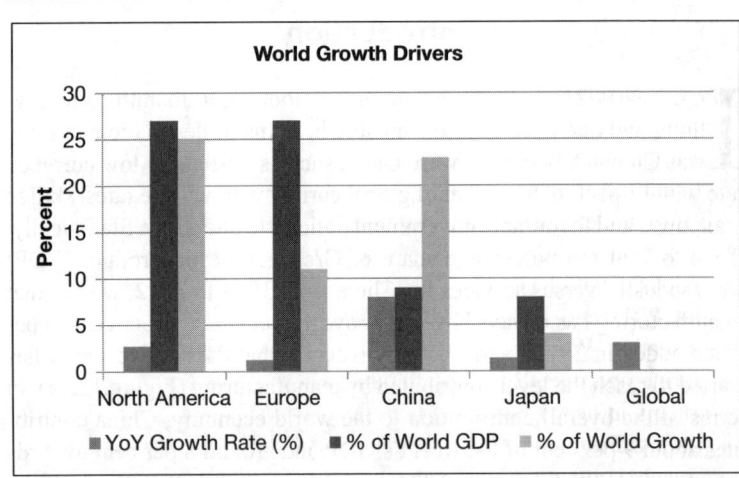

Source: The Economist

world GDP, 2 per cent of the world's manufacturing value and the sector itself barely constitutes 15 per cent of India's own GDP as of 2012. The numbers for India look worse if we compare them with the National Manufacturing Policy, and its stated objective that the manufacturing sector should be contributing about 25 per cent of the overall Indian GDP by the year 2022 together with creating 100 million jobs.

Some issues of concern that present themselves before policy-makers today include:

- whether China has achieved the height of manufacturing revolution;
- whether India can ever make a mark in manufacturing given special emphasis on manufacturing by the existing Indian Government;
- what is the way forward for both China and India;
- whether India can utilise its rich service sector to develop the underperforming manufacturing sector;
- whether China can develop an effective services sector building on top of its manufacturing base, etc.
- will the existing political and socio-economic conditions help or impede the development of the two emerging countries?

None of these questions seem to have an easy answer; nevertheless, the success of China has presented some very prominent learning for the world to sit up and take notice. Ours is an attempt to understand and interpret this success from the Indian perspective and in the process present ourselves possibly one last opportunity to transform India into a manufacturing base, inspired by the Chinese success.

In this chapter, we take a critical look at the development strategy for manufacturing followed by China and propose a stage-based framework of understanding the evolution of Chinese manufacturing. This is based on an in-depth analysis of two regions that have shown tremendous development over the last few decades, that is, the Pearl River Delta (PRD) and the Yangtze River Delta (YRD). This is presented in the next section. We also identify problems associated with Chinese manufacturing and overall Chinese model of development which could pose problems in near future, and therefore, would require some thoughtful solutions. From a methodological perspective, we adopt a case study approach, comparing and contrasting the two regions and then moving back and forth between theory and practice as required to develop a perspective on manufacturing trajectory followed by China. Subsequently, in the next section we present an overview of issues plaguing Indian manufacturing; we also suggest certain recommendations based on learnings from China. Last but not the least, in the concluding section we try to develop a symbiotic model that could help both China and India achieve further success and economic transformation of their people.

China and Economic Development

Both China and India are ancient civilisations that have engaged in trade and commerce throughout the known human history. It has been documented that till about 1800, China and India put together constituted 50 per cent of the world's GDP.[4] The situation changed drastically from 1820 to about 1970 when the combined share reduced to less than 10 per cent of the world economy (Maddison 2001). It is only beyond the late 1990s that the combined share again started moving up, reaching a level of about 25 per cent (all these figures are in 1990$ at purchasing power parity). All through the history, China and India have had similar contributions to the world GDP, but in its latest modern avatar, China contributes the lion's share as of 2012.

China started its march towards industrialisation after 1949, when the Communist Party came to power and established the People's Republic of China (PRC). During the phase of 1949–78, China followed the Soviet model of centralised planning (much like India after independence in 1947) in an attempt to pursue self-sufficiency. The focus was primarily on core industries such as steel, capital goods, cement, etc. However, the actual transition was initiated by the vision of Deng Xiaoping starting in 1978–79. Under his leadership, China set out with the objective of achieving economic well-being, which was defined as GDP per capita of $800 for all citizens by 2000 (Hale and Hale 2003). Deng began an era of economic liberalisation in China, which was unique as this was happening under the umbrella of a single party communist regime. What was achieved through the 1980s and the 1990s can be best captured by studying the development of two very prominent industrial clusters of China, that is, the PRD and the YRD. Study of these two regions will help us in developing a list of the drivers for the humungous success achieved by China in manufacturing.

PRD: PRD comprises nine cities, namely Guangzhou (the provincial capital), Shenzhen, Foshan, Zhuhai, Jiangmen, Zhongshan and Dongguan, four districts and counties of Huizhou and four districts and counties of Zhaoqing. The impact of PRD on the overall economy of China can be best gauged by the fact that in 2013, this region alone accounted for 9.3 per cent of China's GDP, 19.6 per cent of the total

Foreign Direct Investment (FDI) in China and 27.5 per cent of China's exports[5]. It is the world's leading producer and exporter of electronic goods, electrical goods, toys, garments and plastic products.

It was in 1979 that PRD was established as a special economic zone (SEZ) that was permitted to follow a much liberal economic policy that included tax incentives, repatriation of profits, duty-free imports, etc. The PRD region being in proximity with Hong Kong and Macau has always nurtured their association through long-standing family-related and cultural ties. The Chinese diaspora in both Hong Kong and Macau had long before the 1970s developed a strong business foundation and were prominent players in international trade. Hong Kong was one of the largest ports, a hub for light manufacturing, financial services centre and a trading hub in the region; while Macau was well known for its garment and textile industry. This diaspora always wanted to bring business to mainland in order to reap the advantage of cheap land and labour present in and around PRD, and to cater to the demand from China, thereby focusing more on the management of production rather than producing themselves. The liberalisation process offered them just the right fillip. Initially, the work that moved to this region was mostly labour intensive, such as toys, clothes, beverages, etc. Initial production was to satisfy the local demand in China but slowly an export-oriented mindset developed more so on the eastern bank of PRD.

Around 1985, a major relocation started happening mostly from Hong Kong. This was due to greater confidence that developed as a result of early success with production across parts of PRD and rich returns earned by the investors from Hong Kong. This was also facilitated by infrastructure development that happened in PRD and that made logistics much easier than before. Moreover, Hong Kong was also home to several multinational corporations (MNCs) with their regional headquarters which were looking for cost-effective procurement from PRD after the success achieved by investors from Hong Kong. During this period, investment from Taiwan, Japan and Korea started reaching PRD, though they were primarily routed through Hong Kong, as the understanding about business in PRD was very high in Hong Kong. As a result, the production capabilities of PRD were deepened with sub-assemblies of electrical and electronic components, labour-intensive hardware assembly and household electrical consumer goods comprising major chunk of manufacturing. This represented a very critical technological input that found its place inside China with Hong Kong playing the intermediary. Although the western bank of PRD was home to state-owned manufacturing units, they were not export oriented or technologically as advanced as Hong Kong promoted units. This marked the proliferation of technology, with many firms in PRD resorting to copying, reverse engineering and innovating on their own to absorb the newly introduced capabilities. During the 1990s, production capabilities were enhanced further with the introduction of highly technologically intensive products such as computer parts and assembled computers, telecom equipment, electronic toys, high-end fine chemicals and precision equipment. During this phase, more and more technology adoption happened in PRD region largely led by Taiwanese, Western and Japanese companies, although still intermediation through Hong Kong helped. Beyond this, with increasing investment, coupled with rich addition of technological inputs, favourable legislations and presence of increasingly skilled workforce; PRD by the 2000s had reached a point where it was hailed as the prime production facility of all kinds of products related to electrical, electronic, footwear, chemicals and toys, supplying its products across the world both through direct connections as well as through Hong Kong. The sheer pace of development since the 1990s can be best captured by the rise of local companies such as Huawei and ZTE that are the leading producers of highest end telecom products across the world today. Table 12.1 captures the extent of production contributed by PRC towards various items.

While in 1978 the majority enterprise was state owned, by 2001, state owned represented less than 10 per cent of the enterprise with balance being contributed by the private sector funded by foreign investment. In 1978, the share of PRD's GDP as a percentage of China was 2.6 per cent, exports as a percentage of Chinese exports were 3.4 per cent and FDI as a percentage of China's FDI was around 3 per cent. The same numbers for the year 2001 paint a picture of comprehensive transformation. The GDP percentage reached 8.7 per cent, export percentage reached 34.1 per cent and FDI percentage reached 28.6 per cent.

YRD: The YRD is located on the eastern coast of China, comprising Shanghai and 15 other surrounding cities including Suzhou, Wuxi, Changzhou, Zhenjiang, Nanjing, Nantong, Yangzhou, Taizhou (Jiangsu Province), Hangzhou, Jiaxing, Huzhou, Shaoxing, Zhoushan, Ningbo and Taizhou (Zhejiang Province). YRD covers about 110 sq. km. and is home to about 115 million residents as of 2013. The share of YRD's GDP in the overall GDP of China was about 18.8 per cent (2007); the GDP per capita of YRD region reached about 2.5 times the GDP of China (2007). The YRD accounted for almost 25 per cent of the total

Table 12.1
Contribution of PRD Towards Overall Production from China (2000)

IT and Electronics		Electrical Appliances	
78.80%	Telephones	88.20%	Electrical fans
60.20%	Printers	80.40%	Hi-fi
55.80%	Fax machines	79.00%	Electric cookers
50.70%	Digital switches	72.10%	Microwave ovens
43.60%	Video recorders	64.30%	Cameras
35.50%	VCD players	58.40%	Gas water heaters
31.10%	LS semiconductors	37.50%	Air-conditioners
24.30%	CRT	34.80%	Colour Televisions
23.00%	PCs	25.10%	Refrigerators
19.10%	Mobile phones	24.90%	Vacuum cleaners

Source: Enright, Chang, Scott and Zhu (2003)

industrial output of China, 50 per cent of all FDI in China as well as 37 per cent of total exports from China (2007).[6]

During the early 1990s, YRD was actively promoted by both central government and the local government as the new growth centre. The initial fillip was given by state-owned enterprises, township and village-ship firms. However, this model soon ran into problems due to inefficiencies and lack of economies of scale. This was followed by active investment by external partners, that is, firms from Hong Kong and (primarily) Taiwan that completely changed the face of YRD since late 1990s and early 2000. Such has been the impact of YRD especially from the Taiwanese IT industry perspective, that during the period of 1990–2006 the total share of Taiwanese investment has moved from 5 per cent to about 67 per cent in YRD while decreasing correspondingly across other parts of mainland (Yang 2009). As an example, during the time period 1997–2002, the output of state-owned and other collectivist firms dropped from almost 60 per cent to 10 per cent in Suzhou (a small town in Jiangsu province in YRD), and this was the case for most of YRD (Chen 2007). An important point of difference between PRD and YRD has been the nature of industry and the intensity of knowledge utilised by the industry. Whereas PRD factories were primarily export oriented, labour intensive, low on intensity of knowledge; YRD had a more diverse mix of industries such as semiconductor design and manufacture, highly mechanised auto design and manufacture and heavy industries such as petrochemicals, steel, machine tools and so on. The level at which YRD-based industry links with the global production networks is fundamentally different from their peers in PRD (Chen 2007; Yang 2009). YRD also seems to have adopted a more balanced approach in terms of manufacturing and services, which possibly have been fed into each other in promoting growth. Shanghai, the core city in YRD region, has a particularly high place in terms of both world-class R&D centres (Du 2005) and other business services such as banking, IT services, accounting, law and so on. Another important observation of scholars vis-à-vis PRD and YRD has been the growing discontent with local authorities in PRD, better transparency and efficiency of local bodies in YRD, better institutional mechanisms especially with regard to intellectual property rights in YRD as well as better infrastructure in YRD; these have all led to higher growth within YRD. Further, most factories that were set up in PRD had 100 per cent re-export orientation and this made transferring of output to Chinese demand rather cumbersome officially. So, Shanghai-based subsidiaries and industries were better suited to fulfil the rising Chinese internal demand for goods (Overholt 2004; Yang 2009). The development strategy for YRD has been more top-down with local authorities dedicatedly trying to develop well-defined clusters such as for notebooks in Suzhou as compared to self-evolving clusters in PRD.

Analysing the Success of China in Manufacturing

We try to map the overall growth trajectory of Chinese manufacturing based on comparison and analysis of PRD and YRD regions, in terms of certain distinguishable milestones or stages, with prominent characteristics of each stage (Table 12.2).

Two drivers of success that have contributed to stupendous transformation in China have been identified further, based on the discussion on PRD and YRD regions and the policies followed in the two regions.

Government Policy: A slew of measures were taken by China over the years beginning in 1978–79 with 'the open door policy' that set the pace for reforms. The most important of these measures was the empowerment of the local government and other local bodies. For example, Guandong province (PRD) was given control over trade and land rights were delegated to local bodies that could decide on land leasing and its price for MNCs or any production work that required

Table 12.2
Manufacturing Growth Phases (China)

		Phase 1	Phase 2	Phase 3
		Simple Contract Manufacturing	Specialised Manufacturing and Assembly	Original In-house Design and Advanced Manufacturing
Parameters	Labour Characteristics	Labour intensive, low skill work	Labour and skill intensive	Highest level of R&D skill required
	Product Complexity	Basic- toys, chemicals, fabrics	Medium- auto components, PC components, electronic toys, precision equipment, tools etc.	High- Notebooks, high end mobile phones, engines, high end machinery
	Requisites	Rudimentary manufacturing should be present	Sustained successful manufacturing of various components	Highest level of shop-floor maturity, proven delivery of assembled products, advanced mechanisation, best practices adopted
	Technology Transfer Process	State owned enterprises in China enabled this basic manufacturing	MNC infused technology building upon rudimentary technology	In house R&D complements and enhances technology adopted or licensed from top companies
	Basis of Competition	Labour based cost arbitrage, locational proximity to regional trade centres	Labour based cost arbitrage, locational proximity to regional trade centres, locational proximity to various component manufacturers for rapid assembly, high capacity	Advanced design skills, well established low cost manufacturing ecosystem

land. Foreign-owned banks were also started in the province ensuring foreign exchange trading and local stock market was established as early as in 1980. All this was almost unthinkable for any mainland province at the time. Although there was an over-the-top control, but provincial and district-level bodies were given sufficient autonomy to plan and chart their course as per the requirements. The local bodies were given sufficient powers and autonomy in order to frame policies and generate conducive atmosphere for business. This process was neither immediate nor automatic. This began as an experiment by the creation of SEZs in PRD subsequently, as the business needs evolved, local bodies were allowed to gain power and prominence. These local bodies had a huge say in the way property rights were defined, land use policies were formulated and leasing structure was defined for leasing land to various export-oriented MNCs that set shops in the respective regions. The revenue generated from these activities was utilised for the betterment of the regions with central body reducing its earnings from the tax that could have been charged. Right from the development of the requisite infrastructure in the region to opening up a SEZ to enable foreign exchange transactions as well as to develop a stock exchange, creation of institutions was well timed to ensure that the development cycle could move on unabated. Infrastructure creation included roads, bridges, ports, better housing, schools and universities in regions that saw huge migration of workers from the central provinces to coastal provinces.

The second important aspect has been the constant infusion of technology. As the firms matured and absorbed higher technological levels, the lower work was outsourced within the region forming clusters within clusters (Figure 12.2), assuring that almost complete product could be assembled within the region. So, it was not that only one company absorbed technology and moved up the ladder, in fact, technology transfer happened not just from MNCs to specific firms but also within regions as well. Thus, the overall technological intensity and capability of the region improved over time gradually.

A very important policy intervention was artificially depressed currency that could favour the exporters. The Chinese government created its own home grown version of competing firms by promoting serious competition between various regions that were vying for investor attention as well as cut-throat competition between firms within the same region. Although within the same region firms with ownership structure varying from MNC owned to state owned to collectively owned were all aligned in terms of creating products of higher value and were feeding on each other's products, at the same time consistent pricing pressure forced

Figure 12.2
Various Clusters in PRD

Clusters in PRD Cities

City	Clusters
Guangzhou	Autos and parts, transport equipment, electrical products, electronics, chemicals, garments, textiles, business services, software, toys
Panyu*	Sports goods, textiles, garments, jewellery, toys, electric supply equipment, shipping containers
Shenzhen	Electronics, computer products, telecom products, ICs, toys, plastics, watches, clocks, oil paintings, port services, logistics, finance, printing, artificial trees
Dongguan	Electronics computers, components, peripherals, garments, furniture, shoes, toys, watches, clocks, cutlery, kitchen tools, soldering machinery, angling equipment
Huizhou	Laser diodes, digital electronics, CD-ROMs, telephones, batteries, circuit boards, precision machinery, plastics, chemicals
Zhongshan	Lighting fixtures, lamps, metal products, motorcycles, casual wear, locks, audio equipment
Foshan	Industrial ceramics, ceramic artwork, needlework, textiles, children's garments
Chencun*	Flower farming, ornamental fish, turf farming
Nanhai*	Textiles, aluminium products, motorcycles, underwear
Shunde*	Electrical appliances, woodworking, shipping containers, furniture, machinery, bicycles
Jiangmen	Textiles, garments, paper, batteries

Source: Enright, Scott and Chang (2005)
Note: *Panyu is a district of Guangzhou. Chencun, Nanhai and Shunde are districts of Foshan

the firms to think of newer ways of cutting cost while upgrading their overall technological content in terms of the process.

Once the regional development and competition took off, the top leadership in China focused on promoting this intense competition on one hand and at the same time creating conditions for extending the SEZ model and carrying the learnings derived from the previous implementations to new regions. For example, the learnings of PRD were utilised in YRD by trying to create a more value-added, high-end manufacturing, together with R&D services and other business services. The regulated capitalism model of development adopted by China was unique, successful and very contextual which could not be directly adopted or copied by any other part of the world.

Low Wages and Consistently Improving Skilled Manpower: The wages in China have been historically low as compared to the existing manufacturing hubs of the 1990s which included the USA, Japan and Europe. This factor proved decisive in overall cost competitiveness of China that set the Chinese juggernaut on course for achieving peak position in manufacturing. Moreover, skilled manpower available in China further contributed to the development of manufacturing ecosystem there. Here too, government policies played an important role. A special emphasis was laid on high-technology-intensive industry such as semiconductor manufacturing; and establishing links between universities and state-owned enterprises to focus on research and development in order to develop newer technologies in house. Chinese engineers with specialised skills, which they developed either through training abroad or through working in factories of MNCs in China, were given special incentives to start out on their own as entrepreneurs. This ensured that the skill that was acquired was not only sustained but further transferred to more graduates. Overtime, such skills led to internal innovation and high-end products too were developed in China which could compete with global products. Their work on the transfer of technology in China (Hu, Jefferson and Jinchang 2005) point out that both in-house R&D and external infusion of technology by MNCs is complementary to each other as in-house R&D was primarily responsible for developing the absorptive capacity (Cohen & Levinthal 1989) among the Chinese companies. As the market within China evolved, the Chinese Government leveraged the huge potential by promoting home-grown standards (e.g., in the 4G standard for mobile telephony) which had a positive impact on the existing manufacturing base enabling them to develop world-class facilities and scale.

Possible Problems China May Encounter in Future

China has undoubtedly made great progress and results are for everyone to see and analyse. However, as with any coin there are two sides. The negative side of Chinese development is also a reality that China has to possibly deal with in near future. Some of issues that we could point out are discussed as follows.

- Uneven development, with coastal regions moving way higher on all parameters of development as against the internal regions posing a huge threat to the stability of the existing model. Some very serious issues include: ultra-high urbanisation of coastal areas leading to high pollution, huge pressure on resources and destruction of croplands in the fertile delta regions impacting food production in the long run.
- China effectively created high competition between cities and even municipal regions that were vying for FDI. However, this created a unique problem of similar industry clusters across the regions with minimum divergence and, hence, all regions that were trying to woo same firms and FDI in one region meant loss for another region.
- Improving economic conditions and better standards of living may bring with it a requirement for higher autonomy by the next generation putting the existing political system under scrutiny and putting the single party system under stress.
- Artificially lowered currency may be questioned by world order prompting a response that seeks to put a higher value to Renminbi.
- Anti-dumping issues might threaten to derail the Chinese wagon, thereby throwing certain industries either out of business or making certain industries unviable. Therefore, it is essential to balance business such that it caters to both internal demand as well as exports rather than a purely export orientation.

Overview of Problems Associated with Indian Manufacturing

Given the scope of this chapter, we keep ourselves limited to summarising major problem areas with Indian manufacturing rather than developing detailed discussion. Relevant scholarly work related to strategy and practices in Indian manufacturing of recent origin is a rarity. Most quoted works include Chandra and Sastry (2002) and Dangayach and Deshmukh (2003). Although these works are almost a decade old, they are still relevant; especially so as evidenced from various industry reports prepared by the likes of PWC (FICCI & Price Waterhouse Coopers 2014); BCG (Bhattacharya, Bruce and Mukherjee 2014) and many others which emphasise upon the following points about Indian manufacturing.

- Lack of highly skilled (MTech, PhD, etc.) workforce within the manufacturing sector across the spectrum.
- Lack of synchronised supply chain and logistic policies across the board especially among the unorganised players.

- Lack of standardised tools on shop floor, and lack of integration between IT tools and manufacturing in general including design.
- Lack of local standards, low acceptance of Indian standards among global peers and low R&D expenditure.
- Lack of labour reforms, changing tax structures based on tax holidays for specific locations that prove unviable once the tax holiday ends and minimal focus on labour safety and labour training.
- High material cost as a percentage of the overall product cost, lack of vendor development practices and lack of long-term contractual arrangements.
- Minimal benchmarking efforts.

Apart from the Indian auto industry and auto component industry, others seem to have made little impact on the global scene (Dangayach & Deshmukh 2003). However, if we compare with China, in 1991 India actually produced more passenger cars as compared to China, but by 2013 the scene was completely different. China not only overtook India in passenger car production, but in 2013 itself the volumes produced by China were almost six times that of India.

Conclusion

A comprehensive analysis of relative strengths keeps India primarily a services destination and China a primarily manufacturing base for near future. China seems to be making good progress towards services as apparent from R&D and banking centres developed in YRD region especially. India on the other hand does not seem to be making very significant progress in manufacturing, although huge push has been present since last few years. Things seem to be improving but as the previous section summarises, many issues need to be taken care of. Both India and China face rising wages in their respective strongholds, with new players coming into picture that are better placed to take advantage of labour cost arbitrage. Again, this problem is less pronounced for China as value addition and high-end manufacturing are well established. In India on the other hand services (IT and ITES) have not been able to rapidly move up the value chain, so with cost advantage gone, India faces greater pressure to sustain its services economy.

There are some interesting ways by which India and China could create a symbiotic ecosystem. As China develops newer products, it would need access to Indian market and thereby Chinese companies could join hands with Indian service companies to provide various customer services for their products. This would provide a good exposure to Chinese companies with ambitions across the world. Indian markets offer tough competition with American, European, Japanese and Korean products ruling the roost, and this could prove to be the external test that could help Chinese products develop a brand image and reputation for quality. Besides India, specific products, which could be produced at a lower cost in India, could be outsourced to India especially at the component level. This is especially relevant for the Chinese capital goods and machinery industry, electronic products, etc. Indian software capabilities put together with Chinese hardware and manufacturing capabilities could help in developing better products for future that could enable products from Asia to compete with the likes of Apple, Microsoft, etc. India itself is looking at potential electronic imports worth $400 billion[7] by 2020 and China is well placed to play a major role in catering to this demand both through imports as well as setting up Chinese-owned manufacturing units in India.

Last but not the least, Chinese companies have a proven expertise in implementing large infrastructure projects (roads, bridges, ports, railways, power plants, etc.). This expertise could be effectively utilised by the Indian companies in the form of joint ventures for such projects, thereby providing a greater market share to China as well as scope for further future growth outside China. Such joint ventures would involve not just the export of machinery but also the export of services in the form of consulting activities by the Chinese infrastructure companies. Besides the above-mentioned areas, rich collaboration could be explored in the areas of joint exploration in the energy sector (both offshore and onshore) as well as the development of renewable and sustainable energy sources which would be a great boon for both the energy-starved countries for times to come.

Notes

1. See https://www.mapi.net/china-has-dominant-share-world-manufacturing (accessed on 28 February 2015).
2. https://www.bluenomics.com/data#!data/national_accounts_gdp/key_indicators_2/structure_of_gross_value_added_by_sectors_gva_/901686967|chart/line&countries=china (accessed on 5 April 2016).
3. http://www.ft.lk/2013/12/17/us-and-china-will-set-global-growth-pace-in-2014/ (accessed on 28 February 2015).
4. See http://www.economist.com/news/finance-and-economics/21572236-services-are-poised-become-countrys-biggest-sector-served-china (accessed on 28 February 2015).

5. See http://china-trade-research.hktdc.com/business-news/article/Fast-Facts/PRD-Economic-Profile/ff/en/1/1X000000/1X06BW84.htm (accessed on 1 March 2015).
6. See http://info.hktdc.com/mktprof/china/yrd.htm (accessed on 9 March 2015).
7. See http://archive.financialexpress.com/news/electronics-imports-to-reach-400-bn-by-2020-it-ministry/1074652 (accessed on 8 April 2015).

References

Bhattacharya, A., Bruce, A., and Mukherjee, A. 2014. *Make in India: Turning Vision into Reality*. CII and BCG. Available at http://www.manufacturingchampions.in/Document/NewsLetter/CII-BCG%20Report%20on%20Make%20In%20India%20-%2013th%20Manufacturing%20Summit%202014.pdf

Chandra, P., and Sastry, T. 2002. 'Competitiveness of Indian Manufacturing: Findings of the 2001 National Manufacturing Survey'. Working Paper 2002–09–04, 1–42, IIM Ahmedabad.

Chen, X. 2007. 'A Tale of Two Regions in China: Rapid Economic Development and Slow Industrial Upgrading in the Pearl River and Yangtze River Deltas'. *International Journal of Comparative Sociology* 48(2–3): 167–201.

Cohen, W.M., and Levinthal, D.A. 1989. 'Innovation and Learning: The Two Faces of R&D'. *Economics Journal* 99(397): 569–596.

Dangayach, G.S., and Deshmukh, S.G. 2003. 'Evidence of Indian Manufacturing Industry: A Survey." *International Journal of Production Economics* 83(3): 279–98.

Du, D. 2005, August 4. *Shangai: An Emerging Global R&D Base of Multinationals*. Shangai, China: Session on Urban Progress and Governance, the 4th International Convention of Asian Scholars.

Enright, M.J., Chang, K.-M., Scott, E.E., and Zhu, W. 2003. *Hong Kong and Pearl River Delta: The Economic Interaction*. Hong Kong: The 2022 Foundation Ltd.

Enright, M. J., Scott, E. E., and Chang, K. 2005. *Regional Powerhouse: The Greater Pearl River Delta and the Rise of China*. John Wiley & Sons (Asia) Pte Ltd.

FICCI, and Price Waterhouse Coopers. 2014. *India Manufacturing Barometer 2014: Turning the Corner*. Price Waterhouse Coopers Ltd. Available at http://ficci.in/spdocument/20279/ManufacturingBarometer-FINAL.pdf (accessed on 15 April 2015).

Hale, D., and Hale, L.H. 2003, November–December. China Takes Off. *Foreign Affairs* 82(6): 35–53.

Hu, A.G., Jefferson, G.H., and Jinchang, Q. 2005, November. 'R&D and Technology Transfer: Firm Level Evidence from Chinese Industry'. *The Review of Economics and Statistics* 87(4): 780–786.

Maddison, A. 2001. *The World Economy: A Millennial Perspective*. Paris: Development Centre Studies, OECD.

Overholt, W.H. 2004 (May/June). 'Hongkong or Shangai?' *The China Business Review* 31(3): 44–47.

Yang, C. 2009 (April). 'Strategic Coupling of Regional Development in Global Production Networks: Redestribution of the Taiwanese personal Computer Investments from the Pearl River Delta to the Yangtze River Delta, China'. *Regional Studies* 43(3): 385–407.

13

Corporate Social Responsibility Practices
A Comparative Study of India and Asia

Paramita Mukherjee and Rajashri Chatterjee

Introduction

Corporate Social Responsibility (CSR) is a familiar term nowadays. It is primarily concerned about how businesses may take into account the possible economic, social and environmental impact of their operations on the society. Businesses, since ages, have been engaged in philanthropic activities with varying degrees. But, the concept of CSR was formalised not very long ago. After its emergence as an important concept only in the last century, CSR was initially practised in developed countries for quite long. It is only recently that it has become a common concept as far as the businesses are concerned in the emerging economies. In recent times, some emerging economies have even enacted laws or provisions to make CSR practices mandatory as it is perceived as a contribution of the corporates in the upliftment of the quality of life in a country.

However, still there is a lack of understanding of the issues related to CSR in emerging economies in the literature (Kisenyi and Gray 1998). There are contentious issues even in defining the areas and activities of CSR. The European Union has defined CSR as 'a concept whereby companies integrate social and environmental concerns in their business operations and in their interaction with their stakeholders on a voluntary basis'. But the World Business Council for Sustainable Development (WBCSD) defines it as 'the continuing commitment by business to behave ethically and contribute to economic development while improving the quality of life of the workforce and their families as well as of the local community and society at large'. The early writings mostly referred to the concept as social responsibility rather than CSR. The book by Bowen (1953) is regarded as the beginning of the modern period of literature on the subject. Others including McGuire (1963), Walton (1967), Davis (1967), Carroll (1979, 1999) also made significant contributions. So far, the Organisation for Economic Co-operation and Development (OECD) guidelines for multinational enterprises and the goals embodied in the United Nations Global Compact are among the most prominent CSR standards in the world.

In the last few decades, developing countries all over the world have experienced remarkable economic growth. But, many of them have lagged behind in terms of human development (Table 13.1). It is evident that most of the developing countries across the world especially China, India, Argentina, Mexico and Philippines have accelerated their economic growth over the decades. But, Philippines and India along with two other countries still remain in the category of medium human development and do not figure in the top 100 countries. India is in the 135th position out of 186 countries, as on 2013. Notably, the ranks of even the countries in the high human development category range between 57 and 91. Given this background of widespread poverty, growing inequality, lack of education and employment and negligible improvement in the parameters related to human development; environment and social transformation, growing awareness is observed among companies and the society as a whole about the role of the businesses in the development process of an economy by contributing in the progress of economic and social sectors and mitigating the environmental concerns. The transformation of CSR activities and practices in such countries also involved integrating CSR into sustainable business strategy, apart from the traditional engagement in charity and philanthropic activities.

Asian emerging countries are no exception to this phenomenon. Emphasis on CSR disclosure/reporting and making the provision for CSR as a part of profit mandatory are the recent developments and the extent of such activities, in many instances, are dependent on the socio-economic as well as cultural factors of the country. In India, mandatory

Table 13.1 Trend in GDP Growth and Human Development Index in Select Developing Countries

HDI Rank 2013		Human Development Index (HDI)							GDP Growth (CAGR, per cent)			
		1980	1990	2000	2005	2010	2012	2013	1981–1990	1991–2000	2001–05	2006–10	2011–13
	Very high human development: group average	0.76	0.80	0.85	0.87	0.88	0.89	0.89					
49	Argentina	0.67	0.69	0.75	0.76	0.80	0.81	0.81	−1.5	4.5	2.0	5.7	4.1
	High human development: group average	0.53	0.59	0.64	0.68	0.72	0.73	0.74					
57	Russian Federation		0.73	0.72	0.75	0.77	0.78	0.78	—	−3.9	6.1	3.5	3.0
62	Malaysia	0.58	0.64	0.72	0.75	0.77	0.77	0.77	6.0	7.1	4.7	4.5	5.2
69	Turkey	0.50	0.58	0.65	0.69	0.74	0.76	0.76	5.2	3.6	4.6	3.2	5.0
71	Mexico	0.60	0.65	0.70	0.72	0.75	0.75	0.76	1.8	3.6	1.6	1.9	3.0
79	Brazil	0.55	0.61	0.68	0.71	0.74	0.74	0.74	1.5	2.5	2.8	4.5	2.1
89	Thailand	0.50	0.57	0.65	0.68	0.72	0.72	0.72	7.8	4.5	5.1	3.6	3.1
91	China	0.42	0.50	0.59	0.64	0.70	0.71	0.72	9.3	10.4	9.8	11.2	8.2

(Continued)

Table 13.1 (Continued)

HDI Rank 2013		Human Development Index (HDI)							GDP Growth (CAGR, per cent)				
		1980	1990	2000	2005	2010	2012	2013	1981–1990	1991–00	2001–05	2006–10	2011–13
	Medium human development: group average	0.42	0.47	0.53	0.56	0.60	0.61	0.61					
108	Indonesia	0.47	0.53	0.61	0.64	0.67	0.68	0.68	6.4	4.2	4.7	5.7	6.2
117	Philippines	0.57	0.59	0.62	0.64	0.65	0.66	0.66	1.7	2.9	4.6	4.9	5.9
118	South Africa	0.57	0.62	0.63	0.61	0.64	0.65	0.66	1.5	1.8	3.8	3.1	2.5
135	India	0.37	0.43	0.48	0.53	0.57	0.58	0.59	5.6	5.6	6.7	8.3	6.2
	Low human development: group average	0.34	0.37	0.40	0.44	0.48	0.49	0.49					

Source: http://hdr.undp.org, World Development Indicators, The World Bank

provision, reporting and supervision of CSR is just coming up with the enactment of the New Companies Act, 2013.

The Asian Sustainability Rating list of 2011 shows that among the ten Asian countries, namely South Korea, China, Hong Kong, India, Indonesia, Malaysia, Taiwan, Philippines, Singapore and Thailand, India ranked 4th preceded by South Korea, Thailand and Malaysia and followed by Singapore (6th) and China (7th). The ratings are computed on the basis of public disclosure on environmental, social and governance (ESG) issues.[1]

The reasons for CSR adoption, determination or voluntary disclosures in CSR are studied globally by many, but it remains inconclusive to some extent. For example, industrial affiliation, culture, level of corporate governance, firm size and business risk are the determinants of the level of CSR in different parts of the world (Gao et al. 2005; Haniffa and Cooke 2005; Naser et al. 2006). The impact of CSR is also explored and it is observed that CSR predicts innovation climate (Ubius and Alas 2012) and the firm can use CSR communication at the times of difficulty to shape a distinctive corporate brand personality (Mishra et al. 2013).

There are a few studies in the last two decades that examine the status of CSR activities in India, China and other Asian economies. For example, Rosario Sr., Herrera and Roman (2011) found that along with the presence of strong authoritarian states and multinational companies, business associations and groups helped in the spread of CSR practices in the Southeast Asian countries. But, the challenge in this region is that the MSMEs which constitute the majority of the businesses, may find it difficult to adhere to environmental and labour laws when CSR legislation becomes effective. Williams (1999) studied seven Asia-Pacific nations and argued that socio-political and cultural factors like uncertainty avoidance influence countries on voluntary CSR disclosures. Chambers et al. (2003), based on an analysis of web reporting of CSR of top 50 companies of seven countries including India, observed that CSR levels in Asia lag behind those in the West and Asian countries have developed their own systems of CSR and globalisation plays a major role in the spread of CSR practices. In another study, Shaba and Meuter (2013) pointed out that the formation of CSR network by Association of Southeast Asian Nations (ASEAN) countries in 2011 is likely to have a far-reaching implication on CSR in future. Chapple et al. (2014) found that, between 2002 and 2009, there has been a significant increase in the levels and depth of reported CSR, suggesting an increase in CSR initiatives in six Asian countries. However, there is no standardised pattern.

Thus, there are very few studies on the trend of CSR practices or activities in emerging Asian countries. This chapter tries to fill the gap by finding out the recent trends and developments in CSR activities in emerging Asian economies with special focus on India. This is because India is in a transition phase with the introduction of new CSR norms under the New Companies Act, 2013, that involves mandatory CSR reporting and provisioning for a large number of companies. The CSR landscape in the country, thus, is believed to change with important implications for social sectors in the near future. This process has already started in the last 5–10 years in other Asian developing countries. So, it will be interesting to find out the position of India vis-à-vis other Asian economies in the recent past with regard to the CSR practices and framework.

The analysis is based on the scores and rankings of the companies in the Asian countries provided by agencies. For India, based on the listed firms' CSR reporting for the recent financial year, an analysis is done to find out the possible impact of the CSR mandatory provisions in the near future. From the analysis, a clear scenario on the type of companies going for CSR and the areas of CSR emerge. For this analysis, apart from India, we consider select countries, namely China, Indonesia, Malaysia, Thailand, Singapore, Philippines, South Korea and Taiwan.

The rest of the chapter is structured as follows. The next section describes the trends in Asian emerging economies followed by the section on the assessment of the possible implications of the new CSR framework in India. The following section compares the results and the final section concludes.

Trends in CSR Practices in Asian Economies: An Overview

The CSR initiatives, practices and framework are described separately for India, China and other Asian emerging economies in the following sub-sections. This is because China and India are emerging as stronger economies in the region, compared to other developing countries considered in this study.

Asian Emerging Economies

Among the Asian emerging economies, the two promising economies, namely China and India have experienced remarkable economic growth in last decade; but in terms of CSR practices, China has started the transformation a little earlier than India. Other countries are more or less on the same boat. Belal and Momin (2009) provided an excellent account of the research areas and findings related to CSR in Asia-Pacific economies in the last few decades. There are only 20 studies on Asian countries excluding India since the 1980s, some of which are quite old. Based on these studies (Rosario Sr., Herrera and Roman 2011; Chapple et al. 2014), we summarised the emergence of the CSR practices, areas of CSR and current trends in CSR in the countries mentioned above. It should be noted that, in most of these countries, cultural factors were one of the important drivers of the emergent practices of CSR.

In Thailand, Buddhism and monarchy play a crucial role in the development of CSR as companies in Thailand practice philanthropy as a way of giving back to the community and loyalty to the monarchy constitutes the social structure. In terms of CSR activities, environmental concerns and poverty alleviation are the priorities. The focus is gradually shifting from philanthropy to strategic CSR.[2] Being Islamic countries, Malaysia and Indonesia link Islamic values and national traditions with CSR practices, which is an important aspect in the implementation of CSR framework. While both the countries have CSR-related policies, Malaysia has Islam-based laws for foundations and donations as well as a CSR framework for publicly listed companies. On the other hand, Indonesia has mandated CSR recently and now is in the process of setting implementation rules. Poverty alleviation, education and health issues are the key CSR concerns in these countries.

Philippines is a predominantly Roman Catholic country and philanthropy continues to be the main form of CSR while a growing interest for corporations to integrate CSR into their business strategy is observed in recent times. Notably, large local and foreign companies operating in the country participate actively in CSR activities. Singapore is a more developed country compared to its neighbouring countries and the set of considerations for CSR are different. Singapore does not have a CSR-specific law but the government has enforced a wide range of labour and environmental laws that Singapore-based corporations follow. The government also actively supports the practice of CSR for companies practising it with the help of a reward system.

In South Korea, the companies started taking greater interest in CSR since the mid-1990s with the occurrence of series of scandals and specifically the Asian financial crisis which disclosed the weakness of business system and corporate governance in the country. During this time, the corporations took social responsibility as a strategy to improve their social image, stressed on code of ethics and initiated social contribution. In 2002, the ministry of commerce, industry and energy established the Business Institute for Sustainable Development under the Korea Chamber of Commerce, developed Korean Sustainability Report Indicators in 2006 and held awards ceremony to honour sustainability management practices (for details, see (Nam 2011)). In 2008, the Federation of Korean Industries (FKI) established a CSR committee to monitor member companies' economic, legal moral and social responsibilities and supervise on the disclosure/reporting on the CSR activities of Korean corporations. Most of the corporations however still perceive CSR activities as an act of philanthropy. However, there is also a lack of understanding of the concept in South Korea as many companies include activities like sponsorship of sports games and other events with purely public relation functions for example within the ambit of CSR.

Taiwan has taken significant steps towards promoting CSR to a great extent in the recent past by emphasising on international practices (Taiwan Stock Exchange 2014). The Financial Supervisory Commission (FSC) has gradually revised the scope of CSR disclosure and instructed the Taiwan Stock Exchange (TWSE) and Taipei Exchange (TPEx) to launch 'Corporate Social Responsibility Best Practice Principles for TWSE/TPEx-Listed Companies' and 'Ethical Corporate Management Best Practice Principles for TWSE/TPEx-Listed Companies' in 2010. The FSC announced the 'Corporate Governance Roadmap 2013' as a guideline to promote corporate governance and CSR policies in Taiwan, and has also been guiding the TWSE and TPEx in hosting the 'Business Integrity and Corporate Social Responsibility for Listed Companies Forum' since 2011. The Taiwan Stock Exchange works closely with the GreTai Securities Market, Taiwan Business Council for Sustainable Development and the Taiwan CSR Institute to draft CSR guidance for companies. In 2014, the TWSE joined the World Federation of Exchanges' sustainability working group. Importantly, the Taiwan Stock Exchange Corporation recently announced that from 2015, it is mandatory for specified listed companies to start CSR reporting annually. With this initiative in place, Taiwan will be the first country in the Asia-Pacific region to implement mandatory CSR reporting that adheres to internationally recognised Global Reporting Initiative (GRI) G4 principles (*The China Post* 2015).

As a part of ASEAN, Indonesia, Malaysia and Thailand governments also have engaged in Responsible Business Conduct (RBC) initiatives since 2006–07. Such initiatives include requirement of CSR reporting, provisioning of 2 per cent tax on profit for natural resources companies, computation of Socially Responsible Investment (SRI) index and CSR awards in Indonesia; CSR awards, CSR framework and reporting requirement for listed companies in Malaysia and CSR guidelines, CSR awards, CSR research and reporting guidelines in Thailand.[3]

CSR Practices in China

At the back of increasing awareness about the adoption of CSR practices in different parts of the world, in 2006, CSR was formally included in the Chinese corporate law. The Chinese stock exchanges gradually started encouraging CSR disclosures initiatives. In 2008, the State-owned Assets Supervision and Administration Commission (SASAC) of the state council issued a policy directive on guidelines to the State-owned enterprises directly managed under the central government regarding fulfilling corporate social responsibilities.[4] The Chinese Labour Contract Law also addressed CSR issues in the same year. Subsequent to a natural disaster in China, the number of CSR reports published by the companies increased substantially in 2009 compared to the previous year. Currently, the Chinese companies are also giving serious thought to integrate CSR dimensions with their core business strategies.

Very few studies are available on CSR in China. Sarkis, Na and Zhu. (2011) found that, over the past few years, news reports have highlighted various incidents that demonstrate poor CSR practices in China.[5] However, in recent times, the institutional pressures from government, business organisations, international clients, community, media, NGOs and unions are the main drivers of CSR initiatives. For example, in 2012, the China Banking Regulatory Commission released its Green Credit Guidelines' environmental principles and rules across its banking sector as a pre-condition for China's sustainable practices. Chinese companies tend to adopt one of the three major approaches to CSR communication, treating CSR as ad hoc philanthropy, strategic philanthropy or ethical business conducts (Tang, Gallagher and Bie 2015).

Moreover, China, being one of the USA's largest trading partners, is trying to develop a CSR framework on the Western lines with some unique characteristics of its own. A study based on the companies in China has put forth that the multinational corporations (MNCs) usually have clear sustainability strategies and are good at integrating CSR into their daily operations.

CSR Practices in India

Long before the enactment of the new Companies Act, certain companies (e.g., Tata Group, ITC and so on) were involved in socially responsible activities. Traditionally, Indian CSR was mostly based on philanthropy and being voluntary on the part of the companies. In 2009, the government through its Ministry of Corporate Affairs (MCA) made its first formal CSR-related effort with the introduction of the voluntary guidelines for CSR. In 2012, the Securities and Exchange Board of India (SEBI) issued a circular mandating that the top 100 listed companies based on market capitalisation have to submit Business Responsibility Reports (BRR) regarding their social, environmental and economic responsibilities or initiatives. After the emergence of the New Companies Act, 2013, CSR is going to be an integral part of the sustainable business practices for a considerably larger number of companies.

As per Section 135 of the Act, every company having a net worth of ₹500 crore or more, or a turnover of ₹1,000 crore or more or a net profit of ₹5 crore or more during any financial year shall constitute a CSR committee consisting of the members of the board that will formulate a CSR policy, indicate the activities to be undertaken by the company as specified in Schedule VII of the Act and also recommend the amount of expenditure to be incurred on such activities. The board of every such company shall ensure that the company spends, in every financial year, at least 2 per cent of the average net profits of the company made during the three immediately preceding financial years, in pursuance of its CSR policy.

Thus, the CSR provisions as mandated in the new Act are likely to have significant implications for the development of a country like India. In this perspective, it has been mentioned that the company shall give preference to the local area and areas around it where it operates for spending the amount earmarked for CSR activities. CSR as per Schedule VII of the Act includes activities like eradication of hunger, poverty and malnutrition; promotion of preventive healthcare, sanitation, education, employment enhancing vocation skills; gender equality, women empowerment; setting up homes and hostels for women and orphans, elderly people; making available safe drinking water, ensuring environmental sustainability, ecological balance, conservation of national heritages and also contribution to the Prime Minister's National Relief Fund or any other fund set up by the central government for socio-economic development and relief and welfare. It is estimated that, out of the 1.3 million companies in India, about 6,000 to 7,000 companies will be covered under the new CSR provision and an estimated ₹27,000 crore will flow into the social development every year (*Hindustan Times* 2013).

Implication of the New CSR Framework in India

In order to find out the trends in the CSR practices observed by the companies so far and assess the possible implication of the new CSR norms, we analyse the disclosures on the amount of CSR spending in various specified activities with reference to companies listed in the Bombay Stock Exchange (BSE) and constitutes BSE 100 index. The year 2012–13 was the last year with no mandatory requirements related to CSR and we analyse this year's CSR activities by companies. Data was mostly extracted from their respective annual reports or the business responsibility/sustainability reports; however, in a couple of cases other web-based reports had to be consulted. Data relating to the list of BSE companies and data on profit after tax (PAT) was collected from the CMIE database Prowess. We analyse the information on the amount of CSR spending for 71 companies.[6] The analysis has also focused on all the broad categories of CSR activities undertaken by the firms during the period 2012–13. The CSR spending as a percentage of average PAT during the three immediately preceding years were calculated for each company. Two per cent of the average net profits (PAT) were calculated for each company in order to find out the possible gap between what the CSR norm mandates now and what they have actually practised in the absence of such mandate. Table 13.2 provides the summary of the findings. It is observed from Panel A that even in the absence of mandatory CSR contribution, there are some companies, as many as 15, out of 71, that have spent more than 2 per cent of their last three years' average profit to CSR activities. The top five companies on the basis of their CSR spend as a percentage of average profits of the last three years are Tata Steel Ltd. (7.59 per cent),[7] Adani Enterprises Ltd. (5.29 per cent), Adani Power Ltd. (4.87 per cent), Reliance Power Ltd. (3.74 per cent) and Dabur India Ltd (3.6 per cent). It may be concluded that very few companies have been engaged in CSR willingly as most of the companies (nearly 80 per cent of the companies sampled) contribute very small amount of their profit towards CSR (as low as only 0.04 per cent). During 2012–13, the average expenditure on CSR as percentage of average profit ranged between 1.3 to 1.5 per cent only. ITC, which is well known for its CSR initiatives, has spent 1.62 per cent of its average profit on CSR. The companies which have made contributions of more than 2 per cent of their average PAT include Ultratech Cement, Ambuja Cement, Nestle, Coal India and ICICI Bank among others.

Panel B of Table 13.2 provides some idea about the private sector's contribution in the social sector. In 2012–13, while the government

Table 13.2
Summary of Findings on CSR Spending by Indian Companies during 2012–13

PANEL A: Analysis of CSR Spending

	Figures[1]	Company	Per cent of PAT	Company
Max CSR spending by a company	4,707.6	Tata Steel Limited	7.6	Tata Steel Limited
Min CSR spending by a company	1.8	GMR Infra Limited	0.04	Union Bank of India
Median CSR spending by a company	168.3	Dr. Reddy's Laboratories Limited	1.3	Axis Bank Limited
Average CSR spending by a company	417.1	–	1.5	–
CSR Spending as Percentage of Average PAT during last 3 years	No. (Per cent) of Companies			
More than 2%	15 (21.1%)			
Between 1–2%	25 (35.2%)			
Less than 1%	31 (43.7%)			

PANEL B: Contribution of Private Sector and Government in Social Sector

	Amount (₹ Million)	Per cent of GDP	Per cent of GDP from Social Services[2]
Total CSR spending by all the 71 companies	29,613.4	0.03	0.22
Govt Spending on Social Sector (Education, Health etc.)	65,46,020	6.90	50.0
Total of Average Profit after tax of all 71 companies	20,85,118.9	2.22	15.5
CSR Spending if all companies spent 2% of their average PAT during last 3 years	41,702.4	0.04	0.31
CSR Spending if 15 companies spend more than 2% and rest spent 2% of their average PAT during last 3 years	46,674.6	0.05	0.35

Notes: [1] In ₹ Million unless otherwise specified.
[2] Includes Community, Social and Personal Services.

Source: Handbook of Statistics on Indian Economy, Reserve Bank of India (various issues); The Economic Survey, Ministry of Finance, Government of India; and authors' computation.

Figure 13.1
Number of Companies Contributed in Different Sectors

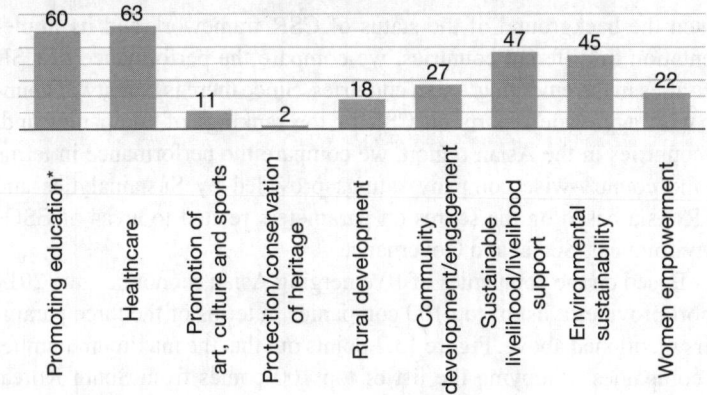

Source: Author's computation
Note: * includes special education and employment enhancing vocational skills/courses

expenditure on social sector is more than 6.5 per cent of GDP and 50 per cent of GDP from community, social and personal services, the expenditure on CSR by the companies in the sample is not even 0.1 per cent of GDP and only 0.22 per cent of GDP from community, social and personal services. However, the share of the total PAT (average PAT for last 3 years) in GDP is 2.2 per cent and that in GDP in social sector is 15.5 per cent. Given this scenario, if all the companies contribute 2 per cent of the average profit towards CSR or if the companies conform to 2 per cent norm and some companies continue to spend more than 2 per cent (15 such companies in our sample), even then the private sector's contribution may increase to at most 0.05 per cent of GDP and 0.35 per cent of GDP from social sector.

Figure 13.1 presents the sectoral contribution of CSR by the companies which have contributed in more than one sector. It is observed that most of the companies (85 to 89 per cent) have contributed in education and healthcare, followed by livelihood support and environment (63 to 66 per cent companies) and community and women development (31 to 38 per cent). Around 25 per cent of the sampled companies contribute for rural development, 15 per cent for promotion of art, culture and sports and only 3 per cent for protection or conservation of heritage.

CSR Performance: Comparison of Asian Countries

Given the background of the status of CSR framework and its implementation in different countries, we compare the performance of CSR activities in the emerging Asian countries. Since there is paucity of country-wise aggregate reports on CSR or the rankings of companies and/or countries in the Asian region, we compare the performance in terms of the country-wise company ratings provided by Sustainalytics and CSR Asia based on the scores on parameters related to areas of ESGs (Environment, Social and Governance).[8]

Based on the companies of 10 emerging Asian economies, the 2014 report provides a list of top 100 companies in terms of the three parameters mentioned above. Figure 13.2 points out that the maximum number of companies occupying the list of top 100 comes from South Korea, followed by Taiwan, India and Hong Kong. Philippines and China have only one or two companies, respectively, in the top 100 list. Interestingly, the sectoral composition of these top 100 companies reveal that 33 per

Figure 13.2
Distribution of Top 100 Companies

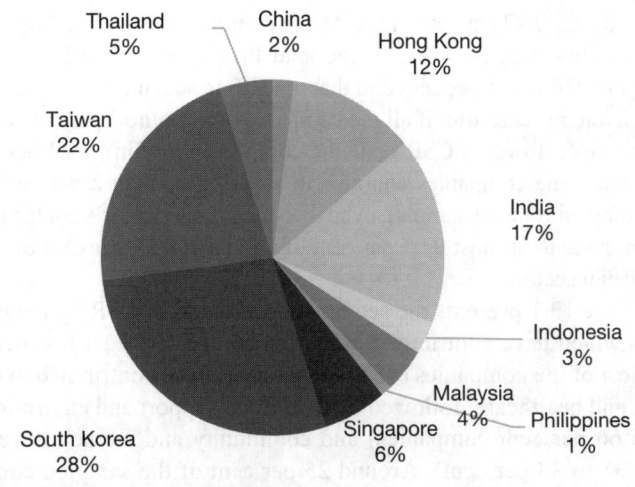

Source: Authors' computation

cent of them are technology firms, out of which 20 are from Taiwan; 13 per cent of them are from materials sector, out of which 6 are from India followed by 10 per cent from energy sector across different countries. Out of 7 real estate companies, 4 are from Singapore. It is only in South Korea that representation of companies from almost all the sectors (except real estate) is there. The sectoral representation is also quite good from India and Hong Kong (companies represent 7 out of 10 sectors).

The 2014 report has also identified the regional leaders in corporate sustainability in different countries, if we take into account the ranks of those companies (Table 13.3). The ASR Asia ranking of the top three companies in the countries considered here clearly points out that India has performed the best with all three companies within the top 10 of the Asian companies, followed by South Korea, Taiwan and Thailand with all the companies in the top 20. The worst performers are China and Philippines with ranks of companies close to 100 or not even within 100. It is quite interesting that even when India started quite late in enforcing a CSR mandate, it has done quite well.

Figure 13.3

Sectoral Distribution of Top 100 Companies

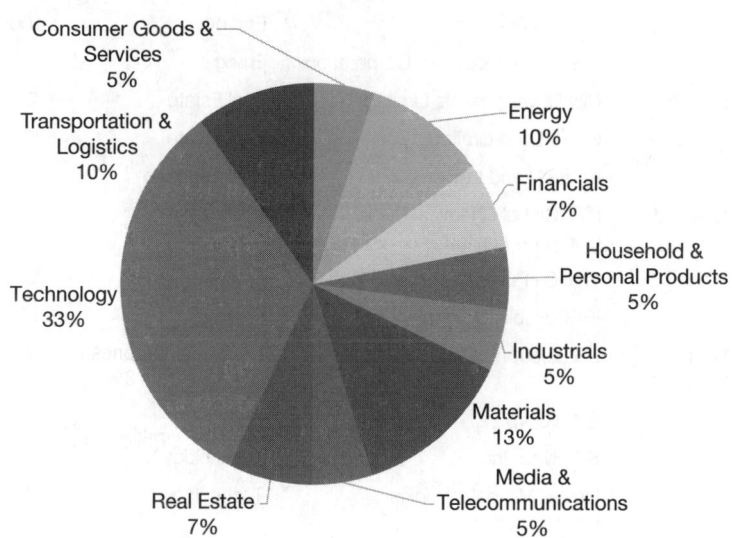

Source: Authors' computation

Table 13.3
Top Three Companies Countrywise from ASR 2014 Ranking

Country	Companies	Sector	Asia Rank
China	China Vanke Co. Ltd.	Real Estate	77
	BOE Technology Group Co. Ltd.	Technology	90
	Trina Solar Limited	Technology	>100
India	Tata Consultancy Services Limited	Technology	1
	Wipro Limited	Technology	6
	Infosys Limited	Technology	8
Indonesia	Unilever Indonesia Tbk PT	Household & Personal Products	3
	PT Vale Indonesia Tbk	Materials	34
	PT Bukit Asam (Persero) Tbk	Energy	54
Malaysia	Digi.com Bhd	Media & Telecommunications	32
	Bursa Malaysia Bhd	Financials	55
	Malayan Banking Bhd	Financials	59
Philippines	Ayala Land, Inc.	Real Estate	81
	Manila Water Co Inc.	Energy	>100
	Energy Development Corporation	Energy	>100
Singapore	City Developments Limited	Real Estate	2
	CapitaLand Limited	Real Estate	17
	Keppel Land Ltd.	Real Estate	25
Thailand	PTT Global Chemical Public Company Limited	Materials	11
	Thai Oil Public Co Ltd.	Energy	18
	IRPC Public Company Limited	Energy	19
South Korea	LG Electronics Inc.	Consumer Goods & Services	7
	S-Oil Corp.	Energy	10
	SK Hynix, Inc.	Technology	13
Taiwan	United Microelectronics Corporation	Technology	4
	Qisda Corporation	Technology	12
	Taiwan Semiconductor Manufacturing Co. Ltd.	Technology	14

Source: http://sustainability-ranking.channelnewsasia.com/

Conclusion

This chapter has made an attempt to find out the status of CSR activities, regulations and performance of Asian emerging countries including India. An analysis of the Indian listed companies in BSE during 2012–13 along with the comparison of CSR activities between the Asian countries on the basis of ASR reports provide some useful insight at the moment as it was not at all explored in this way. First, even without the mandatory CSR provisions, in 2012–13, Indian companies have made contributions towards CSR and around 21 per cent companies have made contributions more than stipulated 2 per cent of their average profit for last three years. Second, the analysis reveals that on an average the Indian companies (among the sampled ones) contributed 1.3 to 1.5 per cent of their average PAT towards CSR before the introduction of New Companies Act, 2013. Third, most of the companies have contributed mostly on education and healthcare, followed by livelihood support and environment and community and women development. Fourth, among Asian emerging economies, India fared quite well with three companies featuring among the top 10 of top 100 companies in Asia with regard to CSR activities. South Korea and Taiwan have made even greater development in this regard. Finally, China and Philippines are the countries lagging behind. However, increasing awareness regarding CSR is observed in all the countries and authorities are taking appropriate steps to encourage such activities by implementing a proper framework in most of the countries.

It is observed that India has outperformed China and other developing economies in CSR contributions and activities although the mandate has just come up recently and yet to be implemented. However, all the countries have started taking initiatives to move towards more CSR in the form of not only philanthropy but also strategic CSR. This is likely to affect lives of a large section of the people and hence has implications for the development process of the country. But there is no denying the fact that there are constraints and challenges in the implementation of CSR framework, as it may also affect the interest of the businesses, as believed by the Singapore government. A strong collaborative effort is required among the various stakeholders, namely government, industry and civil society in all the emerging countries. The countries are also characterised by corruption and lack of accountability on the part of the stakeholders, which are also to be taken care of. So monitoring of the compliance has to be stringent. It is too early to comment on the success of the CSR framework adopted by the emerging economies in Asia as they are quite recent. We all have to wait to see how the private sector becomes an integral contributor, in a more direct way, to the development process in the region.

Notes

1. Computed by CSR Asia. The parameters are governance, codes and policies, CSR strategy and communication, marketplace and supply Chain, workplace and people, environment and community and development.
2. Strategic CSR implies integration of CSR into core business processes and stakeholder management by which organisations can achieve the ultimate goal of creating both social value and corporate value.
3. For further details, see Shaba and Meuter (2013).
4. For details of such initiatives, see Afsharipour and Rana (2014).
5. It should be kept in mind that various cultural sensitivities and political biases are major hindrances in the research on CSR practices in China.
6. For others, information was either not available or they registered losses and hence excluded.
7. Amount spent during 2012–13 to ensure environmental sustainability has also been considered as specified in Companies Act 2013 as an activity included in CSR.
8. For details on sample and methodology, see http://sustainability-ranking.channelnewsasia.com/ (accessed on 30 April 2015).

References

Afsharipour, A., and Rana, S. 2014. 'The Emergence of New Corporate Social Responsibility Regimes in China and India'. *UC Davis Business Law Journal* 14(2): 175–230.
Belal, A.R., and Momin M. 2009. 'Corporate Social Reporting (CSR) in Emerging Economies: A Review and Future Direction'. *Research in Accounting in Emerging Economies* 9:119–143.
Bowen, H.R. 1953. Social Responsibilities of the Businessman. New York: Harper & Row
Carroll, A.B. 1979. 'A Three-dimensional Conceptual Model of Corporate Social Performance'. *Academy of Management Review* 49(4): 497–505.
———. 1999. 'Corporate Social Responsibility. Evolution of a Definitional Construct'. *Business & Society* 38(3): 268–295.
Chambers, E., Chapple, W., Moon, J., and Sullivan, M.2003. 'CSR in Asia: A Seven Country Study of CSR Website Reporting'' ICCSR Research Paper Series No. 09-2003, International Centre for Corporate Social Responsibility, Nottingham University Business School, Nottingham University.
Chapple, W., Moon, J., Slager R., and Herzig, C. 2014. 'The Dynamics of Corporate Social Responsibility in Asia: A 6-country Study', Paper to Academy of Management Annual Conference. INSEAD, France. Available at: http://centres.insead.edu/social-innovation/what-we-do/documents/The_Dynamics_of_Corporate_Social_Responsibility_INSEAD.pdf

The China Post. 2015 (20 February). 'Taiwan to Begin Mandatory GRI G4 CSR Reporting'. The China Post. Available at http://www.chinapost.com.tw/taiwan/business/2015/02/20/429350/Taiwan-to.htm (accessed on 25 April 2015).

Davis, K. 1967. 'Understanding the Social Responsibility Puzzle: What Does the Businessman Owe to Society?' *Business Horizons* 10(4): 45–50.

Gao, S.S., Heravi, S., and Xiao, J.Z. 2005. 'Determinants of Corporate Social and Environmental Reporting in Hong Kong: A Research Note'. *Accounting Forum* 29(2): 233–242.

Haniffa, R.M., and Cooke, T.E. 2005. 'The Impact of Culture and Governance on Corporate Social Reporting'. Journal of Accounting and Public Policy 24(5): 391–430.

Hindustan Times. 2013 (21 September). 'Estimated by Indian Institute of Corporate Affairs (IICA) in CSR Spending May Pump in ₹27,000 Cr a Year'. *Hindustan Times*. Available at http://www.hindustantimes.com/business/csr-spending-may-pump-in-rs-27-000-cr-a-year/story-CWIuKDZdtrpope1oULHmfO.html (accessed on 30 April 2015).

Kisenyi, V., and Gray, R. 1998. 'Social Disclosure in Uganda'. *Social and Environmental Accounting* 18(2): 16–18.

McGuire, J.W. 1963. *Business and Society*. New York: McGraw-Hill

Mishra, M., and Mohanty, S. 2013. 'Impact of Corporate Social Responsibility Communication on Corporate Brand Personality Assessment'. *IUP Journal of Management Research* 12(4): 26–38.

Nam, Y. 2011. 'The changing landscape of Corporate Social Responsibility in Korea'. *Revista de EDUCAÇÃO do Cogeime* 20(38): 145–158.

Naser, K., Al-Hussaini, A., Al-Kwari, D., and Nuseibeh, R. 2006. 'Determinants of Corporate Social Disclosure in Developing Countries: The Case of Qatar'. *Advances in International Accounting* 19: 1–23.

Rosario Sr., Ramon V. del, Herrera, M., and Roman, F.'2011. 'Corporate Social Responsibility in Southeast Asia: An Eight Country Analysis'. Report of the Center for Corporate Social Responsibility, Asian Institute of Management, Philippines.

Sarkis, J., Na, N. Zhu, Q. 2011. 'Winds of Change: Corporate Social Responsibility in China'. *Ivey Business Journal,* January/February issue. Available at http://www.iveybusinessjournal.com/topics/social-responsibility/winds-of-changecorporate-social-responsibility-in-china

Shaba, L., and Meuter, J.B. 2013. 'RBC Initiatives in Southeast Asia: An Overview'. Anakout Report, Singapore.

Taiwan Stock Exchange. 2014. Corporate Social Responsibility Overview. Corporate Governance Centre. Available at http://cgc.twse.com.tw/frontEN/responsibility (accessed on 28 April 2015).

Tang, L., Gallagher, C., and Bie, B. 2015. 'Corporate Social Responsibility Communication Through Corporate Websites: A Comparison of Leading Corporations in the United States and China'. *International Journal of Business Communication* 52(2): 163–247.

Ubius, U., and Alas, R. 2012. 'The Impact of Corporate Social Responsibility on the Innovation Climate'. *Engineering Economics* 23(3): 310–318.

Walton, C. 1967. Corporate Social Responsibilities. Belmont, CA: Wadsworth Publishing

Williams, S. 1999. 'Voluntary Environmental and Social Accounting Disclosure Practices in the Asia-Pacific Region: An International Empirical Test of Political Economy Theory'. *The International Journal of Accounting* 34(2): 209–238.

14

Health Care Sectors of India and China
A Comparative Study of Performances and Challenges

Paramita M. Nag

Introduction

India and China are two very similar countries, especially in terms of a shared history, a glorious past and now, a very fast developing economy. Yet there are differences which are also deeply rooted in history, especially China's regimented and closed communist past, one language and a single political party and no religion state pitted against India's multi-cultural, multi-religious multi-language democracy.

With slackening of the regimental hold of the communist party in China (post-1980s) and liberalisation of the Indian economy (post-1990s), both the Chinese and Indian governments had decided to allocate substantial funds to the development of the health sector and subsequently healthcare facilities. Both the countries face similar challenges that put huge burden on their health system, especially in terms of meeting the demands of an increasing (rapid growth) population. Epidemiological and population transitions have resulted in a growing ageing population. This along with a huge spurt in income growth has been instrumental in creating a high-consumer expectation and a requirement (demand) for high-quality healthcare service. Yet it is found that there is a widening gap (rapidly increasing) between income groups, especially between the rich and the poor and urban and rural populations for both the countries. To understand the functioning of the health system of these two countries, this chapter starts by looking into the historical, social and political development which has shaped the current status.

Historical Evolution of Health Systems

China

The People's Republic of China came into being in 1949. At that point in time, the country was going through a period of internal chaos and a long external strife with Japan, resulting in a huge decline in health conditions. The communist party, along the stringent lines of the communist ideology, eschewed all roles of the private sector. Thus, all healthcare facilities including large urban hospitals and small village clinics were owned and operated by the government. The main motto at this time was prevention and it was done for the first time by combining Western and Chinese methods of practice. The government took care of planning the entire revenue expenditure of the system. In urban areas, residents had to pay an insignificant 'registration' amount to avail services in times of need. In rural areas, healthcare requirements were met by a 'cooperative medical system' which was financed through a 'commune'.

During the period 1950–90, the economy grew very slowly but the healthcare system achieved enormous gains. Life expectancy grew from 35 years to 68 years, infant mortality fell from 200 to 34 per 1,000 live births (Blumenthal 2005), and infectious diseases decreased radically (polio was almost eradicated). At this time, healthcare delivery was based on a three-tier, bottom-up system where at the lowest tier, the village or urban street clinics provided the basic preventive and curative care followed by the township or community health centres. The district or urban hospitals provided specialised care to those needing intensive treatment and special attention. In this period, special training was provided to thousands of village doctors who were formerly 'barefoot doctors' (people with basic healthcare training) to upgrade their skills (Hsiao 1995). Primary healthcare, all in all, achieved tremendous gains in upgrading health indicators of China.

Even though healthcare improvement achieved enormous gains, it might have been overemphasised greatly. First, it is easy to improve when one starts at a very low point, and China at the time of independence was at an abysmally low-health status. Second, care is not the only factor of improving health conditions but it is a function of hygiene, education and living standard, which too, improved dramatically during this time. Finally, it is the question of equity, which was certainly not big during this time and the lack of transparency hid this and other shortcomings from public view.

Since the early 1980s, China underwent huge socio-economic transformation. Privatisation became legal and this led to the start of private practice in medicine. China made a dramatic move in healthcare financing shifting a huge portion from the central government to private companies and individual consumers. The central government also transferred funding of rural healthcare services to provincial and local authorities. In spite of relaxing control largely, it did not relinquish all responsibilities in as much as it maintained tight regulation on prices of medicines and medical procedures. This led to the growth of black market, overuse of high-end technology and an overuse of prescription drugs. In the rural areas, the 'commune' was dismissed in favour of individual household control leading to the rapid decline of the Community Medical System (CMS) as it lost its source of funding. Chinese peasants lost their means of availing affordable healthcare. Barefoot doctors lost their employment and started practising privately, changing their focus from doing good to raking in profits. In urban areas, hospital visits decreased by 5 per cent whereas profits for these hospitals increased by 70 per cent (Lim, L. 2006).

India

India's health policy originated with the Bhore Committee report (report on the health survey and development committee). The report laid down some fundamental rights of the Indian population with regard to healthcare. It said that all Indians have the right to and should have an access to primary healthcare irrespective of their socio-economic conditions. A three-tier healthcare system, like China, came into being, yet, unlike China; India never abolished private healthcare. In fact, public sector involvement became imperative only because involvement of the private sector in the Western form of medicine at that time was low.

PHCs (Primary Health Centres) were at the lowest rung of the three-tier system. They were located mainly at the village (rural) level and are still entrusted to provide health education, prevent diseases and provide basic healthcare. At the next level were the sub-centres located at the district headquarters followed by the district hospitals or urban hospitals. There was a strong referral system in place. By the end of the 1980s, this infrastructure was strengthened and a large number of healthcare personnel received in-depth training. By the 1990s, PHCs almost tripled in number and the number of doctors too increased by almost a lakh (Quadeer 2000).

Healthcare delivery, in India, is a state responsibility. The central government is responsible for providing a national strategic framework, defining policies and imparting medical education (Ibid. 2000). Though the Indian Government vowed to provide healthcare to all its citizens, the picture at the state levels was different. The states were responsible to deliver effective healthcare to the poorest of the poor of the population, yet they had to depend on central funding for the procurement of necessary medicines and infrastructure. The reason behind this was that nearly 70–80 per cent of the state's spending on health was used up to pay salaries to the workers, thus reducing the effectiveness of delivery. Thus, India has a top-down decision-making process which includes vertical disease control programmes sponsored again entirely by the centre but implemented by the states.

Since the late 1980s and early 1990s, the middle class has emerged strong. People's expectation from the health system also increased and the private sector in healthcare received a huge push in response to this demand for better and higher technology-based medical care. Health sector reforms were put in place around 1992 which saw international donors like International Monetary Fund (IMF) and World Bank playing a crucial role. They introduced user charges and private investment in public hospitals among others. As a direct result of this, PHCs received a huge setback and were relegated to the background. Funds got redirected and reduced for infectious diseases control programmes from 14 to 7 per cent (Ibid. 2000). Focus then mainly shifted to family planning, improving water supply and introducing proper sanitation. Small pox, polio and guinea worm disease were eradicated; HIV and cancer were on the rise. Diseases such as tuberculosis and malaria once considered controlled have made a reappearance in a mutated form and is a larger threat to public health concerns.

Even though both India and China face very dissimilar demographic and health challenges, both countries have made great inroads in achieving their public health goals. The above retrospective view has been provided to reflect the current healthcare condition as a function of the historical past of both the countries. The developments over time have been summarised in Table 14.1.

Comparison of Overall Achievements

The World Health Organisation's (WHO) report 'The World Health Report 2000 – Health Systems: Improving Performance' suggests that a health system of any country must seek to address three basic objectives. They happen to be the following:

- Improving the health condition of the population it serves
- Responding to people's expectations
- Providing financial protection against the costs of ill health

In this section, this study tries to find out how India and China have fared in achieving these goals.

Table 14.1
Summary of Historical Developments

Period	Indicators	China	India
Late 1940 – early 1980s	Strategies or policies	Priority given to preventive care and health education	Priority given to curative care
	Providers or entities	Completely publicly owned: CMS delivers care in rural areas: a three tier delivery system in place	Public and private providers co-exist: a three tier system is established
	Health gains	Substantial	Moderate
Early 1980s to early 2000	Disease trend	Chronic disease replaces infectious diseases as top cause for mortality; increasing aging population	Infectious disease still top cause for mortality; HIV and Cancer related diseases on the rise
	Providers or entities	CMS collapse; private players emerge	Increasing privatisation; PHC suffer setback
Early 2000s to present	Policy context	Health system reform	Health sector reform but not much change

Source: Hafner and Pop (2008)

Health Status

Performance of Key Health Indicators

In general, people live a healthier and longer life in China than in India (Table 14.2). A woman born in China in 2004 has a life expectancy of 74 years as compared to 63 years for an Indian woman. An Indian male is expected to live up to 61 years whereas a man born in China has a life expectancy of 70 years (WHO 2006).

It is observed that the life expectancy is greater for females than males and it is also documented that there exists a high maternal death rate during child birth for Indian women as compared with their Chinese counterparts. In addition to this, the Indian population as a whole suffers from a higher mortality in both childhood and infancy than do the Chinese citizens. It was evidenced in 2004, by a WHO study, that nearly 30 per cent of infants in India were born with Low Birth Rates (LBW <2,500grams at birth) (WHO 2006) as compared with 6 per cent of Chinese infants. Other than life expectancy and infant mortality rate differences between India and China, overall mortality rates are also worse for India compared with China. Cause-related mortality shows that more deaths in India occur from communicable or infectious diseases whereas mortality in China could be blamed on lifestyle disorders or non-communicable diseases. Table 14.3 provides a summarised picture of infectious as well as non-infectious disease related mortality.

Table 14.2
Performance of Key Health Indicators

				Probability of Death, 2004[a]						
	Life Expectancy in Years, 2004			≤1 Year	<5 Years		15 to 60 Years		Maternal Death Rate, 2000[b]	LBW Rate 1999[c]
Country	M/F	M	F	M/F	M/F	M	F	M	F		
China	72	70	74	27	31	27	36	158	99	56	6
India	62	61	63	58	85	81	89	275	202	540	30

Source: Hafner and Pop (2008)
Notes: M = male; F = female
[a] Per 1,000 persons
[b] Per 100,000 women
[c] Per 100 newborns

Table 14.3
Mortality from Infectious and Non-communicable Diseases

	Death Rates by Cause	
	Mortality (per 100,000 persons)	
Cause of Death	China	India
All causes	**701.5**	**988.8**
Lower uncertainty bound	669	950.8
Higher uncertainty bound	731.7	1017.4
All communicable, maternal, perinatal, and nutritional conditions	**83.7**	**401.9**
Infectious and parasitic diseases	39	197.3
Tuberculosis	20.8	34.8
HIV/AIDS	3.3	33.4
Diarrhoeal diseases	8.3	43.5
Childhood-cluster diseases	1.6	27.4
Meningitis	0.6	5.1
Respiratory infections	22.4	107
Maternal conditions	0.8	12.7
Perinatal conditions	20.9	72.6
Nutritional deficiencies	0.6	12.3
All non-communicable diseases	**541.4**	**486.9**
Malignant neoplasms	133.5	71
Other neoplasms	1.2	1.2
Diabetes mellitus	9.6	14.9
Endocrine disorders	2.4	1.5
NeuroPsychiatric conditions	8.4	17.4
Sense organ disorders	NA	0.1
Cardiovascular diseases	230.5	267.7
Respiratory diseases	110	58.1
Digestive diseases	27.9	32.6
Genitourinary Diseases	10.7	11.2
Skin Disease	NA	0.7
Musculoskeletal Disorder	1.9	0.7
Congenital anomalies	6.6	9.9
Injuries	**76.3**	**100**
Unintentional Injuries	52.3	76.2
Intentional Injuries	24	23.8

Source: WHO (2006)

In China, about 77 per cent of the deaths could be attributed to non-communicable diseases like Chronic Obstructive Pulmonary Disorder (COPD), cardiac disorders and cancer. On the other hand, India suffers most from communicable diseases; mortality is vastly attributed to HIV/AIDS, diarrhoea and respiratory infections.

HIV/AIDS and cancer have made inroads into the deepest corners of Asia and are increasing their digits rapidly. China had around 650,000 patients suffering from HIV in 2003. In 2005, India's figure for HIV positive citizens reached 5.7 million and was on an increasing trend. Malaria has become an increasing menace in India.

As far as lifestyle health problems are concerned, about 7.1 per cent of the Chinese population were obese as compared to 32 per cent among women and 50 per cent among men in India. (Gupte 2001).

Protection against Financial Disaster

Health is a state of mental and physical well-being. Poor health reduces physical well-being and as a direct result of which there is a worsening of mental well-being. In other words, illness leads to increased medical expenses and infrequent labour market participation which often causes loss of savings, incurring of debt and overall poverty to rise. WHO feels that the most important aim of the health systems of the world should be to reduce and also distribute some of the risks for all sections of the society (WHO 2000).

Both India and China, unfortunately, are unable to provide much protection against the financial disaster of illness. In China, sickness-related expenses have become the most important cause of transient poverty relegating 44 per cent of rural households to below the poverty line (Liu et al. 2003). Often in China and as well as in India, households are known to borrow money and also to sell off assets to pay for medical expenses. In India, cost of healthcare is the single most reason for families becoming destitute or pushing 'above poverty line' families to 'below poverty line'. Moreover, health expenses are most effective in 'crowding out' other essential heads of expenditure like education. More often than not, high medical expenses are a deterrent to seeking timely medical advice leading to a very high curative care for both the countries, as deferred preventive care leads to chronic illness in addition to overutilisation of care facilities.

Performance of Healthcare Accessibility, Efficiency and Quality

Accessibility

Accessibility in other words can be called 'effective availability'. This refers to the ease of availability of healthcare services to the general public, overcoming the barriers of cost, time and service. Both the countries have seen a deterioration of healthcare services to the common people even though basic healthcare is recognised as a fundamental right of all.

As discussed in the previous sections, for post-liberalisation (for both India and China) there has been a shift in the focus from preventive to curative healthcare. Although by the time this shift took place in China, control infectious diseases have progressed well and they were in a much better position to concentrate on curative care. Even then, access to basic healthcare (which includes immunisation) took a direct hit and thus declined quite rapidly. Control and prevention of infectious diseases were made paid services and this impacted hugely on the accessibility to basic healthcare. Furthermore, rural urban inequalities increased rapidly; there was also a huge exodus of medical personnel from rural areas to the towns and cities of China. Paying capacity started determining the levels of care received. There have been instances where the rural people have been denied hospitalisation due to the lack of funds.

In India, on the other hand, it was found that there was a huge shortfall of healthcare workers for the rural areas. Trained medical personnel from government hospitals though were forced to travel to rural areas, would soon quit the service and join private hospitals in the cities where the pay was substantially higher and there was better technology available to treat patients. Lack of a competitive pay structure and paucity of medical appliances and technology often left the government health service starved and thus rural healthcare declined. Physical access to healthcare, that is, accessible distance to health facility also increased over the years. Out-of-pocket expenses also increased for both the rural and urban areas, thereby increasing destitution and poverty.

Quality

Maintaining the quality of healthcare service meted out to patients is an important criterion for measuring the health status of a country. Both India and China sorely lack a proper evaluation mechanism for assessing, maintaining and controlling the quality of healthcare. There is a tendency to overutilise facilities coupled with over prescription of drugs and unnecessary interventions among the medical personnel of both the countries. It is noticed that the majority of the out-of-pocket expenses are made for medicines and doctor fees.

Efficiency

There are two different kinds of efficiencies; allocative efficiency and technical efficiency. Allocative efficiency stands for maximising collective gains by producing the 'right outputs' while technical efficiency would mean using minimal cost to produce outputs the 'right way'. Following these definitions, measuring efficiency is next to impossible for either China or India. China has, in recent years, developed some vertical agencies following closely the pattern of Centres of Disease Control (CDC) and Prevention in the USA. Due to the lack of well-defined roles and lack of coordination between these agencies, they lost much of their effectiveness. In India, due to the federal system of government and state centre sharing of the subject health, something similar too happened where horizontal healthcare services (basic health services) became largely delinked from vertical national programmes (disease control programmes). Even though the vertical disease control programmes are expected to reduce the burden of disease, there is not always the expected level of outcome as the horizontal agencies do not function to its full capacity always.

Understanding the Poor Performance of the Health System

Financing of the Healthcare system

Post-liberalisation, for both the countries, government spending on healthcare as a proportion of the country's GDP has gone down drastically and is steadily declining over the years now. This, in addition to the lack of proper health insurance for all strata of the society, has led to an increase in out-of-pocket expenses. The poor of both the countries seem to be the worst affected by this, resulting in poverty and destitution. Throughout this transition period, the subject of healthcare has been treated by both the governments as non-productive and relegated as low-priority in government spending.

Insurance coverage for the population, both Indian and Chinese, is very limited. Before economic liberalisation, that is, pre-1979; China had an insurance package in place for nearly all its citizens and was covered by the co-operative medical scheme in rural areas and by the Labour Insurance Scheme (LIS) and Government Insurance Scheme (GIS) in the urban areas. These schemes lost their finance base and ceased to exist in the post-reforms' period, leaving millions uninsured and open to out-of-pocket expenses. In India, only about 15 per cent of the population have health insurance coverage and this is being provided by their employers. This, in most cases, does not cover family and dependents. The private insurance agencies have stepped into this void, but covers only about 1 per cent of the population that comprises those living in the urban areas that are concentrated mainly among the rich and the middle class. This leaves the urban poor and the rural population largely insurance free and prey to high-medical expenses.

Lack of proper insurance coverage along with reduced government spending has left the citizens of both the countries to rely heavily on out-of-pocket payments (OOPs). India has a higher level of OOPs but the rate of increase of OOPs for China is higher than in India and is expected to overcome India very soon.

Limited government funding had left a vacuum in provision of proper healthcare in both India and China. This has paved the way for the entry of private players, especially in India where the government followed the policy of benign neglect. China, on the other hand, maintained governmental control of urban hospitals and made public provisions of healthcare, although accessibility was a major issue with most of the people. Even though there were public provisions in the rural areas, these centres became defunct with the huge exodus of health professionals to the cities. Thus healthcare delivery became a huge public health concern especially for the poor of both India and China. China developed a unique method of cross-subsidisation, whereby they kept the prices of basic health services below cost prices but increased the prices of high-technology diagnostics, while keeping a 15 per cent margin on drug costs. But this system had negative fallout as physicians felt encouraged to prescribe expensive diagnostics as they had to offset the loss from basic services. Thus, there was rampant overutilisation of high-tech facilities, overprescription of drugs and underutilisation of public services. These doctors, in both urban and rural areas, no longer served the interest of the public but became profit-seeking individuals. In India, the bulk of the public hospitals received their funding from the state or the central government. With reduction of public spending on this head, these hospitals began to suffer from the lack of good physicians, proper caregivers, high-tech diagnostic facilities and were short of correct and free drugs.

Table 14.4 gives an overall comparative picture of the impact of financial factors on accessibility and affordability of healthcare of the two countries.

Table 14.4
Policy Factors Impacting the Chinese and Indian Health Systems

Factors	Indicators	China	India
Financing	Total per-capita expenditure on health (2003)	$61	$27
	Percentage of national GDP spent on health (2003)	5.6	4.8
	Out-of-Pocket Expenses as a percentage of total medical spending (2003)	56.0	73.0
	General government contributions as a percentage of total medical spending (2003)	36.0	25.0
	Health Insurance Composition	Reliance on public insurance	Emerging private micro-insurance
Payment	FFS	Dominant; Government sets prices	Dominant; Providers set price
Organisation	Public Providers as a percentage of total medical service provision	96 (2002)	21 (2003)
	Private Providers as a percentage of total medical service provision	4	79
Regulation	Enforcement	Coercive	Laissez-Faire
	Regulatory Structure	Diffuse	Highly diffuse
Behaviour	Education and Promotion Campaigns	Somewhat Effective	Limited by Illiteracy

Source: WHO (2006)

Policy Interventions

Some of the major characteristics of the health systems of both the countries are dominated by huge out-of-pocket payments, overutilisation of services and lack of accessibility faced by the poor. These are some of the ills plaguing the system. Thus, strong and explicit policies are now being framed by both the countries to channelise governmental funds and target spending. Yet, neither of the two countries have any regulation to control quality and efficiency or even manage health-spending inflation. This paper concludes by understanding some of the main challenges and thereby identifying the policy interventions required for both India and China.

Reduction of Burden of OOPs on Individuals

It is the opinion of all leading researchers over the world that there is a need to reduce OOPs in order to avert financial catastrophe and destitution. A way to avoid this is maybe to follow the example of a lot of European countries where this challenge is generally met by social or national insurance or by going the American way of encouraging private insurance at an affordable cost. India seems to be following the American path where private insurers are seen to make slow but steady inroad. China, on the other hand, is still leaning towards greater governmental control.

Lowering Overutilisation of Services

The problem of overutilisation of services is prevalent in both the countries. This can only be controlled to some extent by separating user charges from drug prescription, followed by a method of reimbursement as practised by Medicare in the United States. Moreover, a cultural change should be initiated among the medical practitioners encouraging professionalism and loyalty in their service. One hopes that this might also pave the way for quality control and improvement in efficiency. Meanwhile, governments of both the countries should be encouraged to develop evaluation and monitoring agencies as an integral part of the medical system.

Increasing Accessibility for the Poor

The population of both India and China faced and is still facing tremendous adversities and disadvantages over the years. There are issues of supply-induced demand in both the countries, resulting in overutilisation of services in some areas along with large portion of the poor going underserved. Even at this stage of health transition, both the countries need to pay attention to preventive care along with specialised attention to curative care. Primary health agencies should be revived and their outreach improved and increased especially in the rural areas.

Addressing Capacity Building Requirement

India and China have agencies at both the provincial and central levels, with several programmes addressing various health issues separately. The major issue with these agencies and programmes is that they do not have a strong coordination among themselves, nor do they cooperate to address important health problems. This strongly affects the efficiency of delivery and impact on the people. Thus, the most important requirement is a strong integration of both vertical and horizontal branches of the system and improving surveillance and control of communicable diseases. China needs to increase data transparency while India needs to improve disease surveillance.

Even after a couple of years of implementation of health sector reforms in both the countries, it is still too soon to feel a measurable impact of regulated and coordinated government health sector spending. Though the governments have tried to streamline proper insurance coverage and strengthen health infrastructure, improve outreach and reduce financial disasters; it is not enough to make the impact felt from these initiatives. More needs to be done in terms of companion policies in order to improve delivery accessibility and efficiency.

References

Blumenthal, D.W. 2005. 'Privatisation and its Discontents: Evolving Chinese Health Care Systems'. *New England Journal of Medicine* 353 (September): 1165–1170.
Gupte., D.M. 2001. 'Epidemiological Profile of India: Historical and Contemporart Perspectives'. *Journal of Biosciences* 26(4): 437–464.
Hsiao, W.C. 1995. 'The Chinese Health Care System: Lessons for Other Nations'. *Social Science and Medicine* 41(October 1995): 1047–1055.
Lim, L. 2006 (2 March). 'The High Price of Illness in China'. *BBC News.*
Liu,Y., Rao, K. and Hsajo, W.C. 2003. 'Medical Expenditure and Rural Impoverishment in China'. *Journal of Health, Population and Nutrition* 21(3): 216–222.
Hafner. T. and Pop, D. (2011). 'China and India as Suppliers of Affordable Medicines to Developing Countries'. Working Paper no. 17249. National Bureau of Economic Research, July 2011. Available at HYPERLINK "http://www.nber.org/papers/w17249" http://www.nber.org/papers/w17249

Quadeer, I. 2000. 'Health Care Systems in Transition III: India, Part I. The Indian Experience'. *Journal of Public Health Medicine* 22(1): 25–32.
WHO. 2000. *The World Health Report 2000: Health System: Improving Performance.* Geneva: World Health Organisation.
———. 2006. *The World Health Report 2006: Working Together for Health.* Geneva: WHO.

15

Social Responsibility Strategies in China and India

A Comparative Exploration

Tirthankar Nag, Arindam Banik, Miao Pang and Chen Jixiang

Introduction

Over the last two decades, research literature has placed due emphasis on corporate sustainability obligations of firms (Quinn, Mintzberg, and James 1987). Recognising this view, organisations have also been spending voluntarily on various sustainability activities. In countries like India and China, similar arrangements have been in vogue.

Studies find corporate responsibility and sustainability research in China lacking in English language journals (Belal and Momin 2009) with the first quality research being that of Kuo et al. (Kuo, Yeh and Yu 2012). At present, most of China's CSR-based (Corporate Social Responsibility) discussions are qualitative in nature, with a scope of quantification only through the CSR Development Index Report for the top 100 organisations. In India, there has been a long-standing feeling that companies were not doing enough for sustainability issues (Hadfield-Hill 2014). Ultimately, this has led to the introduction of the Companies Act 2013, which mandates companies to spend at least 2 per cent of their net profit on CSR issues.

Though researchers have been studying about CSR for about last 50 years, only recently has there been a shift in setting from Western to emerging economies (Murthy 2008). Thus, it becomes important to examine CSR taxonomies and explore linkages if any, between CSR strategies followed by organisations and corporate returns.

The study examines explicit CSR strategies followed by corporations in developed economies as disclosed in annual reports and compares it with the practice followed in China and India. The study explores CSR strategies in India and China and carries out a comparative analysis between India and China.

Literature Review

Global Context

Starting with a limited reference by Ansoff, research on CSR has grown rapidly with the works of Freeman, Mintzberg, Donaldson, Preston, Carroll, Mendelow and others. Howard Bowen's '*Social Responsibilities of the Business Man*' (1953) was perhaps one of the initial texts to initiate this area and he put forth that large businesses actually impacted lives of citizens (Carroll 1999). Focusing more specifically on social stakeholders, researchers have tried to examine the social and economic performance of firms and explore whether firms performing well on social measures also have better economic performance (Berman et al. 1999). The theoretical challenges range from relating social and economic performance, developing a fine grained understanding of stakeholder groups and finally questioning whether normative and descriptive research can be viewed separately (Harrison and Freeman 1999).

The results of empirical research into CSR and its linkages with firm performance, carried out mostly in developed countries have surprisingly failed to reach any particular conclusion. Some studies have suggested a negative association between CSR activities and the firm's financial performance mainly due to increased costs which could have been better utilised elsewhere in the value chain of the firm. Other studies have reported a positive association in terms of employee and customer goodwill. Some studies have even suggested that future research can focus on prior firm performance influencing the CSR agenda and not the other way around (McGuire, Sundgren and Schneeweis 1988).

India

In early ages, social responsibility by organisations was in the form of donations to institutions and social causes. Post-Independence in 1947, social responsibility by corporates were ensured by standardised norms for labour and environmental performance. In the past two decades, academic research has placed due emphasis on corporate social responsibility, though the gains for corporate are not short term and often remained within the boundaries of the firm (Nag and Bhattacharyya 2012). The Ministry of Corporate Affairs (MCA), Government of India, had published two voluntary guidelines:

- Corporate Social Responsibility Voluntary Guidelines, 2009
- National Voluntary Guidelines on Social, Environmental and Economic Responsibilities of Business, 2011

The latter lists down 9 principles to be followed by businesses:

1. Businesses should conduct and govern themselves with ethics, transparency and accountability.
2. Businesses should provide goods and services that are safe and contribute to sustainability throughout their life cycle.
3. Businesses should promote the well-being of all employees.
4. Businesses should respect the interests of and be responsive towards all stakeholders, especially those who are disadvantaged, vulnerable and marginalised.
5. Businesses should respect and promote human rights.
6. Business should respect, protect and make efforts to restore the environment.
7. Businesses when engaged in influencing public and regulatory policy, should do so in a responsible manner.
8. Businesses should support inclusive growth and equitable development.
9. Businesses should engage with and provide value to their customers and consumers in a responsible manner.

However, with the introduction of Companies Act 2013, CSR compliance has shifted from voluntary to mandatory for the business firms. According to the Companies Act, 2013, section 135, every company having a net worth of ₹500 crore or more or a turnover of ₹1,000 crore or more or a net profit of ₹5 crore or more, during any financial year, shall have to ensure that the company spends at least 2 per cent of the average net profits of the company made during the three immediately preceding financial years, on CSR IN (KPMG 2015).

The revised schedule VII of the Companies Act 2013 for India lays down certain areas for CSR activities, though there are no such rules for Chinese companies.

- Eradicating hunger, poverty and malnutrition, promoting preventive health care and sanitation and making available safe drinking water
- Promoting education, including special education and employment enhancing vocation skills especially among children, women, elderly and the differently abled and livelihood enhancement projects
- Promoting gender equality, empowering women, setting up homes and hostels for women and orphans; setting up old age homes, day care centres and such other facilities for senior citizens and measures for reducing inequalities faced by socially and economically backward groups
- Ensuring environmental sustainability, ecological balance and protection of flora and fauna, animal welfare, agroforestry, conservation of natural resources and maintaining quality of soil, air and water
- Protection of national heritage, art and culture including restoration of buildings and sites of historical importance and works of art; setting up public libraries; promotion and development of traditional arts and handicrafts
- Measures for the benefit of armed forces veterans, war widows and their dependents
- Training to promote rural sports, nationally recognised sports, Paralympic sports and Olympic sports
- Contribution to the Prime Minister's National Relief Fund or any other fund set up by the central government for socio-economic development and relief and welfare of the Scheduled Castes, the Scheduled Tribes, other backward classes, minorities and women
- Contributions or funds provided to technology incubators located within academic institutions which are approved by the central government
- Rural development projects

Source: (Ministry of Corporate Affairs 2014)

China

Though most emerging economy CSR studies have focused on the Asia-Pacific region, very few have focused on mainland China (Belal and Momin 2009). CSR was perhaps introduced in China in the early 1990s with the increase of disasters and accidents (Guan and Noronha 2013).

SOCIAL RESPONSIBILITY STRATEGIES IN CHINA AND INDIA

Some of them are Yingze Park lantern festival stampede in Shanxi (1991), Gouhou dam burst disaster in Qinghai (1993), explosion in the basement of an apartment building in Hunan (1996), collapse of under construction Baikong bridge in Shaoguan (1996) and a number of coal mine accidents in the early 1990s.

However, Chinese CSR research from then on has grown rapidly in Chinese language and not necessarily in other languages like English (Lu and Li 2010). CSR was one of the most important focus areas in the 11th Five-Year Plan released by the central committee of the ruling Chinese Communist Party (Zheng 2006). Sustainability reporting guidelines was first published by GRI (Global Reporting Initiative) in 2002. In 2006, the Shenzhen Stock Exchange released the 'Guidelines on corporate social responsibility of listed companies', followed by the Shanghai Stock Exchange's issue of 'Environmental information disclosure direction for listed corporations in the Shanghai stock market' in 2008.

Increasingly, the Shanghai and Shenzhen stock exchanges required listed companies to publish their CSR practices through CSR reports. Thus 2009 onwards, CSR reports were issued by Chinese companies (Figure 15.1) and especially the state-owned ones have gone up significantly.

Studies in both countries have explored the linkage between CSR and firm performance. A study in China constructed a CSR index for major Chinese listed companies. The study points out that overseas-listed

Figure 15.1
CSR Reports Issued in China

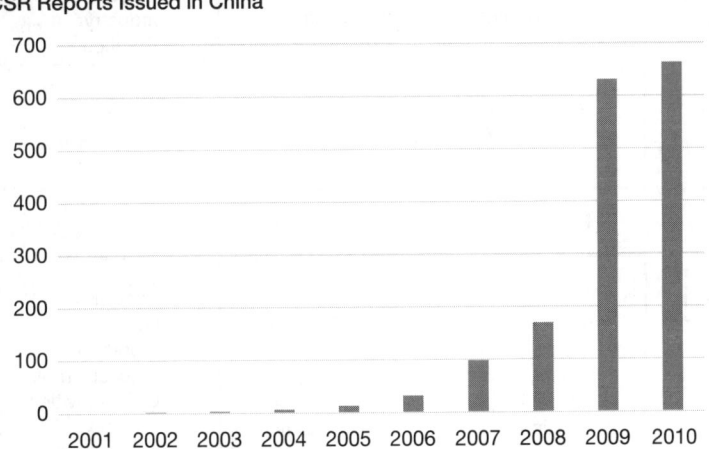

Source: CSR Report Research 2010 by China WTO Tribune, Other Reports

and comparatively profitable companies improved CSR practices and the market rewarded these improvements (Cheung, Jiang and Tan 2012). Another study carried out in China reports that CSR and financial performance mutually influence one another significantly (Chen and Wang 2011). Studies carried out in India are mixed with some finding positive linkages between CSR and firm performance. One recent study carried out reports that CSR activity reporting does not significantly influence firm performance, with the only exception in case of environmental CSR (Nag and Bhattacharyya 2012).

Methodology

The study carries out a brief comparative analysis between India and China on CSR reporting. The data for such a comparison is based on secondary sources.

Field case studies in four sectors based on primary data and personal interviews were developed for China. Indian companies in corresponding sectors were compared with, to get an idea of the CSR efforts being undertaken. The study provides ample opportunities for inter-case and intra-case comparisons to reach initial conclusions.

The methodological framework adopted for our research is provided here.

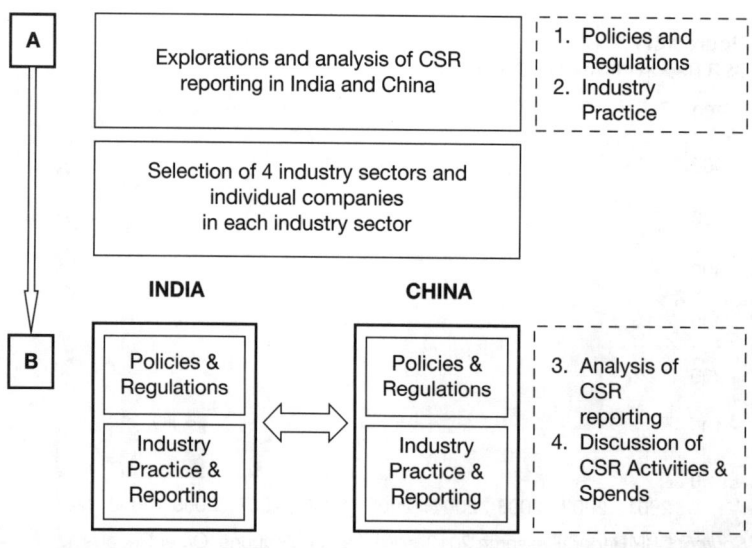

Comparative Analysis and Case Studies

CSR reporting has been growing very fast in Asia because of the introduction of new regulations and push by individual country governments. Especially, CSR reporting has seen very high growth rates in India and China. The rate of corporate social responsibility reporting is provided in Figure 15.2.

For the study, four different sectors of the economy were selected as follows:

- Pharmaceuticals
- Manufacturing
- Paper & Pulp
- Oil & Gas

A global review of CSR reporting across these four sectors are provided in Figure 15.3.

The companies chosen for the study are provided in Table 15.1.

The top management in Chinese companies were interviewed for understanding the motivation for CSR and investments carried out. Similarly, Indian companies reported CSR were identified and compared

Figure 15.2
Percentage of Companies Reporting CSR in China and India (100 Largest Companies in Countries)

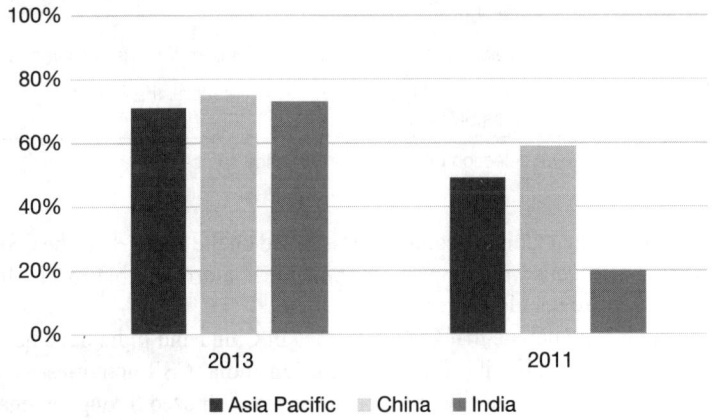

Source: KPMG (2013)

Figure 15.3
Percentage of Companies Reporting CSR (100 Largest Companies in Countries)

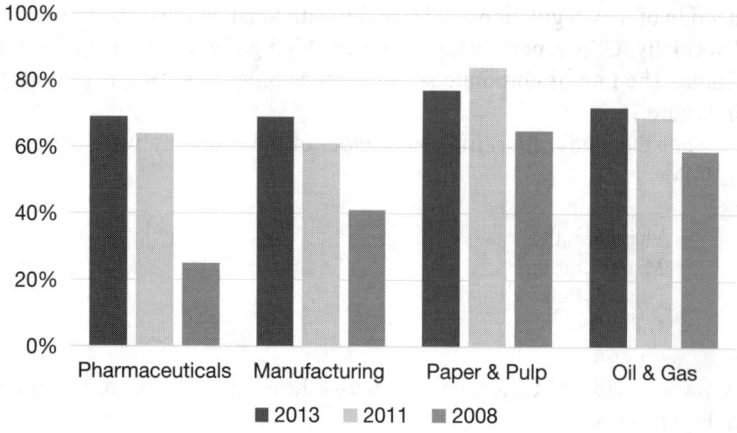

Source: KPMG (2013)

Table 15.1
Firms in India and China Selected for Understanding CSR Investments

Sector	China	India
Pharmaceuticals	Sichuan Yuanda Shuyang Pharmaceutical Co. Ltd.	GlaxoSmithKline Pharmaceuticals Limited
Manufacturing	Sichuan SUNFOR Light Co. Ltd.	Havells
Paper & Pulp	Tibet Yuanzheng Group	Ballarpur Industries Limited
Oil & Gas	Sichuan China Natural Gas Sales Co. Ltd.	Indraprastha Gas Ltd.

Source: Author's own selection based on convenience sampling

with those of their Chinese counterparts. Based on the above data, the CSR reporting and focus was compared for both the countries (Table 15.2). The case studies are not elaborated.

There is no debate that CSR activities in China and India have been increasing and continuing for some time. In India, CSR activities have been carried out voluntarily earlier and later on imposed through a legal

Table 15.2
CSR Activities in Selected Chinese and Indian Firms

Sector	CSR in Chinese Firms	CSR in Indian Firms
Pharmaceuticals	• Producing High quality health products • Assistance in natural disasters – financial contributions as well as products • Setting up charity fund for plasma donors	• Investing in Healthcare Projects • Developing Healthcare Delivery Systems • Training Community Workers • Volunteering by employees
Manufacturing	• Innovation for affordable quality product • Energy efficiency and energy savings • Regular visits and training of school students	• Focusing on Child nutrition though own kitchens for improving school attendance • Mobile Healthcare van
Paper & Pulp	• Recruiting some workers from children of farmers • Donated money to earthquake in Sichuan • Environmental protection • Contribution to Children's organisation in villages • Employees volunteering for poverty alleviation activities.	• Rural employment, health & agricultural improvement • Community based health and education
Oil & Gas	• Sustainable Development Through Technology • Energy conservation and emissions reduction	• Reducing the pollution levels • Proposed in areas of health, education, environment and empowerment of women & underprivileged.
Key Observations	**CSR Obligations:** There is no regulatory or mandatory obligation for CSR in China **CSR Spend:** Companies do not have any fixed percentage of their turnover or profits earmarked for CSR. **Activities:** Companies are interested in product related developments that indirectly help the society or cash contributions to social causes.	**CSR Obligations:** Mandatory CSR obligations for companies meeting prescribed criteria **CSR Spend:** Companies to spend 2% of average net profits **Activities:** Companies to follow Schedule VII to the Companies Act, 2013

Source: Based on author's interviews with top management of firms in China, annual reports and secondary sources in India.

Table 15.3
Firms Reporting CSR in Shanghai Stock Exchange [Companies Reporting CSR (% of Total Sample in Sector)]

Sector	2008	2009
Conglomerate	6 (3.28%)	7 (3.41%)
Cultural	2 (1.09%)	2 (0.98%)
Social Services	4 (2.19%)	4 (1.95%)
Real Property	15 (8.20%)	15 (7.32%)
Retail and Wholesale	8 (4.37%)	8 (3.90%)
Information and Technology	6 (3.28%)	5 (2.44%)
Transportation	16 (8.74%)	17 (8.29%)
Construction	5 (2.73%)	6 (2.93%)
Utilities	12 (6.56%)	10 (4.88%)
Manufacturing	103 (56.28%)	120 (58.53%)
Mineral	3 (1.64%)	6 (2.93%)
Agriculture	3 (1.64%)	5 (2.44%)

Source: Wong (2012)

mandate. In China, such activities have been totally voluntary in nature and there is evidence that such activities are increasing over time as shown in Table 15.3.

Conclusion

The study reaches a number of significant conclusions based on case studies of Indian and Chinese companies. First, companies are increasingly focusing on CSR and CSR reporting both in India and China. Companies in India are more driven by policies and regulations whereas companies in China are motivated by increasing requirements from stock exchanges and regional programmes. Second, CSR obligations on firms are mandatory in India but they are still voluntary in China. Third, while CSR spend have been fixed as a percentage of their average net profits in India, Chinese companies are free to choose their level of CSR spend. Finally, Indian companies follow government prescribed legal guidelines for their CSR commitments. Chinese companies face no such guidelines and mostly focus on output products or services and related aspects.

References

Belal, A., and Momin, M. 2009. 'Corporate Social Reporting (CSR) in Emerging Economies: A Review and Future Direction', In M. Tsamenyi, and S. Uddin (Eds.), *Accounting in Emerging Economies. Research in Accounting in Emerging Economies* 9: 119–143.

Berman, S.L., Wicks, A.C., Kotha, S., and Jones, T.M. 1999. 'Does Stakeholder Orientation Matter? The Relationship between Stakeholder Management Models and Firm Financial Performance'. *Academy of Management Journal* 42(5): 488–506.

Carroll, A.B. 1999. 'Corporate Social Responsibility: Evolution of a Definitional Construct'. *Business and Society* 38(3): 268–295.

Chen, H., and Wang, X. 2011. 'Corporate Social Responsibility and Corporate Financial Performance in China: An Empirical Research from Chinese Firms'. *Corporate Governance* 11(4): 361–370.

Cheung, Y., Jiang, K., and Tan, W. 2012. 'Doing-good and 'Doing-well' in Chinese Publicly Listed Firms'. *China Economic Review* 23(4): 776–785.

Guan, J., and Noronha, C. 2013. 'Corporate Social Responsibility Reporting Research in the Chinese Academia: A Critical Review'. *Social Responsibility Journal* 9(1): 33–55.

Hadfield-Hill, S. 2014. 'CSR in India: Reflections from the Banking Sector'. *Social Responsibility Journal* 10(1): 21–37.

Harrison, J.S., and Freeman, R.E. 1999. 'Stakeholder, Social Resonsibility and Performance: Empirical Evidence and Theoretical Perspectives'. *Academy of Management Journal* 42(5): 479–485.

KPMG. 2013 (24 May). *The KPMG Survey of Corporate Responsibility Reporting 2013.* Retrieved from KPMG: http://www.kpmg.com/global/en/issuesandinsights/articles publications/corporate-responsibility/pages/default.aspx (accessed on 25 February 2015).

———. 2015 (24 May). *Corporate Social Responsibility in India.* Retrieved from KPMG: http://www.kpmg.com/CH/Documents/Blog/pub-20140430-csr-india-2014-en.pdf

Kuo, L., Yeh, C.C., and Yu, H.C. 2012. 'Disclosure of Corporate Social Responsibility and Environmental Management: Evidence From China'. *Corporate Social Responsibility and Environmental Management* 19(5): 273–287.

Lu, X., and Li, J.M. 2010. 'A Research on the Environmental Information Disclosure of Chinese Listed Companies: A Case Study of the Listed Manufacturing Industry of A-shares Firms During the Period 2007–2008 in the Shanghai stock market'. *Journal of Audit and Economics* 25(3): 62–69.

McGuire, J.B., Sundgren, A., and Schneeweis, T. 1988. 'Corporate Social Responsibility and Firm Financial Performance'. *Academy of Management Journal* 31(4): 854–872.

Ministry of Corporate Affairs. (2014, February 27). *Ministry of Corporate Affairs Notification.* Retrieved from Ministry of Corporate Affairs Website: http://www.mca.gov.in/Ministry/pdf/CompaniesActNotification3_2014.pdf (accessed on 25 February 2015).

Murthy, V. 2008. 'Corporate Social Disclosure Practices of Top Software Firms in India;. *Global Business Review* 9(2): 173–188.

Nag, T., and Bhattacharyya, A.K. 2012 (November). 'Does corporate Social Responsibility Yield Returns? A Study of Indian Firms'. *Financial Management*, Chartered Institute of Management Accountants UK, London, 50–53.

Quinn, J., Mintzberg, H., and James, R. 1987. *The Strategy Process*. Englewood Cliffs, N.J.: Prentice-Hall.
Wong, Y.H. 2012. 'Corporate Social Responsibility and Firm Performance: Evidence from China'. Thesis, Lingnan University, Hong Kong.
Zheng, Y. 2006. 'Why China Lacks the Right Environment for Corporate Social Responsibility'. *China Policy Institute* Issue Brief 6. Available at https://www.nottingham.ac.uk/cpi/documents/briefings/briefing-6-china-csr.pdf (accessed on 15 March 2015).

About the Editors and Contributors

Editors

Paramita Mukherjee is Dean (Academics) and Associate Professor (Economics) at International Management Institute (IMI), Kolkata. She is an alumnus of Presidency College, Kolkata, has completed MS in quantitative economics from the Indian Statistical Institute, Kolkata, and PhD in economics from Jadavpur University, Kolkata. She has more than 18 years of varied experience in industry, research and teaching. She has worked with AC Nielsen (formerly ORG MARG), ICRA and reputed business schools such as IBS, Kolkata, and Institute of Engineering and Management, Kolkata.

She teaches courses on economics, statistics, business analytics, financial econometrics, financial institutions and markets and time series analysis. She has conducted management development programmes (MDPs) with Confederation of Industries in India (CII), Kolkata. She also has experience of handling consulting assignments in the power sector.

Her research interest lies in applied financial economics and econometrics. She has worked on contemporary issues in the financial sector, for example, foreign institutional investors, mutual funds, stock return volatility, volatility spillover, gold prices and share repurchases. She has authored a number of research papers in international journals such as *Asia-Pacific Development Journal, Applied Financial Economics, Emerging Markets Finance and Trade* as well as in books and national journals such as *India Macroeconomics Annual* and *Economic and Political Weekly*. She has presented papers in several conferences and seminars in India as well as at Katholik University Leuven, Belgium; Borsa Istanbul, Turkey; National Taiwan University; Sichuan Academy of Social Sciences, China and University of Sophia Antipolis, Nice, France.

Arnab K. Deb is Assistant Professor at the International Management Institute, Delhi. He holds doctorate in economics from University of Connecticut, Storrs. He earned his BSc (Honours) and MSc degrees from University of Calcutta. His research interest includes applied microeconomics, data envelopment analysis, mathematical economics and applied econometrics.

He has around eight years of experience in teaching and research. He has worked on 'District Level Monitoring of All Programs of Ministry of Rural Development, India' project, funded by Ministry of Rural Development, and World Bank-sponsored project 'Moving Out of Poverty: Growth & Democracy'. He has also worked on a National Science Foundation (NSF)-funded project 'Economic and Social Rights: Obstacle or Handmaiden to Growth?' Presently, he is working on an Indian Council of Social Science Research (ICSSR)-funded project on evaluating the performance of Indian manufacturing sector. He has attended and presented multiple research papers, both at national and international conferences.

He has received multiple fellowships and awards in his career. He has been awarded the 'Pre-doctoral Fellowship' and 'Doctoral Dissertation Fellowship' by University of Connecticut, USA. He was also recognised with the 'Abraham Ribicoff Graduate Fellowship' by the Department of Economics, University of Connecticut, in 2011.

Miao Pang is currently working in the Research Management Department of Sichuan Academy of Social Sciences. She specialises in forest resource management and is from the University of Philippines, Los Banos. She has been a visiting scholar at the University of California, Berkeley. Her research interests include rural community development, rural environmental protection and forest economics. She has co-authored two books—*Methodology Used in Rural Community Survey* and *Community-based Natural Resource Management*. She was involved in a national project of social sciences titled 'Ecologically-Vulnerable Communities' Adaptation to Climate Change in Western China' in 2012 and also in China's national project of social sciences titled 'Ecological Compensation in Post Era of Conversion Farmlands into Forestlands in China' in 2010.

Contributors

Prageet Aeron is Assistant Professor at Management Development Institute (MDI), Gurgaon. He is the coordinator for the computer centre, website, ERP & IT at the institute. A fellow of Management (computers and information systems) from Indian Institute of Management (IIM), Ahmedabad, his primary areas of research have been technology entrepreneurship, technology strategy, telecom policy and network economics. His teaching interests include management information system (MIS), IT security and numerical methods for management. Before joining MDI, he was an Assistant Professor at IMI, New Delhi.

Prior to his doctoral education, he was working as a scientist at Defence Research and Development Organization (DRDO), High Energy Materials Research Laboratory (HEMRL), Pune, on explosives and propellants (with a focus on gun propellants). He holds a Bachelor's degree in chemical engineering and technology from Indian Institute of Technology-Banaras Hindu University. At IIM Ahmedabad, he was a recipient of the IDEA IIMA Telecom Centre of Excellence Research Award. He has publications in journals of international repute and has several working papers to his credit.

Arindam Banik is Director at IMI, Kolkata. He holds a PhD from the Delhi School of Economics. He has been with IMI since 1994. Earlier, he was with American Express Bank, Dhaka. He is a member of the American Economic Association, Euro-Asia Management Studies Association and Global Awareness Society International, USA. He has taught international finance, development economics, development planning and project appraisal and macroeconomics at the Department of Economics, University of West Indies, Barbados, during 2001–05 as a visiting faculty. He holds the position of Associated Cement Companies Chair Professor in International Finance and Business at IMI. He has authored more than 100 scientific articles on international economics, macroeconomics and economic development in journals of national and international eminence. He is the editor of the SAGE journal, *Global Business Review,* and the International Advisory Board Member of *Asian Business and Management*. He has been a consultant to companies, the Government of India and multi-lateral institutions such as Associated Cement Companies, Ministry of Rural Development, World Bank, ILO-SAAT, International Development Research Centre (IDRC), Canadian International Development Agency (CIDA) and United Nations Industrial Development Organization (UNIDO).

Xiang Baoyun is Secretary of Discipline Inspection Commission of Sichuan Academy of Social Sciences (SASS) and Director of Center for Indian Studies of SASS, China. He is a professor with a PhD in Arts. Furthermore, he is Executive Vice President of Sichuan Research Institute of Theory of Literature and Arts. He specialises in literature and arts with a focus on Chinese modern literature. He is a leading researcher for many national and provincial projects. He has publications in reputed journals such as *Xin Hua Digest* and *Academic Monthly* and has also published books such as *Study on Cao Yu's Tragic Aesthetic Ideology*.

Sriparna Basu is Professor at FORE School of Management, New Delhi. She has a Masters and a PhD in Cultural Studies from University of Illinois at Urbana-Champaign, USA. Her research contributions include articles, research papers, cases and book chapters published in several national and international peer-reviewed journals and books. Her current research contributes to the interdisciplinary scholarship on globalisation by examining the multiple forms of globalisation and evolving cultural and national identities as exhibited by the Asian economies. She is also interested in exploring the interaction between post-colonial cultural theory and organisational communication and the widening of reflexive practices in cross-border mergers and acquisitions.

Her training interests span the domains of HR and communication and she has conducted training workshops on change communication, cross-functional team work, interpersonal communication, assertiveness, cross-cultural communication in international business and issues of gender in the workplace. She has been involved in training and consulting activities with a number of public and private sector organisations such as Oil and Natural Gas Corporation Limited (ONGC), Power Grid, NHPC, Indian Oil, Tata Motors, Food Corporation of India (FCI) and Border Security Force (BSF) along with many start-up organisations.

Rajashri Chatterjee is Senior Research Officer at IMI, Kolkata. She has completed her Masters in finance from the University of Calcutta and MBA (finance) from West Bengal University of Technology. She is currently pursuing PhD at the University of Burdwan. Prior to joining IMI Kolkata, she has worked as a Finance Executive at Rabindranath Tagore International Institute of Cardiac Sciences and AMRI Hospitals Ltd in Kolkata. She is the Editorial Assistant of 'IMI Konnect', the scholarly management magazine of IMI Kolkata. She has been actively engaged in organising various national and international conferences at IMI Kolkata. She has contributed articles for *IMI Konnect*, co-authored one book chapter and has papers to her credit that have been presented in conferences in India and abroad.

Xie Jing is Lecturer at SASS. Educated at Sichuan University Institute of South Asia, her research interests include international relations, India's foreign policy, interaction between China and India in the Indian Ocean region, the Pakistan–Afghanistan relationship and the 'One Belt, One Road' initiative.

Li Jingfeng is Assistant Researcher at SASS. His research interests include foreign affairs and security issues in South Asian countries. He has published several papers in various professional publications.

Chen Jixiang is Vice-Director of Indian Research Center at SASS. He has published numerous papers on the economy of India as well as a book based on employment of rural labour force in India.

Jian Li is Associate Researcher at SASS. She specialises in communication and cultural studies.

B.A. Metri is currently Dean (Academic and Alumni Relations) and Professor of Operations Management at IMI, New Delhi. He also served as a professor and Dean at MDI, Gurgaon and as In-charge of PhD Programmes at Birla Institute of Technology and Science (BITS), Pilani. He has more than 25 years of experience in teaching, training, research and consulting. An authority in the field of project management, quality and supply chain management, he has published over 100 research articles in international and national journals and proceedings and co-authored six books. He is on the editorial advisory boards of national and international journals. He has also organised a number of national and international conferences.

He is deeply involved with executive education including international training with leading organisations of government, public sector (Maharatna and Navaratna companies) and private sector. He has trained senior executives and chief engineers of several leading organisations including ONGC, Bharat Electronic Ltd. (BEL), Sona Koyo, Bharat Heavy Electricals Limited (BHEL), National Thermal Power Corporation (NTPC), Reserve Bank of India (RBI), Fortis, Jindal Stainless Steel Ltd., Power Grid Corporation of India Limited (PGCIL), NHPC, HCL, Punjab National Bank (PNB), Construction Industry Development

Council (CIDC), ASEA Brown Boveri (ABB), Nestle, DCM Shriram, Cairn Energy, New Holland Fiat India, Department of Atomic Energy (DOAE) officers, Indian Army officers, Indian Technical & Economic Cooperation Programme officers (under the purview of the Ministry of External Affairs, from 16 countries), Afghanistan government Officers, top business managers from Mauritius, Ministry of Health & Family Welfare as well as Indian Administrative Service (IAS) officers.

He has carried out consulting projects with various organisations. He is a PhD from IIT Bombay, a civil engineering graduate of Government College of Engineering, Karad, and holds a Master's degree in civil-construction & management from KBP College of Engineering, Satara. Currently, he serves on the Board of Directors of Decision Sciences Institute (DSI) and is the first Indian elected as Vice President (Asia–Pacific Division), Decision Sciences Institute (DSI), Houston, Texas, USA.

Sanjoy Mukherjee is a faculty of business ethics and corporate social responsibility at IIM Shillong. He is the Chairperson of the Fellow Programme in Management (FPM) and also the Chairperson of the Institute's Annual International Sustainability Conference (SUSCON). A mechanical engineering graduate from Jadavpur University he did his post-graduation in management from IIM Calcutta and PhD from Jadavpur University. After a corporate experience of nearly seven years, he had a long stint as a faculty at the Management Centre for Human Values of Indian Institute of Management, Kolkata. His areas of interest and research include enlightened leadership, management by human values, Indian ethos in management, management and liberal arts and alternative sources and methods of learning. He has lectured and presented in conferences worldwide including prestigious forums such as Aspen Institute, Oxford Roundtable, Globethics Geneva, International Society for Business Ethics and Economics, Harvard Business School, Copenhagen Business School, Stockholm Business School, Corvinus University of Budapest, Norwegian School of Economics at Bergen, UNESCO, Paris, and China Europe International Business School among others. For nearly a decade, he was the Editor-in-Chief of *Journal of Human Values*, the bi-annual international journal from SAGE Publications. He has published several papers and articles in national and international journals. He has jointly edited two books, *Corporate Governance, Economic Reforms and Development* and *Sustainable Ethics: Ecology and Ethics*.

Paramita M. Nag currently is the Head of Research with Whitebox Research Solutions (a research organisation working mostly in the infrastructure sector). She has the overall responsibility of research and publication. Before joining here she was working with Unitedworld School of Business where she was responsible for executive education and research. She had been associated previously with ICFAI Research Center as a Consulting Editor. Prior to that, she was a consultant with a market research firm, where she had the independent charge of all social development projects, especially dealing with the health sector. Also during her tenure at Indian Institute of Public Administration (IIPA), she was responsible for handling research projects ranging from rural development to public administration and economics. Furthermore, she has also handled several research projects as an independent consultant.

She has obtained her MA, MPhil and PhD degrees from Jawaharlal Nehru University, New Delhi. Her area of research pertains to public health. She has also qualified the National Eligibility Test/Junior Research Fellowship (NET/JRF) under the University Grants Commission (UGC) scheme and has also been awarded the Indian Council of Social Science Research (ICSSR) Fellowship under the All India Central Scheme.

Her areas of research interest include all facets of societal development, especially the domains of public health, environmental health, policy research and analysis essentially pertaining to public health and epidemiology.

Tirthankar Nag holds a doctorate from IIM Ahmedabad. He is Dean (research and international relations) and Associate Professor (strategy) at IMI, Kolkata. He has been advising doctoral courses at institutes of national repute. He is also involved in guiding and examining doctoral candidates working in the area of strategy/policy at several universities and institutes. He has authored several books, book chapters, peer-reviewed papers in international journals and a number of papers in collaboration with Stanford University. He has received several awards and recognitions from IIM Ahmedabad for his academic work (Chaudhary Padmanabhan Pant Award, Sahir Memorial Award, 'Contribution to developing entrepreneurial ecosystem in India') and holds a certificate from the World Bank Institute. He is a mentor for CIIE (Centre for Innovation, Incubation & Entrepreneurship) at IIM Ahmedabad. He also holds a bachelor's degree in electrical engineering from Jadavpur University.

He has been an advisor to the top management of various companies on behalf of PricewaterhouseCoopers, KPMG and SBICAPS, dealing with strategy and policy advisory. He also has a considerable experience of working with Calcutta Electric Supply Corporation (CESC) Ltd as a power professional. Overall, he has 19 years of experience across management consulting, investment banking, utilities and research. Some of multilateral agencies he has consulted for include the World Bank, United Nations Environment Programme (UNEP), Department for International Development (DFID), United States Agency for International Development (USAID) and Asian Development Bank (ADB).

Huang Weimin is Associate Researcher at the Research Institute of Literature, SASS. As a PhD student, she is mainly interested in Chinese classic literature, cultural industry and cultural tourism and has published many articles in *Modern Literary Magazine* and other Chinese Social Sciences Citation Index (CSSCI) journals. In recent years, she has focused on the comparative study on religion, public opinion, tourism and cultural industry in China and India, and also composed several articles. Currently, she is focusing on contemporary and modern Chinese travel notes about India (1840–1949), and attempting to explore Chinese people views about India in contemporary and modern times with an aim to make an academic contribution to improve the mutual understanding between the Chinese and the Indian people.

Zou Yiqing is Researcher at the Institute of History, SASS. He focuses primarily on the Bashu culture and the Southern Silk Road and has published a significant number of research papers.

Duan Yu is Professor and Researcher at the Institute of History, SASS, and is also Director of the Bashu Cultural Research Center of Sichuan Normal University. Additionally, he is the Vice President of the Pre-Qin History Association of China and Vice President of the minorities in Southwest China Research Institute. His areas of interests include Chinese ancient civilisation, history of pre-Qin period, Bashu culture and the Southern Silk Road. He has published a significant number of research articles and a number of monographs.

Index

above poverty line, 195
advanced civilisations, perception of China and India as, 133
aesthetics, 50
Afghan National Security Force (ANSF), 116
Afghanistan, 17, 75, 76
   benefits from China-India cooperation in, 115
   challenges before China-India cooperation in, 116
   China's interests in, 110
   Chinese silk unearthed at, 22
   cooperation between China–India for reconstruction of, 112
   economy, 116
   geographical location of, 108
   India's interests in, 111
   Islamic extremist organisations in, 110
   regional conflicts in, 108
   US planning to withdraw forces from US war against terrorism, 116
Afghanistan Watt Khan Corridor, 86
Africa-Persian Gulf-Xinjiang energy corridor, 99
aggressive materialism, 43
Al-Qaeda, 109
allocative efficiency, 197
Ancient Chinese Note, The (Henry Yule), 19
Anglo-French agreement, 144
anti-dumping, 165
anti-imperialist ideology, 133
Armenians, 26
Arthashastra, 14, 17

artificial irrigation system, 4, 5
artificially depressed currency, 162
artificially low currency rate, 153
Aryans, 26
asceticism, 25
ASEAN, 173, 176
Asia-Pacific region
   close connection with China, 79
Asian economies, 38
Asian financial crisis, 175
Asian voice, 45, 49
Asian voice. *See also* Tagore, Rabindranath
Asian voice
   against western capitalism, 43
   Tagore as champion for cause of rasing, 41
Asiatic mode of production, 133
Aspirations, 81
ASR Asia ranking, 183
atheism, 25
audience experience-driven, 80
Austerity Plan (1993) of China, 137
Australian aborigines, 26

balance-of-payment crisis in 1991, 133, 135
Bangladesh, 60, 83, 85, 88–91
Bangladesh, China, India and Myanmar - Economic Corridor (BCIM-EC), 84, 97
   aim of, 83
   constraints of, 90
   current status of, 91
   driving force of, 88

economic cooperation significance within, 84
implications of, 86
barriers to trade, 144
BCIM Kolkata to Kunming (K2K) Rally, 84
Beautiful Daughter-in-law, 81
Beidi ethnic minorities, 16
Beijing Normal University, 44
Beijing Olympic Games 2008, 80
belief, 25
below the poverty line, 195
benevolence, 25, 78
Bengala (Bangladesh), 60
big bath structure in Mohenjo-daro, 6
big unification ideology, 25
BJP, 89
bodhidharma, 25
British culture, 26
Bronze Age, 10
bronze culture of Shu civilisation, 4
Buddha, 26
Buddhism, 63, 65, 73, 76, 175
Buddhists, 73
bureaucracy, 133
Burma, 13, 85, 86
    political transition and national security issues, 90
Business Ashram, concept ot, 48
business opportunities, 35
Business Responsibility Reports (BRR), 178

Calicut (Kozhikode), 60
business trade between Ming dynasty and, 67
    Hindu beliefs of, 64
Calicut Manuscript Library, 67
capital adequacy, 143
capital flows, 144
capitalism, 133
castle, 9
Catholicism, 73
Centres of Disease Control (CDC), 197
ceremony, 78
Cheena Bhavana (the Chinese Quarters), 38, 42, 44, 52, 54
Chengdu, 17
Chengdu city, 10, 11

Chengdu Plain, water conservancy project on, 6
Chengdu
    silk, 18
Chidambaram, P., 133
chiefdom system, 10, 12
children of immortality (Amritasya putrah), 51
China Banking Regulatory Commission, 177
China Metallurgical Group, 109
China Tibetology Research Centre, Beijing, 67
China-Pakistan economic cooperation, 100
China-Pakistan Economic Corridor, 97, 99, 100
China
    foreign policy of, 106
    Pakistan, re-orientation of relationship with, 101
Chinese culture
    after the rain comes the sunshine ideology, 26
    attention towards worldly happines
    characteristics of, 25
    components of
    ethical centring of
Chinese monks, 76
Christianity, 73
Cina, 18, 21
    transcription or reincarnation of Chengdu, 18
Cinathana, 19
city construction, comparison between Indua Valley and Shu civilisation, 12
closed door policy, 133
Cochin, 60
    Hindu beliefs of, 64
Coefficient of Variation, 145
Cold War, 105
colonialism, 133
Communist Party of India (Marxist) (CPI[M]), 128
Communist Party of China (CPC), 136
Communist Party of India (CPI), 133
community development, 54
Companies Act 2013, 170, 174, 178, 185, 203, 205, 206

INDEX

conflict management, 51
Confucian culture, 25
Confucianism, 69, 73
Confucius Institute, 80
Confucius morality, 25
Congress party, 133
consumerism, 42, 46
corporate brand personality, 173
corporate governance, 175, 176
corporate returns, 204
corporate social responsibility (CSR), 52
China, practices in, 177
    activities of Indian compnies, 206
    Chinese companies activities, 209
    contribution by Indian companies, 185
    definition of, 170
    emergence of, 169
    emphasis in Asian emerging countries, 170
    India vs developing economies, performance of, 185
    India, practices in, 178
    practices in global world, 204
    research methodology, 208
    trends in Asian economies practices, 176
Corporate Social Responsibility Voluntary Guidelines, 2009, 205
corporate sustainability, 183, 203
corporatisation, 136, 150
cost competitiveness, 164
Country Year, Sino-Indian, 35
Covey, Stephen, 48
crisis of civilisation, 37, 55
cross-cultural awareness, 35
cultural brands, 80
cultural differences between China and India, 25
    areas for cooperation, 35
    culture of optimism vs culture influences by spirituality and afterlife myths, 26
    ethical vs religious culture, 25
    methodology to deal with, 34
    tourism, positive and negative impact on, 31
    unitary culture vs multi-culture, 26
cultural exchanges, 4, 13, 14, 17, 83
cultural homogenisation, 44

cultural industry, 76, 77, 82
cultural interactions, 39
cultural nationalist position of self valorising autonomy, 133
Cultural Revolution, 130
cultural soft power
    China englightment from Indian strategies for promotion of, 82
    definition of, 72
    resources for development by India, 75
    strategies for development by India, 77
cultural values
    China's traditional, 78
culture communication, 82
culture diplomacy, 75
culture of optimism, 26
culturology, 27
customer goodwill, 204

decadal average growth rates, 138
decentralisation, 147, 150
decision making, 51
Deng Xiaoping, 133, 136
deprivation, 134
deregulation policies, 138
Desikottam award, 45
dharma, 52
Dharmarakshsha, 39
diplomatic corps, 60, 63, 64
direct tax rates, 143
Discovery of India, The (Jawaharlal Nehru), 103
disease control programmes, 191
Doctrine of the Mean, 25
dollar colonisation, 94, 96
dollar dominance of U.S., 95
domestic security, 98, 100
dominant culture, 75
drainage system, 3, 5, 6, 8
Dravidians, 26
drug trafficking, 110, 113
dual economy dynamics, 134
dual nationality, 77
Dujiangyan irrigation project, 8
Durand line, 115

East Policy, 88
economic colonisation, 44, 94
economic development, 133

of China, 160
economic growth, 134
　alleviation of poverty and income inequality
economic integration, 86, 97, 99, 107, 133
economic interdependence, 86, 104, 105
economic reconstruction, 114
economic reforms
　in China, 133, 137
　in India, 136, 138
economic sovereignty, 133
economies of scale, 159
economy of India, liberalisation of, 188
education, changing paradigm in, 49
egoistic spirit of separateness, 41
elite class of America, 95
emotional quotient, 50
emotions
engineering technology, 8
environmental performance, 205
environmental, social and governance (ESG), 173
equitable development, 205
Eritrea Voyage, 19
ethical culture, 25
Eurasia Land Bridge, 99
Eurasian civilisation, 4, 15, 23
Europe, 133
exchanges between China and India
　Chinese envoys to Indian kingodm, 72
　Indian kingdoms tribute to China, 71
　origin of, 59

Fa Xian, 39
factor mobility, 135, 144
Fairbank, John K., 133
federal economy, 138
Federation of Korean Industries (FKI), 176
Finance Commission, 140
Financial Supervisory Commission (FSC), Taiwan, 176
firm performance, 204, 207
First Opium War in China (1839–42), 133
fiscal deficit, 143
five Indias, 58, 60
folk Tantrism, 65

foreign direct investment (FDI), 137, 144, 148, 149
foreign exchange transactions, 162
free market, 133
free trade zones, 99, 100, 101
French revolution, 133

G7 (Group of 7), 102
Gambari, 60
Gandhi, Mohandas K. (Mahatma Gandhi), 26, 52, 79, 133
GATT
Gelb, Michael, 48
Geling people, 63
gentleness, 78
geo-civilisational paradigm, 46
Ghani, Ashraf, 116
Gilani, Yousuf Raza, 101
Gini coefficient, 138, 144, 145
global capitalism, 133
global economic meltdown of 2008
　impact on West, 38
global financial crisis, 138
global political economy, 102
Global Reporting Initiative (GRI), 176
global restructuring of capital, 133
globalisation, 40, 81, 135, 136
　advantages of, 133
　counterbalanced by globalisations waves of, 144
Government Insurance Scheme (GIS), 198
Grassland Silk Road, 23
Great Depression, 133
Green Credit Guidelines, China, 177
Gross State Domestic Product, (GSDP) 138

Haas, Ketai, 21
Haj Gac iron mines, 111
Han Dynasty, 21, 22
Harappa/Harappan civilisation, 3, 5, 8, 9. *See also* Indus Valley civilisation, 3
health care system of China
　historical evolution of, 190
　performance of healthcare, 197
　policy interventions, 201
　protection against financial disaster, 195

INDEX

health care system of India
    performance of healthcare, 197
    policy interventions of, 201
    protection against financial disaster, 195
health status of China and India
Hexi Corridor, 86
Hind Swaraj, 133
Hindi Chini bhai-bhai (India and China are brothers) slogan, 128
Hindu Saktism, 66
Hindu Tantrism, missionary activities of, 67
Hinduism, 25, 63, 64, 73
    doctrine of, 25
    in China, 69
History of Ming Dynasty, 63
holistic management philosophy, 50
honesty, 78
Huanghe River Basin, 25
Huangrunxibu, 22
Hui Hui people, 63
Huis people, 63
human-orientation, 25
humanism, Tagore's voice of, 46

illegal
    immigrants, 88, 89, 90
    immigration, 89
import
    liberalisation, 136
    substitution, 133
inclusive thinking, 52
income distribution, 134
Independent Election Commission of Afghanistan, 116
Indian Council for Cultural Relations (ICCR), 76, 77
Indian Council of World Affairs (ICWA), 89
Indian culture
    characteristics of, 25
    components of
    ethical centering of
    myths about afterlife, 26
indigenous manufacturing base, 133
indirect tax rates, 143
Indo-China bonding, Tagore's role in, 47

Indus Valley civilisation, 4
    and Shu civilisation, comparison between, 15
    declining of, 4
    feature of
    origin of, 3
industrial
    civilisation, 50
    dynamics, 133
inequality
    and economic growth, relationship between, 134
    changing tolerance for, 133
    increase as a result of growth, 134
Institute for Defence Studies and Analyses (IDSA), 104
institutional leadership, 53
instrumental rationality, 50
interconnection system in China, 83
international cultural exchanges, comparison between Indus Valley and Shu civilisation, 15
international trade theory, 134
interprovincial inequality, 146
interregional inequality, 145–146
intraregional inequality, 145, 147
invasive colonial powers, 133
investment environment, 112
Islam, 26, 73
Islamic extremism, 115

Jainism, 26, 73
Ji Xianlin, 44
Jiechi, Yang, 87
jihad, 109
Joshi, M.C., 22
Journey to the West, 81
Judaism, 73

Kaiming Dynasty, 7
Karzai, Hamid, 110, 112
Kasyapa Matanga, 39
Kazakhstan, 97
King Yu, 7
Korean War, 133
Kyrgyzstan, 97
Kyunki Saas Bhi Kabhi Bahu Thi serial, 76

Labour Insurance Scheme (LIS), 198
labour migration, 149
Land Silk Road economic belt, 97
Laufer, B., 18
Legend of Zhen Huan, 81
Leonardo da Vinci, 48
Li Keqiang, 84
Li Na, 80
Liang Chi Chao, 44
liberalisation, 136
localisation communication strategy
  of tantrism and Hinduism
  in China, 69
low-income category states of India,
  growth rates of, 140
loyalty, 78

Made in Cheng (Made in Chengdu), 17
Madison, Angus, 133
Mahavira, 26
management education, 39
management learning, 48
management thinking, changing paradigm
  in, 49
manufacturing sector in China
  growth phases of, 164
  industry versus services sector, 153
  problems to be encounter in future, 165
  value of, 153
manufacturing sector in India
  problems faced by, 166, 155
Mao Zedong, 133
Maoism, 128
Maritime Silk Road, 23, 97
market orientation, 34
marketisation, 137, 150
martial art, Chinese, 80
materialism, 41
meditation, 51
Mediterranean ethnics, 26
Mencius, 25
Mesopotamia, 12, 14
Middle East, 73
migration, 144, 149
Ming Dynasty, 59, 67
Ministry of Corporate Affairs (MCA), 177
Minjiang River, 7
Minshan mountain, 7

Mitroff, Ian, 47
moderation, 78
modern management, 53
modernisation, 133
Modi, Narendra, 89, 105
Mohenjo-daro, 3, 5, 8
Moksha, 73
monarchy, 175
Mongolians, 26
mono-culture, 50
MSMEs, 173
Mughal Empire, 133
Mugong, Qin, 16
multi-culture, 26
multilateral communication, 78
multinational companies (MNCs), 137
Myanmar, 22
myths, about afterlife, 26

Nalanda Monastery, 65
Nalanda Temple, 76
Nandy, Ashis, 133
Nanpi people, 63
Narayanan, M.K., 86
nation, birth of, 133
National Manufacturing Policy, 155
National Voluntary Guidelines on Social,
  Environmental and Economic
  Responsibilities of Business,
  2011, 205
NATO, 116
Naxalites, 133
Negley Indian aborgines, 26
Nehru, Jawaharlal, 103, 133
  Tagore's influence on, 45
  vision of an Asian federation, 133
neo-imperialism, 121
Neo-Taoism, 69
neoclassical growth theory, 138
Neolithic age, 10
non-governmental exchanges between
    China and India, 65
  Hinduism remains of merchants in
    Quanzhou and other places, 68
  missionary activities of Hindu Tantrism
    by western monks, 67
non-resident Indians
  and their values, 75

INDEX

Indian culture, influence on, 77
Northern Silk Road, 23
Nye, Joseph S. Jr., 72

Obama, Barack, 93
Olympic Games, 80
One Belt and One Road strategy, 97
oracle bone inscription, 13
oriental cultures, 24, 78
out-of-pocket payments (OOPs), 198, 200

Pakistan, 13, 20, 98
    China's reorientation relationship with, 101
    geopolitical environment, 98
Pan Pan Kingdom, 59
Panchsheel (the Five Principles of Peaceful Co-existence), 45
Papaw people, 63
Parthia merchants, 18
Pearl River Delta (PRD), 155
    established as special economic zone in, 1979 157
    FDI flow into, 156, 158
    infrastructure development, 158
Pelliot, P., 16, 18
pivot to Asia strategy of US, purpose of, 96
political instability, 100
political sovereignty, 133
popular culture, 74
poverty, 134, 170
Prime Minister's National Relief Fund, 178
Prince Sakyamuni, 26
priority sector, 143
private capital, 133
private investment, 143, 191
privatisation, 136
problem solving, 51
propensity to save, 134
protectionism, 148
PSUs, 143
public diplomacy, 80
public investment, 143

Qian, Zhang, 17, 20
Qin Dynasty, 8
    foundation of, 16
Qin-Han civilisation, 15

Qiong bamboo stick, 17
quality consciousness, 48
quasi-alliance, 103
quasi-Marxist notion of private greed, 133
Quilon, 60

racial system, 25
rational model of governance, 133
Ray, Haraprasad, 22
regional income disparity/inequality, 135, 142
regional inequality
    in China, 149
    in India, 143
regional
    convergence, 146
    cooperation, 86
    disparity, 138, 147
    imbalance, 139, 141, 149, 150
    security, 94
regionalism, 102, 104
religious culture, 25
    spread in China in 15th century, 70
religious diversity, 74
religious extremism forces, 96
religious extremists, 109
reorientation, 133
Responsible Business Conduct (RBC) initiatives, 176
retribution, 25
Return of The Pearl Princess, 81
reverse engineering, 158
Richthofen, F.von, 19
righteousness, 25
Rimland theory, 97
rural–urban inequality, 149

Sadhu, 26
Saktism, Hindu, 65
samsara, 25
Sangrgyas-yeshes-shabs, 65
Santiniketan, 37, 38, 43, 44, 45, 52, 53
Sanxingdui city, 10, 11, 13, 14
Sanxingdui culture period, 17
Scenery of the Christian World, The, 19
seashell money, 17
Second World War, 133
secularisation, 31

Security Council, 133
self-assertion, 41
self-contained villages, 133
self-evolving clusters, 160
self-independence (swaraj), 133
self-realisation, 53
self-representations, 133
self-sufficient villages
Sen, Amartya, 41
sense, 25
separatism, 96
Seres, 21
Serica, 18
Sericon, 18
Sericum, 18
service-driven, 80
Shang Dynasty, 7, 11, 17, 21
Shanghai Cooperation Organization (SCO), 114
Shanghai Expo 2010, 80
Shanhaijing, 17
Sharif, Nawaz, 105
Shihuang, Qin, 16
Shijiedatong (world in grand harmony), 45
Shu civilisation, 4
  Indus Valley civilisation, comparison between, 15
Shu culture, influence on Nanzhong regions, 17
Shu merchants, 22
  arrived in Yunnan, 17
Shu silk, 17
Shu-Hindu Road, 14
Shudu Fu, 21
Sichuan Basin, 4
Siddhartha, Gautama, 45
Sikhism, 73
silence, 51
Silk Road economic zone, 109
silk weaving, 21
Sindabil city, 19–20
Sindifu, 19–20
Singh, Manmohan, 75, 84, 87, 133
Singh, Natwar, 128
Sinha, Yashwant, 77
Sino-India cultural exchanges,
  unidirectional flow, 70
Sino-India relations

India's stance towards, 106
  perceived by India, 104
Sino-India war of 1962, 133
Sino-Indian Cultural Society, 44
Sino-Pakistan Economic Corridor, 83
Sino-Pakistan economic integration, 99
Sino-Pakistan relationship
  India's stand towards, 106
social control system, 10, 11
social empowerment, 52, 54
social responsibility of business, 43
social stratification, 9, 11
socialist ideology, 133
Socially Responsible Investment (SRI) index, 176
soft power
  concept of, 77
  cultural soft power, power, 72
  definition of
  features of
  origin of
Sogodiana merchants, 18
Song Dynasty, 19, 45, 59
South Asian Association for Regional Cooperation (SAARC), 99, 114
southern Silk Road, 13, 15, 22, 23, 83
Soviet Union, 108
special economic zones (SEZ), 162–163
spillover effect, 113
spirit-based leadership, 43
spiritual quotient (SQ), 49
spirituality, 73
Spirituality at Work (SAW), 48
spirituality, culture influenced, 26
Spykman, Nicholas, 97
state-directed capitalism in China, 133
state-owned enterprises (SOEs), 136
Stilwell Road, 83
Stock Exchange (BSE), 179
strategic advantage, 111
strategic collaboration, 116
strategic CSR, 175, 185
strategic partnership, 84, 99
Supervision and Administration Commission (SASAC) of the state council, China, 177

INDEX

Sustainability Reporting Guidelines, (2002) 207
sustainable business strategy, 170
sustainable development, 4
symbiotic model, 156
synchronicity, concept of, 49

Tagore, Rabindranath, 38, 79
  and Indo-China bonding, 47
  leadership of, 54
  modern management, lessons to be learnt for, 53
  relevance in present day scenario, 43
  significant contributions of, 39
Tai Ji Quan, 80
Taipei Exchange (TPEx), 176
Taiwan Business Council for Sustainable Development, 176
Taiwan Stock Exchange (TWSE), 176
Tajikistan, 97
Tang Dynasty, 76
Tang Yijie, 69
Tantrism, 65, 66, 68
Tao Te Ching (Lao Tze), 133
Taoism, 80
Tapovan (forest of askesis) system, 53
Tea Horse Road, 83
technical efficiency, 197
techno-economic identity, 47
technological
  bonanza, 40
  revolution, 133
  transfers, 144
technology intensive industry, 164
technology-driven, 80
territorial integrity, 112
terrorism, 96, 98, 113, 115
Theil index, 145
theocracy, 11
Thinai, 18
Tokyo Imperial University, 41
tolerance, 25
top down decision making process, 191
tourism marketing, 34
Tourism Year, Sino-Indian, 35
tourism, China and India cultural differences impact on
  negative impacts, 31

track one diplomacy, 85
track two diplomacy, 85
trade liberalisation, 133, 134, 143
trade openness, 142
trade partner, 104
Trans-Pacific Partnership (TPP), 102
Transatlantic Trade and Investment Partnership (TTIP), 102, 103
transcendental leadership, 39, 53
transnational crime, 110
Travelogues, The (Arab Maihar), 19, 20
Travels of Marco Polo, The, 19
tributary relations between China and India, 60
tributary relationship, 60
tributary trades, 64, 67
tunnel effect, 133
Turkmenistan, 97
Tzinista/Tzinitza/Tzinist, 19

U.S.
  global hegemony, 97
  pivot or rebalancing strategy to Asia, 93
  war against terrorism in Afghanistan, 98
UN office on Drugs and Crime, 110
unitary culture, 26
United Nations Educational, Scientific and Cultural Organization (UNESCO), 27
unskilled labour, 134
Upanishads, 40
urban civilisation, 3, 8
urban-rural continuum, 11
urban–rural income ratio, 149
USC Marshall School of Business, 47
utilitarianism, 78
Uzbekistan, 97

Vajpayee, Atal Bihari, 103
Vasudhaiva kutumbakam (the world is one family), 45
Visva-Bharati university, 38, 40, 43, 45, 46, 54

Wang Yi, 110
warring states period, 7, 14, 17

water conservancy projects, 4
comparsion between Indus Valley and Shu civilisation, 8
western capitalism, 43, 46
western monks
  dependence on imperial court, 69
  Indian religious cultures brought by, 68
  missonary activities of, 67
win-win cooperation, 105, 107
win-win strategy, 100, 103
wisdom, 25, 78
World Bank, 102
World Business Council for Sustainable Development (WBCSD), 170
World Expo 80
World Health Report 2000, The, 192
world heritage sites
  Italy as home of, 27
World Trade Organization (WTO), 133, 137
worship of spirits, 25
Wudi period, 17

Xi Jinping, 110, 112
Xia Dynasty, 7
Xianlin, Ji, 22

Xu Beihong, 43
Xuan Zang, 39, 76

Yalanggeyueshiliqin, 67
Yangtze River Basin, 25
Yangtze River Delta (YRD), 155, 156, 160
Yao Ming, 80
Yi Jing, 39, 76
Yitongshujin, 22
yoga, 74
Yule, Henry, 18
Yulei mountain, 8

Zanshili, Saha, 65
Zeng Jia Gou, 17
zero-sum game, 112
Zhedi people, 63
Zhenjue Temple, 66
Zhiguang, 65
Zhong, Tan, 20
Zhong-Yin Da Tong, Chinese concept of, 46
Zhou Dynasty, 7, 21, 22
Zhou Enlai, 45
Zhu Di, 58
Zoroastrianism, 73